MAIL ORDER SUCCESS SECRETS

Other Books by Tyler G. Hicks
Published by Prima Publishing & Communications

How to Borrow Your Way to Real Estate Riches

How to Start Your Own Business on a Shoe-String and Make Up to $500,000 a Year

How to Get Rich on Other People's Money: Going from Flat Broke to Great Wealth with Creative Financing

How to Build a Million Dollar Fortune

HOW TO ORDER:

Quantity discounts are available from Prima Publishing & Communications, Post Office Box 1260HE, Rocklin, CA 95677; telephone (916) 624-5718. On your letterhead include information concerning the intended use of the books and the number of books you wish to purchase.

U.S. Bookstores and Libraries: Please submit all orders to St. Martin's Press, 175 Fifth Avenue, New York, NY 10010; telephone (212) 674-5151.

MAIL ORDER SUCCESS SECRETS

How to Create a
$1,000,000-a-Year
Business Starting
from Scratch

TYLER G. HICKS

Prima Publishing & Communications
P.O. Box 1260HE
Rocklin, CA 95677
(916) 624-5718

Typography by Compositors Corporation
Copyediting by Cheryl S. Smith
Production by Bookman Productions
Jacket design by Ad Type Graphics

Prima Publishing & Communications
Rocklin, CA

Library of Congress Cataloging-in-Publication Data

Hicks, Tyler Gregory, 1921-
   [Mail-order success secrets]
   Ty Hicks' mail-order success secrets : how to create a $1,000,000-a-year business starting from scratch / Tyler G. Hicks.
     p.   cm.
   ISBN 1-55958-021-6
   1. Mail-order business.   2. Success in business.   I. Title.
II. Title: Mail-order secrets.
HF5466.H557   1990
658.8'72 – dc20   89-39928
                                               CIP

90 91 92 93 RRD 10 9 8 7 6 5 4 3 2 1

Use This Book to Become a Mailbox Millionaire

Are you tired of cranky bosses, not enough money to pay your bills, disputes at home over who overdrew the checking account? If you have problems like these, you need this book!

Why? Because it shows *you* how to get into the world's best business and become a mailbox millionaire! And it won't take a big investment of cash or years and years to get what you want.

You can start in the world's best business today and be putting money into your bank in less than two weeks! How can I say that? I can say it from real-life experience. And I can show you bank deposit tickets giving *actual* deposits made within days of starting the world's best business! You can have *all* the advantages of this great business:

- *Ease* of starting — just a few pieces of paper is all you really need
- *Speed* in starting — if you can get to (or have someone get to) a mailbox, you can start a lucrative business in just moments (mail deliveries will even pick up mail you leave in your mailbox!)
- *Low cost* — postage is still a bargain and always will be if you sell the types of products or services I suggest to you

To help you see how easy it is for *you* to get into this great business, I'll share the experiences of many of the top mail-order professionals (*pros* for short). Since I know almost all of them, I'm familiar with their success stories. You'll soon see how easy it will be for *you* to start and make a bundle in your own mail-order business.

So come along with me — a self-made mailbox millionaire — and I'll show you:

- *Why* mail order is the world's best business
- *How* to start your own mail-order business for just pennies, in just a few days

- *Where* to find what you'll sell — you'll always need a product or service from which you can make money
- *What* doing your own thing can do for *you* in building your own mail-order fortune
- *When* to start bringing in big money with low-cost publicity and ads
- *What* kinds of profits you can build with big space ads for your products or services
- *How* to use mail-order catalogs to make yourself rich today
- *Why* you should use electronic media to pull millions into your mailbox every year
- *Which* mail-order secret of secrets — adding new products and services — will make you a millionaire soonest
- *How* make *big* sales to build a mega-buck business with just pieces of paper
- *Why* going overseas for your sales can expand your business at little extra cost
- *What* steps to take to run your business at the highest profits possible
- *Which* methods will make you the most money in mail order today
- *What* little-known mail-order secrets can put millions into your mailbox, starting right now!

In my years in the world's best business I've sold millions of items — and I still sell *every* day of the year. To help you succeed sooner, I give *you* on-the-spot ways to bring big bucks into *your* mailbox every day. You get hot new ideas directly from someone who's depositing big checks every banking day of the year.

And you'll see how to price your products or services so more money stays in *your* pocket. Why sell items or services for a few dollars when you can sell almost as many for hundreds of dollars? You'll see the answer to this and many other questions in the pages that follow.

On every page of this book I give you powerful mail-order success secrets never before revealed to anyone. Why don't I keep these to myself and make more money? Because I've made just about all I can sensibly spend. So now it's time to "share the wealth of ideas" so you too can become a mailbox millionaire like myself.

Mail order is growing so fast that there's plenty of room — acres and acres of it — for anyone who's willing to put the time in to build their fortune.

And the future of mail order is only up! Why? Because people everywhere have more confidence in mail-order firms. So millions of people every day pick up their telephone, dial a toll-free 800 number, and order thousands of items by phone. Result? A multi-billion dollar business that grows every year. You can share in some of these multi-billions while building a secure business for yourself. I've done it — and *am* doing it! And I'm ready to help *you* every step of the way with free personal advice on the phone, or face-to-face.

You really can't go wrong in mail order — if you start with good advice. This book *gives* you that advice without any theory or useless thoughts. Instead, you learn exactly how to run a low-cost mail-order business that allows you to put thousands of dollars a week into your bank account.

So come along with me, good friend. We'll see how *you* can get rich in the world's best business — using Ty Hicks' mail-order success secrets. And if there's anything in this book you can't understand, just give me a ring on the phone and I'll answer you clearly, directly, and helpfully. Try me and see!

Good luck — happy mailbox opening — every day!

TYLER G. HICKS

CHAPTER 1

GET INTO THE WORLD'S BEST BUSINESS

ARE YOU BROKE? Locked into a dead-end, boring job? Does your spouse complain about not having enough money to do the things you both enjoy?

If you answer *yes* to these and similar questions, you should consider getting into the world's best business! Why, you ask? For dozens of proven, money-laden reasons. The best of these reasons are:

1. You can start with just a few dollars—less than $100 in most cases.
2. You don't need an office, a staff of people, complex machinery, or other costly items. You can make millions in a "paper business."
3. You can start your business in your home. And you can run it from your kitchen table at the start!
4. Better yet, you can run your business from any city, town, village, or hamlet—anywhere! Truly, it makes *no* difference to your customers.
5. You can start with a product you've dreamed up. Or you can get products from others at low cost and sell them at high prices.
6. You can invest a dollar in marketing your products or services and make much more than you would from a dollar invested in the stock market, real estate, municipal bonds, or any other popular investment.

7. You *can* get free of cranky bosses, threats of firing, low wages, excessive overtime, and an insecure future— forever! All you need do is go into the world's best business!

What Is the World's Best Business?

It's *mail order*! You'll hear other names for this great business. Like:

- Direct mail
- Direct response
- Direct marketing

Each of these names has a specific meaning. But many times people use the overall term *mail order* to cover several types of businesses. Let's see what each term really means:

- *Mail order.* You run classified or space ads in magazines, newspapers, newsletters, and other publications. People respond or order by mail *(mail order)* to obtain more information or to send a check or money order for your product or service.
- *Direct mail.* You send a letter, brochure, flyer, or catalog by mail to potential buyers. They send you an order by mail *(direct mail)* to buy your product or service.
- *Direct response.* You run ads, radio or TV commercials, or mail ad material of any kind to prospects. They respond directly to you *(direct response)* by mail, telephone, FAX, or a direct visit, and order a product or service. You are one-on-one with your customer.
- *Direct marketing.* This term covers *all* the methods you might use to sell and service your customers directly— mail order, direct mail, telemarketing (using the telephone to call prospects or take orders), radio, TV, FAX, satellite communications, etc. You market directly *(direct marketing)* to your customers.

Despite all the recent developments in direct marketing, many newcomers like to think, and talk, in terms of *mail order!* Why? Because that's the way they dream of starting— by sending out letters to sell things or services.

What they really mean, of course, is *direct mail*. But they call it *mail order* because that's the term most of them know. So we'll use the term here somewhat freely but we'll always be careful to tell you what we mean.

Why Mail Order Is the World's Best Business

I'm a mail-order professional with more than a few profitable years in the business. Besides this, I know *every* major mail-order dealer in the business today. And during these years I've known *every* major mail-order dealer who hit it big. Plus plenty of the smaller players. All worldwide!

My experiences with these living, earning, and successful mail-order dealers—plus my own day-to-day trips to the bank to drop the day's proceeds into our business account—show me that:

- *Anyone* interested in mail order can get into the business if he or she uses common sense.
- *There are no restrictions* because of race, color, creed, sex, or product interest! Anyone can make it in mail order today.
- *You can sell* essentially any product or service by mail order! Name almost any item or service needed by people or business and someone is selling it by some form of direct response!
- *You can borrow money* to start your mail-order business! Later in this book I'll show you how—and where—you can apply for mail-order loans up to $500,000. Your check will be sent to you via registered mail, or wired into your bank account (whichever you prefer). You can have your loan approved within one hour (60 minutes) after the lender gets your application.
- *You can keep your business small,* or build it as large as you wish. You're the boss and you can do as you please!
- *You can run your business* at any time *you* like, day or night. The measure—from your customer's stand-point—is how quickly the mail-order business responds to his or her order. So if you work days and respond

quickly, great! But the same applies to night workers. So take your pick.

- *You don't need prior experience* to get rich in mail order. Many of today's mail-order millionaires started with little knowledge of the business. But they quickly learned the basics (as *you* will in this book). Then they went on to great wealth, learning something from each sale and each ad they ran.

Sell What You Like

Thousands of Beginning Wealth Builders (BWBs, I call them) come to me, saying:

- I want to get into mail order,
- Because I want to sell by "remote control"—that is, I hate face-to-face selling, it frightens me—
- But I don't know what to sell by mail order
- What can I do?

There's a simple answer to this question, and to your questions, if you have similar ones. The answer is:

Mail order, or any other version of direct marketing, does not require face-to-face selling! Further, you can decide what to sell by making a simple study of what you like to work with.

In dealing with thousands of BWBs in all kinds of businesses, I see a key idea working out again and again:

BWBs who work with products or services they like, and enjoy, are much more successful than those who sell items or services just for the money they can make from them.

So, *sell what you like!* You'll have more fun. And you'll make much more money from each sale!

Pick What You Like To Sell

There are two broad categories of items you can sell by mail order. They are:

1. Products
2. Services

In the *products* category you have dozens of items that sell well by mail. Like:

- Books
- Courses
- Gadgets
- Clothing
- Specialty items for autos, boats, planes, etc.
- Cosmetics, beauty aids
- Health, vitamin, and natural supplements
- Magazines, newsletters
- Etc.

In the *services* category there are also dozens of items you might sell. Like:

- Income tax advice
- Financial planning help
- Dating, introduction, or marital contacts
- Business advice of many kinds
- Loans, venture capital, and financing help

Since you're the person who'll be making money from what you're selling, ask yourself these simple questions:

1. Do I enjoy working with a product that must be packaged, wrapped, and sent to another person or firm? _____ Yes _____ No
2. Do I have the people (or materials) to provide needed advice to others while earning a profit for myself? _____ Yes _____ No
3. Are there any items I feel good about selling by mail (such as hospital supplies,

health aids, medicines, gour-
met food, etc.)?   _____ Yes   _____ No

4. Would I enjoy working directly with people face-to-
face, over the telephone, or
in some other way if the
amount of money I could
earn was a lot more than by
mail order selling?   _____ Yes   _____ No

If you answer *Yes* to Questions 1 and 3, you should consider selling *products*. But if you answer *Yes* to Questions 2 and 4, *services* will probably be your best and most successful offerings.

Selling what you enjoy working with makes such good sense that you really *must* take time to:

* *Look* into yourself to learn what you *really* want to do in your mail-order business
* *See* yourself in the business you think you'll like
* *Review*—in your mind—a complete probable day in the business, seeing yourself performing various tasks, dealing with customers, etc.
* *Analyze* if your product or service has wide (or narrow) appeal. The wider the appeal, the larger—in general—your market and your profits.

Find the Largest Market Possible

Let's see how the above approach to your becoming a mail-order millionaire might work for you. To give you a real-life example, I'll show you one way I'm using to gross more than $7 million in this great business. The steps I use are:

1. I ask myself the four questions above, and
2. Once I have the answer of *product* or *service,*
3. I pick a product or service with the widest appeal

Thus, I like to provide people with both products *and* services. The type of service I like deals with money. So

I "sell" money in many different forms, using direct marketing to:

- **Offer loans** to qualified BWBs who are two-year, or longer, subscribers to my monthly newsletter, *International Wealth Success.**
- **Offer grants** to sincere, qualified BWBs who are two-year, or longer, subscribers to my monthly newsletter, and who have the need for a grant to provide a needed service that benefits a large number of people.
- **Have loan representatives** (reps for short) who find borrowers and people seeking grants. Each rep is paid a commission when he or she finds a borrower who obtains one of our low-interest loans, or one of our grants.
- **Provide money courses** on a wide variety of profitable topics—financial brokerage, real estate finance, mega loans, international financial consulting, etc. You'll find details about these excellent courses at the back of this book.
- **Consult in person** (because I *enjoy* it) with both BWBs and EWBs (Experienced Wealth Builders) who are subscribers to my newsletter or buyers of one or more of our courses.
- **Pay commissions** to our Executive Reps who sell our newsletters or courses to others by any means they like.

So my "thing" in mail order is *money*. My money courses are both *products* (newsletters, books, and courses) and *services* (consulting and Executive Sales Reps). But *you* might not like to sell both products and services. Great!

I respect your views and will help you reach your goals. But product and service sales by mail order have grossed more than $7 million for me. I want *you* to do better than that! How? By finding the largest market possible for the products or services *you* want to sell!

The reasons I sell money products and services by mail order are:

---

* Available for $24 per year (12 issues) or $48 for two years (24 issues). Send check or money order to IWS, Inc., POB 186, Merrick NY 11566. You do *not* have to be a newsletter subscriber to apply for, or obtain, a loan or grant.

- *Everyone* is interested in money—it's the "engine" that makes business go.
- *Everyone* needs money at one time or another during their lives. Even the largest corporations need money at times during their business activities. So everyone is a potential customer for my money products and services.
- *Everyone* is interested in learning how to earn large amounts of money. Many of our money books, kits, and newsletters show the readers how to earn big chunks of money in their own business. In many cases these large sums are earned using mail-order methods.

So you see, I have found my largest possible market. You may be able to find a larger market for your products or services. If you do, and you have any questions, I will be happy to discuss them with you. And I assure you, good friend, that I will *not* try to sell into *your* market. Why? Because I'm too busy selling into my own large market.

How—and Where—to Find Large Markets

In mail order you try to find the largest number of buyers possible. Why? Because the more buyers you have, the larger the amount of money you'll make from each buyer. We'll see how this works later in this book.

The way to find the largest number of buyers is to figure out people's current "hot buttons." Today the most common hot buttons are:

- *Greed*—that is, the desire to get as much money as possible for oneself.
- *Attractiveness*—that is, the desire to look good to others, to be desirable from a business and personal relationship standpoint. As many mail-order millionaires have proven, selling youth and all it implies is one of the easiest sales ever!
- *Security*—that is, knowledge which will help you cope with earning a living, building wealth, and protecting yourself against all kinds of outside attack.

- *Amusement*—that is, any pleasant diversion that prevents people from becoming bored with life and their situations. You can make millions selling amusement products or services by mail order. For example, the game *Scrabble* has generated many millions of dollars in sales for over 50 years. Imagine the income from such an amusement product!
- *Entertainment*—that is, music, video, and similar products that do more than amuse people. An entertainment product provides an emotional experience which is pleasant, uplifting, informative, frightening, or even educational. Many millions are made each year selling entertainment products and services by mail.

You can probably think of other hot buttons. Why not make a list of them right now? If you don't know any other hot buttons, take these easy steps to find the newest turn-ons of people and business:

1. Read your local Sunday large-city newspaper *every* week. In it you'll find many comments on the current scene in the world and what people are doing.
2. Circle with pencil all popular activities of people. Thus, you might circle items like:
   - Popular dances (dance books sell well by mail!)
   - New automobile crazes—such as driving antique cars (auto parts sell strongly by mail)
   - Changes in living habits—such as people moving from single-family homes to condos (home services sell strongly by mail)
   - Homes being foreclosed because people can't afford their mortgage payments (foreclosure publications and services sell well by mail)
3. See if you can develop a mail order product or service which will appeal to these new hot buttons. Who knows, *you* may come up with the next hula hoop, Pet Rock, or mathematical cube. All have sold in the millions by mail order.

So you see, you *can* find a large market for the types of mail-order products or services you want to sell. It *does* take time but your effort *will* produce results that are well worth your time!

There are many other ways for you to find the latest hot buttons. Thus, be sure to read a weekly news magazine, a good monthly or weekly business magazine if you want to develop products or services in the business field. And if entertainment is your interest, be sure to read one of the many magazines serving this field. Once you get in the habit of looking for hot buttons, you'll find them all around you!

And if you can be the first with a new product or service that appeals to the latest hot button, you can make a million in mail order in less than a year! Plenty of mail-order operators are doing exactly that today. Why shouldn't *you* be next? I'm here to help you every step of the way.

Just keep one fact in mind at all times when getting into the world's best business:

> *At this writing, some $25 **billion** a year is being spent on direct-mail sales letters, brochures, etc., making it the largest single ad medium. People are not spending $25 billion a year on advertising unless they're getting profitable results. Such results are available to **you**—if you pick the right product or service.*

As we near the end of this first chapter in your guide to making millions in mail order—as I have and am—I want you to:

> *Resolve—here and now—that you **will** start your own mail-order business, using the simple guides I give you in this book. If you do as I suggest, I'm certain you'll become wealthy in mail order—much sooner than you think at this moment!*

Since I really don't expect you to believe me unless I can prove what I say, I'm ready to give you the proof you want. How? Read on!

Successful Mail-Order Pros Making Big Money Today

Earlier I told you I know all the big (and small) successful mail-order pros in business today. Here are a few you might know of who are friends of mine. After each name I give you a few words about their money making methods.

> *Don Moore* of Business Opportunity Club. Don started as a subscriber to my *International Wealth Success* newsletter, called me dozens of times to talk business. Today he's a successful, well-known, and highly respected mail-order pro who has a successful business going. Don and I even co-authored a money course together!
>
> *Russ von Hoelscher,* a highly skilled writer, is associated with Profit Ideas, through which he publishes a number of books on success. Russ runs full-page ads in a variety of magazines offering a free book on selling information by mail. Russ and I regularly exchange ideas and meet for lunch when I'm in his area of the West Coast. He's one of the most creative mail-order pros in the business today.
>
> *Jay Reiss,* one of the best mail-order ad copywriters around. Not only does Jay write great ads for dozens of mail-order pros, he also promotes his own services by mail order! So Jay works both ends of the business. Jay and I talk a lot on the phone about making more from every mail-order ad. Fig. 1-1 shows one of Jay's excellent ads.
>
> *Joe Karbo,* now at "the great post office in the sky," was one of the most creative mail-order pros of the 20th century. His "Lazy Man's Way to Riches" has been imitated, copied, and—I guess—lifted by hundreds of people too lazy to think for themsleves. There was only one Joe Karbo. The world suffered a terrible loss when Joe passed on. And I miss the many stimulating conversations I had with him about the world's greatest business. Joe knew what a great business it is, and he never failed to mention it to me!

HOW TO FINANCIALLY SURVIVE IN THE '90'S

You really can become a millionaire and financially prosper in the 1990's. You can travel all over the world; own a new car; wear the best clothes; buy and live in your dream home; enjoy your hobbies to the fullest; obtain the best medical attention; or enjoy a safe retirement. My book, SMART MONEY SHORTCUTS TO BECOMING RICH, shows you how.

START SMALL AND GROW BIG—FAST!

If you're not content with your present salary, let me share with you one of the finest money-making programs you've ever seen. Starting with almost no capital, you can start a business that builds steadily, makes good money week after week, and provides you with the kind of lifestyle most people will envy.

Discover how you can build wealth quickly. Learn about seven people who followed this system and have become rich. You'll receive the step-by-step plan they followed. See page 29.

Establish an action base. Learn how to choose a company name which inspires trust and creates public confidence. Then obtain free subscriptions to magazines I recommend, improve your credit rating and learn how to gain access to important people. See page 49.

Discover how to capitalize on your own ideas. I'll show you how 2 million copies of a book were sold using a clever idea and with almost no investment. I'll verify several million-dollar success plans that you can follow right in your own home. See page 61.

Learn how to seize a wealth-building opportunity. I'll reveal six important steps you must follow in order to build wealth quickly. See page 70.

SPECIAL BONUS!

We're convinced you'll find this incredible 226-page book worth hundreds of thousands of dollars. And to prove it to you, we would like to offer you a special bonus, just for ordering promptly. By sending for this book, SMART MONEY SHORTCUTS TO BECOMING RICH today, you'll receive—absolutely free—a valuable bonus report which will show you how to get a Visa or Mastercard regardless of your credit history! This incredible credit card report sells elsewhere for $20.00—and it's yours FREE—but only while supplies last. Send your order today!

Discover how to start a business using other people's money. Learn how to obtain capital without a credit rating. Learn about hidden ways to borrow money with little if any interest. Read about tax advantages that you can use to your benefit immediately. See page 90.

Turn your skills into great profits. Learn how to get free publicity, and find wealth everywhere. I'll reveal the success stories of 8 people who got rich with work-at-home ideas you can follow on your kitchen table. See page 101.

Learn how to diversify for even greater riches. In my book I'll show you 6 ways to build even a mediocre idea into a fortune. See page 108.

Discover ways to find, and market unique and unusual products. I'll show you ten steps to putting your ideas to work. You'll receive details on 14 proven businesses you can start immediately. See page 127.

VERIFIED TESTIMONIALS

"This book is one of the finest collections of money-making opportunities I've ever received. This book is in a class of it's own — it's light years ahead of the other products you see advertising in magazines today. I highly recommend it to anyone."

JOAN ROBERTSON
LINWOOD, NEW JERSEY

"This book is the most substantial collection of business advice I've ever seen. It contains an entire library of information in one book . . . it's worth 100 times what I paid for it."

STEVEN GORSHEN
CHICAGO, IL

"I have reviewed the material in this 226-page book and have found it to be 100% reliable. In fact, if you follow the advice it contains, you should be able to become a millionaire in less than a year."

Jay Reiss   Money-Making Expert
Goleta, California

Go where the money is, and make it yours. Read about 24 more fortune-building businesses that can be started by anyone. Learn how to raise your income by $90,000.00 a year and love every minute of it. See page 151.

Take 4 important steps to part-time wealth. Learn how to evaluate a part-time business, to see if it's right for you. Read about 25 wealth-building businesses you can start at home, in your spare time. See page 158.

Take advantage of every smart money shortcut to wealth. Learn how to size up a business quickly, to start a business right, and to keep it going strong. Learn how to keep expenses down, to be in control at all times, to use your cash wisely, and to expand when the time is right. See page 182.

Learn the secrets to successful advertising. Build a favorable image for your business. I show you how. Choose the best form of advertising. I reveal 10 valuable advertising methods you must use to make the public aware of your product or service. See page 195.

By sending for this incredible 226-page book, SMART MONEY SHORTCUTS TO BECOMING RICH, you'll learn everything there is about starting and building a successful business. This book is loaded with solid information to help you make the kind of money you deserve.

Figure 1-1

Harvey Brody, whose toll-position* concept broke new ground, is another strong believer in the world's greatest business. Though I could be wrong about this, I do believe that Harvey was the first mail-order pro to "go on computer" with his names. Then he had the genius to make these names available to other mail-order operators—at a profit to himself and his customers! A real pro who has my utmost respect!

Jacque Fiala, a mail-order pro from my neck of the woods, Long Island, is another original thinker. Jac, as I call him, developed his own book on credit and sells it all over the world. And Jac keeps coming up with new ideas—almost every day. Meanwhile, his business continues to grow. Started in his spare time, Jac's business allowed him to leave the work he was doing to concentrate full-time on the world's best business.

As we go along in this book I'll tell you about other mail-order pros I work with and talk to. You'll get good ideas from what they do and how they're making money in the world's greatest business *today!* Remember—a mail-order "pro" is a professional, through and through.

Of course, the ultimate test of any mail-order business is whether its customers are pleased with the products or services provided by the business. Here's a letter from one of my customers** who bought our *Loans By Phone Kit* (Fig. 1-2.) (see the back of this book for more information on it):

"I ordered your "Loans By Phone Kit" about two months ago. I have already made $16,400 from it. And I have projected an income of over $100,000 over the next two months. I want to thank you for your time on the telephone with me; you have been most helpful.

* Where you obtain control of a copyright, patent, or other exclusive right and earn income from the right.

** Every letter quoted in this book is available for free inspection by yourself in my office. Just give me a few day's notice and we'll ready the letters for you!

Figure 1-2

This reader paid just $100 for his *Loans By Phone Kit* and made over $16,000 from it in just two months! I'm sure he feels he got his money's worth! I know I do.

Now let's put *you* into the mail-order business—the world's greatest business—so you can give *your* customers great service while they make you rich!

CHAPTER 2

HOW TO START YOUR OWN MAIL-ORDER BUSINESS

You know which you want to sell—products or services—from Chapter 1. Your next step is to start your own direct marketing business, which you're thinking of as "mail order."

Make Your Decision Now!

Decide to go into the mail-order business *now!* Why? For a number of proven reasons that will put money into your pocket. These reasons are:

- When you decide *now* to go into the mail-order business you gather your energies and direct them toward success.
- Your decision sharpens your mind and keeps you alert to the newest hot buttons that are making millions for mail-order pros.
- Once you decide to go into business it's hard to turn back. And I don't want you to drop your plans because I know what a wonderful life the world's greatest business can give *you*. After all, I'm in the business myself!

To make sure you do decide to go into the mail-order business and make the most money you can, take these easy steps:

1. Get a small notebook that you can carry around without any trouble.
2. Starting on page 1 of your notebook, list the various topics your book will cover, along with the page number on which they'll appear. Your first topic will be "My Business Decision."
3. On page 2 of your notebook, mark the following: "On Sept. 1, 19 ___ I decided to go into the direct response business to sell _____ ."

You've now written your decision down. When you do, you'll be amazed at how it will focus your attention and energies. You're now ready to start your own mail-order business! So let's go.

Pick a Name for Your Business

Picking a name for a business can drive people up the wall. Many people want an impressive-sounding name that will imply a big business. Others like to have their personal name on the letterhead and envelope used in the business. And there are many other likes and dislikes that show up when people are naming a business. Here are some pointers that will work for you:

1. Use as simple a name as possible! Stay away from long, complicated names. They only annoy people when they're thinking of sending you money!
2. Test the initials your name will provide. Thus, my firm, "International Wealth Success, Inc.," has the initials *IWS*. People seem to like them and they're easy to say.
3. Avoid using your own name in the firm's name unless you're well-known in the field in which you'll be selling your products or services.

To show you what I mean by the above tips, here are a few names for mail-order firms that sound good to most people:

Alliance Products Company—for a firm that will be selling many different types of products. The word "Alliance" connotes reliability, stability.

Universal Services Company—for a firm that may offer a wide range of services. The word "Universal" gives a broad-base image to the company.

Business Financial Services Company—tells it all for a firm that will be offering financial services to the business community. Once you see the name, you know what the company does.

Success Publishing Company—for a firm that might publish newspapers, books, newsletters, tapes, etc., on success. The very name tells you that you can't buy books on failure from this firm!

Jones & Associates—for a firm that may sell both products or services. The name "Jones" could be your own, or some other one you like. But the entire name is so general, that any business could be run under it.

World Communications—for a firm that may be in publishing, lecturing, broadcasting, etc. You can replace "World" with any other word you might like for *your* firm.

There are plenty of other names you can pick. To get the best one, label page 3 of your notebook "Possible Names for My Business." Then list every name you can think of. When a new name occurs to you, jot it down in your notebook.

Don't overlook using your own name for your business. It may be the best name you can find! Then, again, a company name might be better—especially if you'll be selling to other companies, libraries, universities, etc. With such sales, it looks more professional and businesslike if your letterhead and billhead contain a company name.

Select Your Business Address

If you spend much time around mail-order pros, as I do, you'll hear almost endless discussions of the "best" address for your business. You can have two basic types of addresses, namely:

- A street number and name, city, and state
- A post office box number, city, and state

Today you'll find a third type of address, which has characteristics of both of the above. This type of address is that provided by a mail box center in which you rent a box. Since your mail box is not in the post office, your address will be:

- A street name and number, city, state, and suite number

Now the suite number is really your mail box number. But some people think that "Suite Number 108" implies you have an office at the street address given on your letterhead.

There are arguments for and against both types of addresses. Here are a few you'll hear. You can decide for yourself. For a street address:

- Implies stability—not a fly-by-night outfit
- Says "I can find this outfit"—they're on a certain street
- Can flavor an ad or a direct-mail piece if the address has a name related to the product. For example, "22 Flower Lane" is a great address for someone selling flowers and tulip bulbs by mail!
- Can add credibility to a company when the address is well-known—such as Wall Street for a firm selling investment advice by mail.

For a post office box, people say:

- Many of the world's largest firms operate from a post office box address—why shouldn't I?
- You can pick up the mail day or night from your post office box—this gives you greater freedom
- You get your mail (and *money*!) sooner in a post office box because you don't have to wait for carrier delivery
- You can get around the credibility problems by telling in your ads and mailings what groups you belong to—

such as the Better Business Bureau, Chamber of Commerce, etc.

From my own experience of nearly 25 years in the world's greatest business, I can say this:

- We have two post office boxes and two street addresses at which we receive mail
- More money flows through our post office boxes than through our street addresses
- We've grown every year—we're so liquid we slosh. And we've *never* been bankrupt like a number of the full-page newspaper advertisers who've operated from a street address!

So take your pick! I vote for a post office box if:

- You expect to be moving about (buying a bigger home from the profits you make in the world's greatest business!)
- Your mailbox at home is not suitable to receive a large volume of mail (such as the small mailboxes used in newer apartment houses
- Your landlord is snoopy and wants to find out about you by reading your incoming mail
- You will be sending large packages through the post office and somebody will be going there every day anyway

If you're still in doubt, consider using one of the mailing services that gives you both a street address and a post office-type box. The cost is higher than a post office box, but you may consider the service worth the extra cost.

Another benefit of a mailbox service is that it will forward your mail to you. Thus, my good friend and mail-order pro, Louis Gorchoff, who's an expert on credit cards, receives mail in Beverly Hills, California, but has it forwarded to him wherever he's residing at the moment. His Beverly Hills headquarters receives mail at a street address.

Register Your Business

Your local County Clerk wants to know what businesses operate in his or her county. So you must register your business name and address and pay a nominal fee ($3 to $25, typically) just once. To register your business:

1. Look up the phone number of your County Clerk in your local phone book
2. Call and ask for a Business Registration Form; it will be sent to you free of charge
3. Fill out the form; have it notarized, if required, and mail it to the address stated on it
4. Post a signed copy of the notice in your place of business (which can be your home), if you're required to do so

You're now in business! You don't have to incorporate at the start, unless your attorney advises you to do so. For instance, if you're selling an item that might explode, catch on fire, cut someone, or do other damage, your attorney may advise you to incorporate. Why? Because you could be saved from personal legal actions in the event someone was injured by one of your products. You will register your corporation in the same way as you registered your sole proprietorship or partnership with your County Clerk.

Mail Order Success Can Be Yours!

For years people have come to my "mail-order school" via the telephone and learned in just hours how to gross as much as $2,000 a week. One such reader writes:

> I just want to thank you for the many free ads you gave me when I was just starting out four years ago. Time flies! You've inspired me.

This reader today has his own quarterly success book newsletter which he mails all over the world. He sells many of my books and kits and earns a 50 percent commission.

We mail the items for him (called *drop shipping*) at *no* cost to him or his customers.

Now that you have the name and address for your business, and have it properly registered, you're ready to pick the products or services you will sell by mail. But before we start doing that, let me tell you what my good friend, David Buckley, told me about one of his mail-order services. David said:

> I dreamt up a mailing-list offer in a matter of just minutes. Then I wrote a mailing piece, had it printed, and got it in the mail. In less than a year I made $100,000 in my pocket from this one idea!

While I can't promise you that you'll make $100,000 "in your pocket" from an idea, I can promise you this:

> *Develop or find a wanted product or service, get some good ads prepared, and start mailing to prospects—not suspects! If you do this as carefully as you can, you're almost certain to make a profit which will help you start building your mail-order riches!*

So let's pick your product or service. I'm here to help you do that—both in this book and at the end of your telephone line. And I *guarantee* that I will *not* market the product or service you have in mind! Let's go.

CHAPTER 3

WHERE TO FIND WHAT YOU'LL SELL

MOST BWBs (Beginning Wealth Builders) seem lost when searching for a product or service to market by mail. This is wasteful. Why? Because you *can* find a good product or service to sell. All you need do is look! But before you start looking I want to give you some million-dollar advice. Here it is.

Develop Your Own Item, or Get an Exclusive

There are thousands of items you can sell by mail. But you'll make the largest amount of money on:

- An item you develop yourself to meet a specific need you've discovered will usually make you much more money than an item you buy from someone else.
- But if you've found an item available from someone else which will make money for you, be certain to get the *exclusive right* to market it. Then your profits are almost certain to be high!

Please get the above points clear! You make *more money*—usually—from items you think up yourself, or on which you get an exclusive distributor deal, than on items you buy from others. But you can still make *big* money

from items you buy from others on a nonexclusive basis.
You just have to negotiate the best price possible!

To develop an item or service you want to sell by mail,
take these easy, quick steps:

1. ***Work on an item you like.*** You'll have more fun, will
   do a better job, and you'll probably make more money!
2. ***Aim for a specific benefit*** for the users of your item.
   Be benefit-directed at all times. Why? Because your
   customers buy your item to obtain the *benefits* it offers
   them.
3. ***Test your idea on strangers,*** not on relatives or friends.
   Why? Because few relatives will understand what you're
   trying to do. And friends will rarely tell you what they
   really think! They'll just "butter you up" with nice
   little nothings that won't help. But strangers—
   especially if you ask them to pay money for your item—
   will quickly let you know what they think!
4. ***Avoid invention advice services***—most are a waste of
   money. If you want, I'll give you a fast, *free* reaction
   to your item if you're a two-year or longer subscriber
   to my newslettter, *International Wealth Success,*
   described at the back of this book.
5. ***Try—if possible—to make the item*** yourself. You'll
   earn much more money and will have many fewer
   headaches.

Now that you know how to develop your own item,
let's see how you can find ones on which you'll have
exclusive rights. We'll put *you* into the big money sooner
than you think!

Where to Find What You'll Sell

I have dozens of ideas on where to find what you'll sell.
And I've used each idea in my own business. So I guarantee
that these ideas can—and will—work for you, if you use
them right.

Run Classified Ads for Your Needs

You can run classified ads looking for products or services. Put these ads in magazines or newspapers read by people who might know of sources of the products or services you're seeking. Here are a few examples of such classified ads. You can use them as is, or change them to suit your needs.

WANTED: Home cleaning products to be sold by mail order. Send samples, prices to ABC Enterprises, 123 Main St., Anytown 00000.

NEEDED—new automotive products and services to be sold to the auto owner by mail order. Send samples and prices to ABC Enterprises, 123 Main St., Anytown 00000.

I CAN MARKET your health service by mail order. Send me full details of what you have and your prices. ABC Enterprises, 123 Main St., Anytown 00000.

WE CAN MAKE YOU RICH if you give us exclusive rights to sell your skin-care produts by mail order. Send full details on prices, along with samples, to ABC Enterprises, 123 Main St., Anytown 00000.

You may have better ads! If so, be sure to use them instead of these. But the above ads *will* get you started! Don't waste time—move ahead.

Visit Free Trade Shows

There are hundreds of trade shows around the country every year. Many feature products you might sell by mail. To use trade shows to your profit:

1. *Decide* which trade shows might be best for you. Pick shows featuring the types of products or services you plan to sell.
2. *Register* for the show by filling out the attendee card. You can get this free of charge from the show promoters. Once your card is received, you'll be sent a badge which entitles you to enter the show free.
3. *Attend* the show. Visit the various exhibits. Collect catalogs and data sheets for the products or services you want to sell.
4. *Study* the information you collected. Decide which items would be suitable for you. Then contact the manufacturer or supplier and work out a suitable price.
5. *Get* drawings, photos, and other sales material from your contact. Use these in your mailings, if suitable. If not, use this material as the starting point for improved mailing pieces.

You can find which trade shows are scheduled by contacting the trade association for your field. They will be glad to supply you with a free list of upcoming shows. Such shows can be your key to finding saleable products or services that can make you a mail-order millionaire!

Use Overseas Source Directories

There are thousands of overseas firms that have ideal products for mail sales. While it will take you longer to contact overseas sources than to attend local trade shows, you may be able to get a lower price overseas. One of my good friends who's selling $10 million a year worth of supermarket and kitchen supplies says:

I buy many of my supermarket items which I sell by mail from overseas suppliers. While I have to wait longer to get the items, my savings are enormous. For instance, on wicker baskets which I sell for use in fruit packing, I save about 50¢ per basket. When you're selling by mail, every penny you save on your product goes into your pocket as profit!

To locate overseas suppliers, take these easy steps:

1. *Refer* to copies of *Worldwide Riches Opportunities,* Volumes 1 and 2, available from IWS, Inc. at $25 per volume. Each volume lists a number of overseas suppliers of a variety of products you can import and sell by mail. See the back of this book for more information.

2. *Contact* the embassies of countries which make the types of products you want to import. The embassy will be happy to supply you with much free information on companies in its country that make the items you seek. Have the embassies contact the companies that interest you. This will be done free of charge and it will save you postage and phone costs! Have the embassy get information on cost, quantity, shipping expense, etc. You'll find that most embassies will be happy to do this work, free. Why? Because it means possible sales for the companies. And, as someone once said—"Nothing happens until a sale is made!"

3. *Check* overseas magazines and newspapers. There are a number of such publications featuring products that might be in the field you want to serve. You can contact the maker directly. Or you can go through the embassy and have them contact the firm for you. This will save you time and money.

Source directories come in all sizes and shapes. Be sure to look over *all* that are available to you. Why? Because one right lead can make *you* a mail-order millionaire faster than you might think!

Check New (and Not So New) Patents

There are thousands of patents available around the world. One of these might give you exactly the product or service you seek. To check patents take these easy steps:

1. *Visit* your local large public library and look in the catalog file under the Patents heading.

2. **Look over** every book the library has on patents. At the larger public libraries you will even find a listing of new patents available.
3. **Choose** those patents that will give you the item you believe you can sell by mail. Pick several so you have the chance for more than one item.
4. **Contact** the inventor by mail or phone. Tell the inventor that you're interested in selling the product by mail. Ask the inventor if he or she is willing to help you make the item, if the inventor does not have a way of building it.
5. **Work out** a suitable way to make and sell the item that interests you. Don't try to take all the profits— give the inventor a fair share. Then the inventor will be more willing to share new developments with you. This could lead to you getting the jump on either new items or improvements of existing items.

In the patent field you'll find two types of patents. They are:

1. Private patents
2. Public-domain patents

When you want to promote and sell an item covered by a private patent you will negotiate with the inventor, as detailed above. This can take time because some inventors think everyone in the world wants their item. This usually isn't the case. But if you ever do find an item that everyone in the world wants, you've got it made!

Public-domain patents are those that anyone can use without charge. They are patents developed using government money. To get a list of such patents, contact your local federal government office. Ask for the list. It will be sent to you free of charge.

Go through the list and check off items you believe you could sell by mail. Write the government; ask for a copy of the patent. When you get the copy, decide if you can have the item made at a suitable cost. If you can, try to get a manufacturer to make the item on a shared-profit basis. Then you won't have to advance any money for having the item made.

Contact Your State Business Development Agency

Every state has a Business Development Agency. The purpose of the Agency is to encourage business development, and jobs, within the state borders. You'll find your state agency is full of useful ideas and help. Thus, typical state business development agencies offer the following *free* services to firms within their borders:

- Small business development ideas and advice
- Business skills and technical assistance
- Seed money to start a new business in the state
- Venture capital for businesses having large growth potential
- Financing via conventional business and real estate loans
- Market information in the state and outside the state
- Location and hiring incentives (loans, grants, etc.)
- Employee training and hiring assistance
- Export-import advice and guidance
- Buying and procurement assistance
- Permit and license assistance
- Plus many other services you might need

Using your state Business Development Agency can be a great idea for you. Why? Because you get a respected and known group behind you. Then if someone should complain about your business practices, you can always say: "I checked with our state Business Development Agency and they said it was acceptable to conduct my business this way." People will often reply: "Oh, I'm glad to know that. I'm sorry I questioned you on this."

One of my readers took my advice and consulted his state Business Development Agency when starting an export company which he runs by mail. He needed a $4 million loan. Here's what he says:

Thanks for your suggestion that I contact the _____ Small Business Development Agency for the loan I needed.

They told me to call their venture capital group. I did but they weren't interested. But they did suggest that I call the finance group; they gave me the phone number. I called the finance group and they said "Sure, we'd be happy to fund a $4 million loan for your exporting company," if I presented a suitable business plan. I got the business plan to them and the loan was approved in just days!

When you know what types of items you wish to sell, your state Business Development Agency can:

1. Give you free lists of firms in your state that make what you seek.
2. Introduce you to the executives in the firms that might help you.
3. Get you discounts or other savings on the items you want to buy.
4. Arrange the financing of your purchases, if you need such help.

Get Help from Importers

Importers have thousands of reasonably priced products ideal for mail sales. And every importer is anxious to make a sale! So you can wheel and deal (which can be fun) to get the best price possible. To find importers, take these easy steps:

1. Look in the pages of *Worldwide Riches Opportunities*, Volumes 1 and 2, listed at the back of this book. You'll see hundreds of importers listed under "Products Available" in these two volumes.
2. Look in the "Yellow Pages" of large city telephone books under "Importers." You'll see hundreds of importers listed by the types of products they handle. Contact those that interest you and work out a suitable price after inspecting samples and data sheets.

When working with importers, be sure to take certain precautions to protect your business, namely:

1. Check the importer's source of supply. If you're selling items by mail, you must be certain that you'll have enough items on hand to meet the demands of your customers who are spending their hard-earned money with you.
2. Find out how long the importer has been in business. If the importer has been around for only a year or so, be on your guard. You don't want to sell a large number of products and then find you can't get them because your importer left for a warmer climate!

Many mail-order fortunes are built on selling imports. You can make your millions from imports, too. But you must be careful to be sure your supply is steady and dependable!

Sell Printed Products

One of the biggest mail-order markets in the world is for printed products—books, reports, newsletters, calendars, appointment books, etc. The printed product has many advantages over others:

1. Printed products don't (normally) break. Nor do they need fuel, oil, maintenance, or painting. And few printed products can injure their user!
2. Printed products are economical to buy—that is, they don't cost you "an arm and a leg." And the more of a printed product you buy, the lower each one will cost. So if you have really large orders, you can earn more from each order since the cost of your product will be lower. This may not be so with other types of products.
3. Printed products go well together in catalogs and multiple mailings. Thus, if you sell books on business and finance via the mail, you can have 10, 20, 30, 50 books on these general subjects in one catalog. The result? You'll sell more books from each catalog or mailing because people will browse through the materials you send them in the form of a catalog or ads.

In my company, International Wealth Success, Inc., called IWS for short, we have sales reps selling our many books, kits, and newsletters by mail. Some of these Executive Reps have sold $2,000 per week of our products. At a 50 percent commission rate, their take is $1,000 a week. Not bad for selling printed products that really help people achieve financial freedom.

There are, of course, other printed products you can sell by mail. Thus, one BWB I know of:

- Sells books, tools, and supplies to plumbers by mail and classified ads
- Concentrating only on master plumbers and their helpers—a market that has clearly defined needs and is reachable through trade magazines, union newspapers, and similar publications
- Sending mailings to independent plumbing firms and to plumbing suppliers

While selling to plumbers might not seem to be an exciting business, it has several clear advantages, namely:

1. You can reach plumbers because their names are available from mailing list houses, union membership lists, and license records.
2. Plumbers need books and other instructional materials to continue to be competitive in today's business world.
3. When mailing plumbing printed material ads to plumbers this BWB is mailing to *prospects*, not *suspects*! Prospects *buy*—suspects just look and toss your ad materials away.

So be sure to consider printed products as a possible avenue for you to great wealth in mail order. You might even wish to consider our *Guaranteed Monthly Income* plan covered in the book of that name described at the back of this book. Under this plan you keep *all* the money you receive on the sale of our products, sending us the name and address of the buyer. We then ship at *no* cost to you or to your buyer for shipping.

Now that you know where to find products to sell, let's take a look at some services you might offer via the mails.

You may be able to make more money selling a service than selling a product.

Profitable Services You Can Sell by Mail

There are a number of profitable services you can sell by mail. †n some of these services you'll be more involved personally than when you sell a product. In others, you won't be too involved. Let's look at a few of the services you might offer by mail.

Financial Brokerage Is Profitable

You may have heard the remark "Water is the universal solvent." Not so! Money *is* the universal solvent! Why? For a number of reasons:

- Every business—from the smallest to the largest—needs money at some time during its life. Most businesses need money several times during their life.
- People who can raise money for others are among the most valued personnel in any business.
- Money is the fuel that makes every business go. The finders and suppliers of this fuel can write their own ticket as to costs and rewards. Why? Because without this fuel, few businesses can survive.

You can sell a financial brokerage service by mail. This service will raise or find money for businesses of all kinds. You can be the financial broker or you can hire others on a fee basis to do the work for you. The services you will sell to businesses by mail are:

- Raising or finding money for business or real estate deals of all kinds
- Taking a company public—that is, getting its stock sold to the public for money that *never* need be repaid
- Acting as a business consultant on financial matters to business and real-estate entrepreneurs.

When selling financial brokerage services by mail you never really need meet your customers. All transactions can be handled by mail and phone. So this is really an ideal service for mail-order dealers.

To get a full knowledge of the financial brokerage field, use the *Financial Broker/Finder/Business Broker/Consultant Kit* described at the back of this book. It can get you started quickly and easily. (Also, see Figure 4-3 in the next chapter.)

Offer An Investment Advisory Service

There are millions of people needing financial advice today. They have any number of questions like:

- Should I invest in real estate?
- Which Certificate of Deposit (CD) should I buy?
- How can I best save for my pension?
- Which stocks should I buy?

People who offer answers to these questions are called Financial Consultants or Financial Planners. You can offer such a service by mail to people needing it. If you don't have the needed experience to advise people as a Financial Planner, you can hire experts to work for you. Then your role will be that of a mail promoter who finds the customers for the experts.

Investment consulting differs from financial brokerage in that you're dealing with individuals who need advice in their personal lives. In financial brokerage you're dealing with companies and helping their business activities.

Before entering any financial planning business, check with your state to see if any license is required. Today, few states require a license. But your state may be one of those that does.

As a financial planner you will meet face-to-face with your clients. So if you're turned off by personal meetings, promote financial brokerage or another service by mail. Then you won't have to meet with clients very often.

Leasing Is an Ideal Mail Service

Today leasing is a popular way for businesses to get use of equipment without laying out big bucks. Thus, if a business needs any of the following equipment, they can easily lease it—by mail:

- Copying machines—desktop to standalone
- Electronic typewriters of all kinds
- Computers—from the smallest business personal computer to the largest mainframe
- Satellite dishes for communications
- Telephone systems of all types
- Laser printers
- Office furniture and store fixtures

The service you'll sell by mail in the leasing field is that of being a lease broker. You connect the business seeking to lease equipment to the firm providing the lease financing. For this you earn a fee of 3 to 10 percent of the lease amount. All by mail! Could you ask for any better business?

Let me give you one of today's secrets of making big money in mail order. This secret is:

Selling items for a few dollars each was the "old" way to make millions in mail order. Today the "new" way to making millions in mail order is to sell items worth hundreds of dollars per sale. While you won't make as many sales, you'll make more per sale and you'll have fewer problems.

So a commission of say $4,000 on one leasing sale will put a lot more into your pocket than a few hundred dollars from each of a number of small product sales. Thus, one BWB mail-order operator told me:

He raised $200,000 from a 20,000 piece mailing for his private bank in just a few weeks. While the $200,000 is in the form of deposits in the BWB's bank, it is money his bank is free to invest to earn interest for the depositors and the bank owned by the BWB.

Leasing *can* give you big mail sales, without ever having to meet the firm leasing the equipment from you. And you can make big bucks in leasing by specializing in certain types of equipment.

Thus, some mail-order pros stick to auto and truck leasing. This focuses their efforts and allows them to become expert in vehicle leasing. You can do this if you wish. The commissions are in the same range as listed above.

To learn more about office equipment and vehicle leasing, see the two kits described at the back of this book— *Phone-In Mini-Lease Program* (Figure 3-1) and the *Auto & Truck Leasing Kit*. You can get into leasing without such kits but you'll waste a lot of time learning the ropes. And you may lose some commissions through poor agreements and botched deals.

Income-Tax Advice Sells Well

Taxes are always with your potential customers. You can help them cope with taxes better by giving them useful advice. And you never meet with your client unless you want to! You just send information back and forth by mail.

To give tax advice by mail, you must either be an expert yourself or hire an expert. If you want to be a mail-order promoter, then your best course is to hire an expert to advise the clients you find. You'll make a little less this way. But your life will be a lot freer!

What you do is this:

- Delegate the detailed parts of your business to experts who like details
- "Farm out" as much work as you can to other experts— that is, letter shops that do mailings, copywriters who write ads, etc.
- You concentrate on marketing—that is, making the sales to prospective customers.
- This is the way to get rich while having a lot of free time to think of new deals to sell to new customers!

DO YOU WANT TO USE
MEGA-MONEY METHODS?
HERE'S HOW:

Do you know that MEGA-MONEY METHODS regularly raise $50-million, $100-million, $150-million for real-estate and business deals?

Such amounts ARE available for the RIGHT deals. And our new KIT--MEGA-MONEY METHODS--shows you how to find, work with, and profit from such deals! These are REAL DEALS--not dreams of some amateur who never put a deal together. Here's what this BIG kit gives you:

1. What MEGA-MONEY deals really are
2. Examples of real-life real mega-money deals and their amounts
3. Selected active MEGA-MONEY funders --people and firms with the money
4. How to structure the MEGA-MONEY deal so it works
5. Fees you earn with MEGA-MONEY deals after funding
6. Where to get as much as 116% no-cash funding! NO CASH NEEDED!

This powerful Kit is the real answer to deals from $5-million to $999-million. It puts YOU in command of methods used by BIG MONEY funders who deal in multi-millions. And it gives you the names, addresses, and telephone numbers of real-life MEGA-MONEY funders--the people really doing big deals today! Written by Ty Hicks, this BIG KIT shows YOU:

**Proven ways to get MEGA-MONEY loans
**Loan package methods for FAST OKs
**Full info on MEGA-MONEY lenders
**Step-by-step borrowing methods
**A turnkey business for you from your own home anywhere
**Steps to earning BIG income

Get dozens and dozens of MEGA-MONEY METHODS like these fundings:

**Long-term mortgages
**Short-term mortgages
**Private money with NO income check, NO credit check, NO points
**Interest-only loans
**Interim bridge loans for real estate
**Equipment leasing to $25-million with 24-hour approval
**We-start-where-banks-stop financing
**Immediate cash for accounts receivable
**Fast closings for all types of loans
**Unlimited funds available

You can run a MEGA-MONEY METHODS business on the side while you hold a normal job or run a small business of any kind.

This is a true spare-time business that can earn you profits if you put effort into the putting through of MEGA-MONEY deals.

Order your MEGA-MONEY METHODS KIT today for:

**Just $100 from IWS gets you started
**Those ordering from this ad get TWO big bonus items: "How to Package the BIG Loan", and "Unique MEGA-MONEY Loan Source Leads".

So get started today! Send check, money order, or call 1-800-323-0548 day or night to order by credit card. Get into the world of BIG $!

There is no other Kit like this available anywhere! If you want to enter the world of MEGA-MONEY METHODS, this kit is for YOU!

Here's $100. Send me my MEGA-MONEY METHODS KIT now! If you wish, you can call Ty Hicks at 1-800-323-0548 day or night to order by credit card. Or enter your card number below and send this coupon to IWS, Inc., 24 Canterbury Rd, Rockville Centre NY 11570. Use this coupon for check or money order orders also.

NAME_____ CARD NO._____

ADDRESS_____ EXPIRES_____

CITY_____ STATE_____ ZIP_____

Telephone number: ___ ___ ___

Figure 3-1

- You'll make more money as a marketing expert than as a subject-matter expert! You can always hire subject-matter experts—marketing pros are much scarcer.

If you don't want to give current tax advice, consider teaching others how to be income-tax advisors. There are a number of mail-order schools teaching this subject. With taxes getting more complex every day, there's plenty of room for new, and better, teaching methods. You can offer these!

Or if you don't want to deal with individuals, think about serving just business clients. While the tax work is a little more complicated, your fees will be higher! Why? Because businesses need reliable tax advice. You can be the person to offer such help—while getting rich in mail order!

Offer a Financial Consulting Service

Many executives and businesspeople today need financial advice. Such help can range from planning for the education of the executive's children, to setting up a retirement plan to cover expected expenses in later life.

You can run such a business by mail. You'll need forms for your clients to fill out, plus sheets of questions to be answered. A number of higly successful financial consulting services are run by mail. To get clients for your service:

- Advertise in quality business magazines, travel publications, religious journals, and other upscale publications.
- Promote reliable, confidential service given personally by mail in the privacy of one's home
- Use experts to advise the executive, if you're not competent to do so
- Call on insurance salespeople, stockbrokers, accountants, and others to prepare the advice for each client

Ask your satisfied clients to recommend friends and relatives who might need your services. Using referrals, you can build up a large list of clients who keep sending you money every month. Price your services according to each client's ability to pay and to the importance of your advice. If you must bring in more experts, raise your price!

Teach a Skill by Mail and Get Rich

Another popular service you can sell by mail is the teaching of a skill. And there are thousands of such skills that sell well by mail. Like:

- Electronics, computers, television repair
- Auto maintenance, detailing, repair
- Writing skills for articles, books, stories
- Carpentry, home repair, other building skills
- Electric wiring, motor repair, air conditioner installation

I've taught writing by mail for years. People like the personal contact I give them. And I guarantee that at least one of their written pieces will be published and that they will be paid for the item!

Since my writing course is only $195, it's a bargain when the payment for the published piece is subtracted. That's why people continue to enroll for the course year after year. See the back of this book for more information.

To make money by mail teaching a skill, take these steps:

1. *Learn* the skill you want to teach if you don't already know it. Better yet, teach a skill you know well.
2. *Devise* a unique way to teach the skill. In my writing course, I use personal consultation on the telephone, plus a complete written analysis of each lesson.
3. *Advertise* in publications most attractive to your potential students. If you think truck drivers might be closet writers, advertise in the magazines they read!
4. *Offer* your students something different from the other mail-order teachers! My guarantee of publication is an example of such an offer. No other mail-order school of which I'm aware at this time makes such an offer.

Yes, teaching a skill can be a great mail-order service for you. It can make you rich sooner than you think. Just be sure you pick a skill that lots of people would like to learn!

CHAPTER 4

DO YOUR OWN THING TO BUILD MAIL-ORDER RICHES

IF YOU MEET as many mail-order dealers as I do, you'll quickly reach one strong view, namely:

Mail-order wealth builders are an independent bunch. They come from many different backgrounds; few have any formal education in the field. What they know, they learned from doing. And they all do their own thing—that's what makes them rich!

In suggesting that *you* do your own thing, I'm relying on these traits in you—a Beginning Mail-Order Dealer (BMOD):

- You are interested in having your own business which you can start and run from home
- You want to earn as much money as you can, as quickly as you can, with little hassle
- You're willing to take chances if the rewards are worth the risk
- You're willing to work hard to earn what you seek in terms of money, prestige, and power

Given these traits, plus plenty of others we don't have room for here, I'm sure you'll be a big success in this business. Provided you do your own thing in your approach to making a mail-order fortune.

One of the most creative young mail-order professionals I know today is David Bendah. David is the author of a number of excellent books which he sells by mail order. Gifted with creativity and courage, David started two great magazines serving the small business fields. These two fine publications contain helpful articles on a variety of topics important to people active in business. And a number of firms offering information and equipment for business advertise in David's magazines. David really knows how to judge a market and do his own thing in a highly creative way.

You have unique talents and a special background. Bring your own thing to the party and you too can get rich

Apply Your View to Your Money Maker

In Chapter 3 you picked either a product or service to market. You know what you want to sell by mail. Starting with the next chapter we'll show you exactly how to sell your chosen item.

But before you start selling, we want *you* to put *your* special appeal on what you're selling. We want you to do your thing! How? By understanding more of the basic principles of mail order, namely:

- The major appeal(s) you'll put on the item you'll be selling
- The characteristic traits of your typical customers who'll be buying from you
- The customer traits you'll appeal to in your mailings and ads

We'll start with the appeals you'll put on your item to make it attract as large an audience as possible. Then we'll match these with the traits of your typical customer.

Get Your Sales Features Clear

Every item you sell has certain features that will appeal to your buyers. You have to isolate these features and point them out—again and again—to every prospective buyer you contact by mail or phone. Typical features that appeal to many buyers include:

- *Economy*—the buyer gets excellent value for the money paid for the item
- *High quality*—the buyer will not be ashamed to use your item in public or among friends and associates
- *Long life*—the item won't fall apart the first week the buyer uses it
- *Wide acceptance*—the buyer won't feel that a mistake was made in choosing the item purchased
- *Reliable source*—the buyer knows your company stands behind the item and is ready to do whatever is necessary to make the item perform its promised function

Now you know your product or service better than anyone else. See how you can apply these features to *your* sales item. That is, do your own thing to make this item and offer unique. *You* can make your item different from anything the world has seen before. Let me give you a few real-life examples:

- In 1963, a friend of mine—Jack Payne—started a new and different newsletter which he named *Business Opportunities Digest*. Jack figured that people all over the United States needed a monthly newsletter giving them a digest (brief descriptions) of business opportunities. Jack's newsletter flourished because Jack did his own thing—he brought business opportunities within reach of the person seeking them anywhere in the United States.
- In 1967, a guy by the name of Ty Hicks (your author), who traveled all over the world lecturing on business and technical topics, decided that there was a need for a newsletter covering international small business financing, business startups, mail-order marketing, financial brokerage, real estate, and import–export. So he founded and began publishing the monthly news-letter, *International Wealth Success*. It boomed, and soon had the largest circulation of any newsletter in the field. Ty did his own thing with his newsletter by offering

readers low-interest business and real estate loans—a feature *no* other newsletter offers to its readers to this day. In 1984 Ty started another finance newsletter, *Money Watch Bulletin.* He did his own thing with it by giving 100 lenders a month (minimum) with their lending criteria that are right up to date (within two weeks of publication). It, too, has boomed.

Both these mail-order entrepreneurs did their own thing with their newsletters. The result? Booming businesses that help people in their efforts to build a fortune today. But newsletters aren't the only way to do your own thing. Here's another real-life example:

• Another mail-order friend, Ted Nicholas, wrote a great book in 1973 titled *How to Form Your Own Corporation Without a Lawyer for Under $50.* Ted did his own thing with the book idea. Then, when publishers wouldn't handle the book (for various silly reasons), Ted did his own thing again—he published the book himself. Sales boomed. Today the book is in its 25th revision and is part of some 45 other business titles Ted publishes under his Enterprise Publishing imprint. Ted's sales features have always been clear—publish practical, useful books that tell the reader what must be done to accomplish a certain goal. Ted's creative and unusual approach to book development and sales has made him an outstanding success in mail-order marketing.

So look at the item you want to sell. Take a pencil and piece of paper and make a list like this:

1. Key sales feature _____
   _____

2. Second key sales feature _____
   _____

3. Third key sales feature _____
   _____

At the start, three key sales features are often enough. But if you can come up with more, fine! The more the better. Why?

- Because when you start to market your item, the more key sales features you have, the stronger will be your sales message. And—in general—the stronger your sales message, the larger will be the sales of your item.

Try to see that your sales features include some of those listed above—economy, high quality, long life, etc. The more such features you can apply to your item, the more likely is it to appeal to the usual mail-order customer. Let's take a look at what most of your customers are like, and how you can make easy sales to them.

Know What Makes Your Customers Act

Mail-order customers are both similar and different in their needs and wants. But their similarities are what make them buy by mail. If you know what makes your customers act, you can:

- Relate your key product or service features to the traits that make your customers buy
- Refine your ads so they emphasize your sales features to appeal to customer needs
- Run your mail sales business on a solid base of known characteristics which help you predict results

So you become more than someone who drops envelopes in the mailbox every day. You become a smart business-person who can predict with accuracy the sales that a given mailing or ad will produce. You can do this because you know that your customers:

- *Are ready to spend money quickly* on items giving results they seek in life
- *Seek quick results* from anything they buy by mail
- *Are ready to accept* new and different approaches to solving problems in their daily lives
- *Strongly believe they're entitled* to the best in life—a good job, superior home, plenty of leisure time, etc.
- *Enjoy using a credit card* to buy the products or services offered by mail because this gets the item to them faster

- *Willingly pay high prices* for items or services they believe will give them the quick financial, health, or happiness results they seek, especially if they can work from their home
- *May be less than fully motivated* most of the time; knowing this, they enjoy being nudged into action
- *Seek the easy way out* in getting things done
- *Don't want to read long books*—prefer short, well-written summaries that give how-to information
- *Avoid risk-taking* unless there's a strong promise of success in the near future
- *Will read both long and short ads* on subjects that promise to solve a problem for them
- *Seek security in life* and in a job or business because security promises relief from fears
- *Can be sold* via clear, simple, and plain ads that give the facts without exaggeration
- *React favorably to special attention* from a business that tries to help solve the customer's problem
- *Will take any needed steps* to get faster results—that is, will order by phone using a credit card and pay extra to have the item or service shipped by overnight delivery
- *Are often impatient with delays,* either actual or imagined. Want everything "yesterday"—especially sources of money!
- *May be suspicious* of every mail-order business because of horror stories told by friends and the press

There are other traits your customers have. But the ones listed above are those I run into almost every day. Let's see how you might relate the sales features of a product you have to these traits. You'll learn how to make big sales with any product or services you want to offer.

How to Make Big Sales of Any Item

I hope that by now you see that you *can* take almost any item and sell it successfully—if you know how! And you're seeing how you can do it in this chapter. Let's put this into real-life terms with an actual example.

You—we'll say—have developed a course showing people how to make money as a financial broker/finder/ business broker/consultant. You feel there's a big market for it. But before you start promoting your course you want to tie its main sales features to the known traits of mail-order buyers. Here's what you do:

1. Using the form given earlier, you list the three main sales features of your course. Your list looks like Figure 4-1. List more than three features, if you can.
2. Next, you relate the features of your course (which you now call a "kit" because it sounds easier to use) to the typical mail-order buyer's traits. You do this as shown in Figure 4-2.
3. With the info from these two reviews you write your first ad for your kit, Figure 4-3. Note how you bring together the items important to your buyer.

Let's take a closer look at your process of bringing together features and traits. You can use this approach for any other product or service.

You isolate the customer traits you think will play a part in the buying decision for this kit. Here they are. The customer:

1. Wants quick results in business activities
2. Wants a better lifestyle for himself or herself

Key Sales Features of Proposed Product

1. Shows how to make big money quickly.
2. Allows people to work from home.
3. Gives 2,500 loan sources of all types.
4. Tells which industries pay big fees.
5. Shows how much to charge for your work.
6. Can be bought using a credit card.
7. Has fast "Speed-Read" books.

Figure 4-1

3. Has a credit card which he or she wants to use
4. Likes to work from home
5. Doesn't want to read long books
6. Avoids risk of all types

Next, you list the features of the kit which meet these customer traits, using the same numbers as in the above list. Here are your features:

1. This kit gives fast results (see testimonials in the ad, Figure 4-3)
2. The kit provides a higher income, allowing a better lifestyle
3. A credit card *can* be used to buy the kit
4. Buyer can work from home using this kit
5. The kit has "Speed-Read" books for fast reading
6. Using the kit does *not* involve a big risk

Bringing these two sets of traits and features together gives you Figure 4-2. Note that the kit offers six features which match nicely with six known traits of mail-order

---

Customer Traits this Product Satisfies

Customer Traits	Product Features
1. Wants quick results	1. Shows how to make big money quickly
2. Wants better lifestyle	2. Shows how much to charge for your work
3. Has credit card—wants to use it	3. Can be bought using a credit card
4. Likes to work from home	4. Allows people to work from home
5. Doesn't want to read long books	5. Has fast-read "Speed-Read" books
6. Avoids risks in life	6. Tells which industries pay big fees

Figure 4-2

MAKE BIG MONEY FROM MONEY! START NOW!

NOW? By becoming a FINANCIAL BROKER/FINDER/ BUSINESS BROKER CONSULTANT! Some people call this the "best business anyone can get into!" Would YOU like to become a Financial Broker/Finder/Business Broker? You can! Now? Read on!

If YOU like money, if YOU have ever had some type of job in business, if YOU want to help others, and if YOU like people, YOU can become a Financial Broker. All YOU need do to start YOUR future in this great career is to use the IWS FINANCIAL BROKER/FINDER/BUSINESS BROKER/CONSULTANT KIT! It shows you the how, where, when, and why of this money-laden career. Here's why YOU need this great KIT. It gives YOU the ideas, methods, forms, and steps which YOU can use to get started. Here are some of the specific topics covered in detail in this great KIT:

* How to prepare your business announcement
* Developing a list of financial and business brokers
* Typical business loan application forms
* How to start your own financial broker office
* Where to locate your business
* Doing business from your own home
* How to get your letterhead and business cards
* How, and where, to contact money sources
* What to charge your clients for your help
* Finding clients all over the world
* 2,500 sources of business loans for you
* How to be a financial broker anywhere without needing a state or city license (this method has never been covered in print before—so far as we can determine!)
* Typical financial broker/finder/business broker forms (115 pages of forms covering every aspect commonly met—from placement and processing agreements to financial statements for borrowers to commercial financing forms. You get a total of 41 forms, many of which you can use directly without changing a word!)
* Complete guide to becoming a highly paid business broker in your spare time
* Fees you can collect as a business broker
* Starting with NO license, NO test, NO exams

* Which industries pay the biggest fees to you
* How to become a highly paid business consultant (fees to $1,000 a day!)
* Kinds of problems business broker/consultants solve (get paid big to suggest ideas)
* Get contracts for annual consulting fees
* How to become a highly paid finder in your spare time (turn leisure into BIG cash)
* What finders do—and where—and for what
* How much to charge for being a finder

* Typical finder-fee agreements you can use today
* How to be a successful business consultant
* How to pick a good plant site, get T&E fees
* Taking a company public—Regulation 'A' offerings
* Terms used in the Regulation; what they mean
* How to write a selling prospectus
* Samples of forms to be used for Reg 'A'

* Irrevocable appointment of you as an agent
* Offering stock through underwriters
* Registering with the SEC for the offering
* Loan packages—how to prepare them for approval
* SBIC—Small Business Investment Companies—what they do; how you can use them
* Advertising and office mailing flyer for your firm
* Typical promissory notes you can use—long & short
* Typical bank letter of credit; typical surety bond for a business loan
* Broker letter seeking lenders for clients
* Standby loan commitment for borrower
* Collateral assignment of policy for a business loan
* Plus four (4) 7 x 10 in. membership certificates in two colors suitable for framing and mounting in your office or den
* Plus much, much more to help YOU get started!

WHAT SOME OF THE USERS SAY ABOUT THIS GREAT FINANCIAL BROKER/FINDER KIT & Ty Hicks:

"Received Financial Broker Kit yesterday morning. Using info in it closed deal for $463,750 yesterday afternoon. Thank you. Best regards." Tennessee

"My financial brokerage business grossed $45,000 in (its first year). I am now working on starting a finance company." Virginia

"It was through your letter that I became a part-time financial broker, have been one for six months and have enjoyed several commissions!" Massachusetts

"...went out and borrowed $10,000 and bought a business brokerage representing small business opportunities. I was recently (1 year later) offered $25,000 for half of my brokerage." Pennsylvania

"My fee between two findings is $180,000." Montana

"I am under way and doing quite well. I have completed 1 merger deal and placed 2 loans for $78,000." Massachusetts

The great KIT contains 12 "Speed-Read" books, each 8.5x11 in., a total of some 500 pages, 4 ready-to-frame membership certificates and costs only $99.50. Send your check or money order TODAY!

IWS Inc., 24 Canterbury Rd, Rockville Ctr NY 11570

Yes, I do like money! And this sounds like the kind of break I've been looking for. Enclosed is $99.50 for the FINANCIAL BROKER/FINDER/BUSINESS BROKER CONSULTANT KIT. Please send it to me as soon as possible. I understand I can consult with Ty Hicks as a bonus for buying the KIT.

NAME _____ Apt/Suite # _____

ADDRESS _____

CITY _____ STATE _____ ZIP _____

To order by VISA or MASTERCARD, call Ty Hicks at 516-766-5850 day or night!

Figure 4-3

buyers. If you wanted to, you could increase this to 12 or 18 matches of traits and features. Doing so would increase your belief that the kit would make you a millionaire.

In real life the kit on which this example is based, K-1 at the back of this book, has sold many thousands of copies via mail order. And it has earned—and *is* earning—millions for its creator, your author. It is updated every six months and has generated countless testimonials like these:

> Received Financial Broker Kit yesterday morning. Using info in it, closed deal for $463,750 yesterday afternoon. Thank you. Best regards.

And

> My fee between two findings is $180,000.

And

> I am under way and doing quite well. I have completed one merger deal and placed two loans for $78,000.

Develop a good product like the *Financial Broker/ Finder/Business Broker/Business Consultant Kit* and it will sell for years, building your mailbox riches! Better yet—do your own thing for a good product and you'll have the whole market all to yourself. With such an approach you'll beat all your competitors every time!

Now that your product has *your* stamp of uniqueness, let's see how you'll sell it to bring cash into your mailbox every day. Because, after all:

> *The true measure of any mail-order business is whether the owner goes to the bank every day to make deposits. Cash flow is the key to success in every business—and especially in the mail-order business! So see that your cash flow is steady and rising.*

You're ready to take your next step in building solid-gold mail-order riches starting with little cash and working from your own home.

CHAPTER 5

START MAKING MILLIONS WITH LOW-COST PUBLICITY AND ADS

To MAKE MONEY in mail order, you must tell the world about your product or service. And the best way to do this is with ads in different media and with publicity.

There's just one small problem. When you start your mail-order business you're short on cash. To build your income you must turn to low-cost ways to tell the world what a great product or service you're offering. Let's see how you can bring in solid-gold profits on a peanut-size sales promotion budget.

Publicity Pays Profits

You can get free publicity for your product or service which will bring direct sales to you. For example:

A magazine writer publishing an article on financing small businesses mentioned our **Small Business Investment Company Directory and Handbook** *as one of several useful books on the subject. Just a two-line mention brought us hundreds of phone calls, almost all of which resulted in* *sales. These results show the enormous power of free publicity!*

How can *you* get free publicity for your product or service? It's easy. You just take these simple steps:

1. *Decide* what types of media (magazines, newspapers, radio stations, TV stations, etc.) would be interested in publicizing your product or service for the benefit of its readers, listeners, or viewers.
2. *Get a list* of the names and addresses of your target media. Do this by going to your local public library and getting a copy of *Standard Rate and Data* for the type of media you plan to use. You'll find this publication full of useful info on print media of many types. And in the same section of the library you'll find *Literary Marketplace*. It gives comprehensive lists of radio, TV, and cable stations you can use for publicity outlets.
3. *Copy* the name, address, telephone number, and name of the individual to address at each of your selected media outlets. Put this information in a file folder you set up for *Publicity*.
4. *Prepare,* or have someone prepare, a *News Release* that gives full info about your new mail-order product or service. The next section of this chapter shows you how to prepare, or oversee preparation of, a winning news release—one that gets you plenty of coverage.
5. *Send* your news release to your selected media. Then watch the orders roll in. A well-prepared news release can bring in hundreds of times its cost in actual sales. The profits on these sales can allow you to expand your publicity and advertising so your sales grow at a spectacular rate!

How to Prepare a Winning News Release

A news release (also called a *press* release) is a short (no more than two pages) description of a new product or service and the benefits offered users of the item or service. *Every news release must be typewritten!* You cannot—and will not—get free publicity with a hand-written or printed news release! Such items automatically go into the "circular file."

Winning news releases start with the benefits users obtain from the product or service. Then the release describes the product or service. The release closes with info on where the item or service can be obtained.

Every news release *must* be typewritten and double-spaced. Editors who work with news releases will often add or delete or rearrange info in the release. This cannot be done conveniently if the release is typed single space. So be sure every release is double-spaced throughout!

To write your news release, or to oversee someone who will write the release for you, take these steps:

1. *Isolate* the benefits of the product or service. Write the benefits out on a sheet of paper. Having the benefits in front of you on paper will often suggest other advantages of owning the product or using the service.
2. *Write a short description* of the product or service. Don't make your description too complex—people won't read your news release!
3. *Include data* on where the product or service can be obtained. If at all possible, be certain to include the price of your offering. This will help you get direct orders from readers of the news release.

You can see an actual example of a winning news release in Figure 5-1. This news release was sent out on a 8.5×11 inch paper—as should be *every* news release you prepare! But in the book it has been reduced in size so it can fit on the page.

As you'll note when you look over Figure 5-1, the news release starts with the benefits of the product. These are drawn in part from Figures 4-1 and 4-2, where they were developed earlier.

INTERNATIONAL WEALTH SUCCESS, Inc.

P. O. Box 186, Merrick, N. Y. 11566

FOR IMMEDIATE RELEASE

Financial Broker Kit Provides Quick Training

Aimed at people seeking to earn large fees quickly while working from home, the Financial Broker/Finder/Business Broker/Business Consultant Kit features easy-to-read Speed-Read manuals. Giving specific fee percentages and amounts to charge borrowers, the Kit also lists some 2,500 lenders. Names, addresses and telephone numbers are given for each lender listed.

People who can profit from this Kit include accountants, attorneys, real estate sales people and brokers, small business owners, and others seeking to raise their income. Financial brokerage is a needed and highly respected business. When acting as a financial broker a person seeks loans, venture capital, or grants for businesses and individuals.

To provide the widest possible income sources, the Kit also shows its users how to earn money as a finder, business broker, or business consultant. It is possible for one person to include all these functions in the services provided businesses and individuals. When doing so, the broker increases his or her income potential.

The Kit features 12 "Speed-Read" books, typical agreements used by financial brokers, four colorful membership cards, data on taking a company public, 2,500 active business and real estate lenders, plus full information on the fees to charge each client. Other data cover: what to name your business; pre-written news release to get free publicity, etc.

The complete Kit is available for $99.50 from IWS, Inc., 24 Canterbury Rd, Rockville Centre NY 11570. To order the Kit by credit card, call 1-800-323-0548. Use this number for orders only; the operators are not qualified to answer technical or business questions.

-30-

Figure 5-1

A number of other points illustrated by Figure 5-1, which will help you write, or supervise the writing of, news releases, are:

1. *Use* a good headline which the editor can insert without having to change it. Thus, the headline, "Financial Broker Kit Provides Quick Training" will probably be used (and was) as is. It's newsy, short, and to the point.

2. *Repeat* features you think will help sell your product or service. While the editor may delete the repeats, my findings show that they're left in more than they're taken out! Thus, the news release in Figure 5-1 repeats the number of lenders in the Kit (a very important *selling* feature), the fees to charge (what the user will earn), etc.

3. *Provide* a list of potential buyers. This defines the market for the product or service. It also tells the editor that the product or service is for the readers or listeners of the media in which the news release appears.

4. *Have the news release typed* on your company stationery. This gives the release greater credibility than when typed on a blank sheet of paper.

5. *Type* "For Immediate Release" at the top of the release. This lets the editor know that the release can be run immediately. Then you avoid having your release pushed aside and possibly lost.

6. *Type* —*30*— at the end of the release. Or just type —End—, whichever you prefer. If your release runs more than one page (it shouldn't), type at the bottom of the first page —More—. Then the editor will know that there's more info on the next page.

7. *Be sure to* give the price of your item or service (if you can), and the name and address where the reader should send the money. If you have an 800 toll-free number, give it too. You'll get a number of credit card orders this way.

Get Your Release Out to Bring in Sales

Once your release is finished, and proofread, take it to a quick-copy shop. Order at least 100 copies of the release printed. Don't be cheap with news releases. If you can't find outlets for at least 100 copies, your product or service probably won't make you rich in mail order!

Send your releases via first class mail. This way, they'll get to the news outlet faster. And you'll be seeing money in your mailbox sooner. That, after all, is the whole purpose you have in doing the news release. You're doing it to make money. And the sooner, the better!

Get Better Results with Your News Releases

News releases can generate many thousands of dollars of income for you—if you use them right! Most Beginning Wealth Builders (BWBs I call them) send a few copies of their news release out and give up. This is wrong, very wrong. To get better results from your news releases:

1. *Send each release* to as many outlets as you can find— magazines, newspapers, radio stations, TV stations, cable outlets, etc.
2. *If in doubt* about whether an outlet will use your news release, send it to the outlet! While your release is in someone's hands it *may* be published. But while the release is on your desk you can be sure it will *not* be published by that outlet!
3. *Remember—at all times—*a release costing a few pennies to send can generate millions of times its cost in sales.
4. *Recognize* that a news writeup for your product or service makes it easier for you to sell to stores and consumers. Why? Because the name of your product or service will have been seen by thousands—and, perhaps, millions—of people. So each news release that's published paves the way for future sales!
5. *Don't overlook foreign* news outlets. There are

thousands of magazines and newspapers around the world that might print your news release. This can bring you extra lucrative business. And—when you are ready to take space ads for your item or service— you can boast that your product or service is used all over the world. Then of course you have the foregin radio and TV outlets. Send them a copy of your news release also.

6. *Reprint copies* of your news release as it appears in a magazine or newspaper. Use this in mailings with the line "As seen in the pages of *Popular Marketing* magazine." Your product or service benefits from the good name of the magazine. If you get TV coverage, run a small photo or drawing of a TV screen showing an illustration from the show. And run the line "As seen on Channel 94 in 45 cities around the country." Again, the good reputation of Channel 94 rubs off on your product or service, giving you instant credibility and acceptance.

7. *Keep sending out copies* of your news release. The more copies that are in the hands of New Products Editors and station personnel, the greater your chances of getting favorable coverage.

8. *Prepare* (or have someone prepare) a complete news release for every new product you put on the market. And keep each news release circulating to every media outlet you can find. Do this and the sales results could astound you and build your bank account to its highest level ever!

9. *Never forget*—the space you get in a publication or on the air for a news release is *free*—it doesn't cost you a dime! So the more you work at getting news releases into the right hands, the greater your sales from this source will be.

To see how effective news releases can be, let me give you a real-life example from my own successful mail-order fortune-building. It will show you the enormous power of free publicity:

As some of my readers know, I'm a "boat nut," having owned several yachts of increasing size. Also, as an

Post Office Box 186 • Merrick, New York 11566

Marine Products & Services Division

HI MARINERS! WELCOME ABOARD! VISIT THE SEAGOING PILOTS SHOP! SEE OUR PRODUCTS!
EXAMINE AND USE THE WORLD'S BEST COASTWISE PILOTING AIDS! WE'RE SURE YOU'LL BUY!
MEET TY HICKS, KNOWN WORLDWIDE FOR EASY, SIMPLIFIED "FIGURING" METHODS THAT WORK
HOURS: Weekdays: 9:00 AM--5:00 PM; 7:30 PM--10:00 PM

   Weekends: 10:00 AM--5:00 PM Sat & Sunday. (Ty is aboard BOTH days).
   7:30 PM--9:30 PM

GET 30 MINUTES OF EASY-TO-FOLLOW INSTRUCTIONS ON HOW TO USE OUR 10 PILOT-AIDS*
AND YOU'LL BE A MUCH BETTER COASTWISE NAVIGATOR. SEE HOW BOTH COMMERCIAL AND
PLEASURE BOAT OPERATORS THROUGHOUT THE WORLD MAKE SAFER COASTWISE PASSAGES AND
LONG TRIPS WITH THE IWS PILOT-AIDS*. KNOWN FOR YEARS AS "The coastwise pilot's
best friend." See how they work under actual sea conditions in the SEAGOING
PILOTS SHOP And while you're aboard, look over our books and courses. We're
so sure that you'll buy that we make this one-of-a-kind offer: GET A QUICK,
EASY COURSE IN PILOTING FREE--JUST FOR YOUR VISIT! In 30 minutes YOU might
learn something which could help you reach SAFE HARBOR sooner, with fewer
worries! So COME ON ABOARD, FRIEND. YOU'LL BE GLAD YOU DID--AND SO WILL WE!
USE THE COUPON BELOW TO ORDER NOW YOUR 10 PILOT-AIDS*--just $24.00; a $1.00
saving for those customers that visit us NOW! Yes--please send P-A, No. 1-10.

NAME_____

ADDRESS_____

CITY_____STATE_____ZIP_____

*Registered Tradename.

SEE ATTACHED SAMPLES OF THE CHARTS!

Figure 5-2

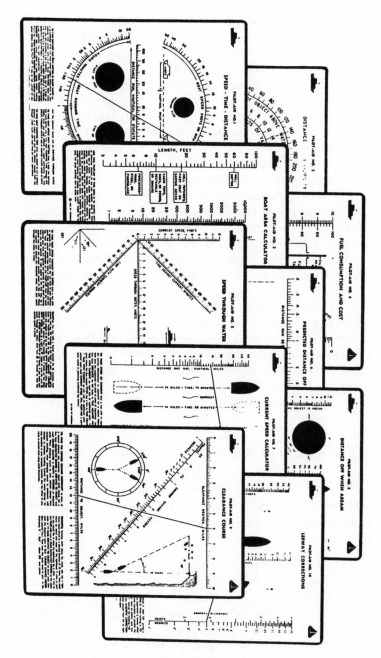

Figure 5-2 a

engineer, I applied my mathematical ability to boating piloting problems. The result was ten charts laminated in plastic, called "Pilot Guides." When we first put these on the market for boaters, our marketing budget was very low. So I decided to get as much free publicity as I could.

Preparing a comprehensive writeup like Figure 5-2, we sent it to every interested publication, radio, and TV station. The response was great. And since we included a photo of one of the guides with the release, we were given more magazine space than if we had just had a writeup without an illustration.

Sales boomed because we gave the price of each item in our group of ten. Orders poured in. We were so busy we had to hire high school kids to come in to open the mail. Once we had so much mail in the living room of my home that we couldn't see the carpet. It was covered with sacks of mail that had just arrived from the post office!

Total sales from our first news release were over $60,000 in just a few months. Following the tips above, we enclosed copies of the new product releases from many boating magazines when we sent ads to mail-order houses whose business we sought. To our delight, they already knew about our "Pilot Guides" and ordered immediately.

This gave another boost to our already strong sales.

Use a Photo or Sketch to Get More Space

In years of sending out news releases on products and services, I've learned a few things which put big money into my deep pocket every day of the week. These basic tips are:

1. *Always use* a photo or drawing with your news release, if you can. You will automatically get more space in the magazine because most submitted pictures *are* run. And editors love drawings. So these are usually also run by the publication.
2. *Submit only* glossy photos. Editors cannot use any other type of photo in most magazines. This means

that four-color photos and non-glossy black-and-white photos are unsuitable. Of course, if a magazine or newspaper uses four-color photos in its New Products columns, you can send such photos. But the usual photo is a black-and-white glossy. Stick with it! Drawings should be in black ink on white paper.

3 *Send only one photo* with each news release. Editors seldom run more than one photo per release. So you're just wasting photos when you send more than one. The same is true of drawings.

4. *Be certain to mark* your product or service name and the company name on the back of the photo or drawing. Then there's little chance that *your* photo will be run with someone else's product description! Use a grease pencil so the photo is not damaged.

The name of the game in publicity is to get as much space as possible. You've no doubt heard the famous quote, "There's no such thing as bad publicity so long as you spell my name right!" In mail order this quote might be changed to read: "There's no such thing as bad publicity so long as you give me a lot of space!"

Thus, suppose a magazine charges $4,200 for a full-page ad. This is a typical going rate these days. If you get a one-column writeup, with photo, of your product or service, this is one-third of a page. So your news release got you $4,200/3 = $1,400 worth of free space! That's a lot of value for just one sheet of paper and one photo. Figure 5-2 shows an illustrated news release.

And the sales which develop as a result of your news release will add to that value. Depending on the price of your product or service, your one-column news release should bring in anywhere from $4,000 to $8,000 in sales. Again, not bad for one sheet of paper and one photo! Now let's move on to your next step in building mailbox millions—low cost ads.

Build Your Sales with Low-Cost Ads

If you're selling by mail order, you'll have to advertise. Publicity can take you just so far. Then you must start to pay for space in a publication. (But there *is* a way to get free ads for your products or services, which we'll show you later in this chapter.)

What kinds of ads are lowest in cost? The quick answer is *classified ads.* You've no doubt read hundreds of such ads when looking for an item you want to buy. Some people spend hours *every* month reading classified ads in their favorite publication. I read classified ads in magazines and newspapers *every* day—just to keep up with who's selling what!

Classified ads—by their name—are run under various classifications like these:

Money Available	Money Wanted
Sales Opportunities	Books and Courses
Finance	Moneymaking Opportunities
Inventions	Mailing Lists
Cash Grants	Business Opportunities
Catalogs	Government Surplus
Personal	Multi-Level Marketing
	Etc.

To make big money from classified ads, take these easy steps once you know what you'll sell by mail order:

1. **Decide** which publications you'll run your ads in, after you've looked over the candidates you think will be suitable for selling your item or service. *Key Idea:* You can get free back issues of any publication that you think you'd like to advertise in by writing the Advertising Manager (or calling on the phone) and asking for their Rate Card and sample issues. The same is true of radio and TV stations, except that they will send you tapes of previous programs.
2. **Select** the classified category under which you want your ad to run. *Key Idea:* If your offering is so unusual that it doesn't fit under any of the regular categories

used for classified ads, ask the publication to use a new and different category just for your ad. This way your ad will be the only one under the new category. As such, it is almost certain to get wide readership—which is exactly what you want!

3. *Write,* or have someone write, your classified ad. For your first few ads, I suggest that you write them yourself. Why? Because you'll learn how important each word in your ad is. *Key Idea:* Write *every* classified ad so it is as short as possible! Why? Because it costs you less to run and it will usually pull better. See the next section of this chapter for tips on writing classified ads that fill your mailbox with inquiries every day!

4. *Place* your classified ads by sending a typed version to each publication in which the ad is to run. Since payment is usually required with the ad, include your check. *Key Idea:* The measure of the effectiveness of your classified ad is the dollar sales it produces. Some large-circulation publications will produce hundreds

| Month of *June*, 19 - -   Product No. 12   List price: $100 |
| Publication Name *Opportunity* Ad Pub. Date *May 1*   Key *M-9* |

Day of Month	1	2	3	4	5	6	7	8		30	31	Total Sales
Sales, Units	10	4	6	3	8	9	5	2		2	1	312
Sales, $	1,000	400	600	300	800	900	500	200		200	100	31,200
Remarks	*This is our first $100 product. It's*											
	doing well in this publication!											

Figure 5-3

(or thousands) of inquiries. But they don't *convert*—that is, send you money when you send them your advertising materials. Yet some smaller publications which produce many fewer inquiries will convert at a 25 percent rate—i.e., 25 out of every 100 people who inquire about your offer will buy it. Such conversions help you take money to the bank every day of the week! This is the ultimate test of an ad outlet—does it put money in your bank. So be careful to place your classified ads in publications that pull for you!

5. *Keep* an accurate record of your ad results. Use a form like that in Figure 5-3. Don't try to slide by without an ad control form. You'll only get very confused and you won't know which ads are making money for you. *Key Idea:* Be sure to figure your Cost per Inquiry (Ad Cost/Number of Inquiries Received from the Ad). The lower the cost per inquiry, the better your business efficiency. Why? Because you can sell your inquiry names in the form of a mailing list and make money from them. Some mail-order dealers make as much—or more—from their list rentals than they do from the sale of product! That's one of the success secrets of this business that few people know.

How to Write Money-Getting Classified Ads

Classifieds can stuff your mailbox with money-getting inquiries every day of the week. But you must follow these general rules if you want the best results:

1. *Don't ask for money* in the classified ad. It's certain to reduce your response rate if you try to sell something for $15 to $100 from the few words in a classified ad. And if you ask for $1.00 for postage and handling (P&H), your response rate will also fall. Build response by being willing to pay the postage cost to get information to people who respond to your ad!

2. ***Offer free information*** to your ad readers. They'll respond "like crazy" and you can always make money renting their names—even if they don't buy from you.

3. ***Make the first few words*** of your ad attention-getting so the reader finishes your ad. You'll see a number of such leadoffs (sometimes called a *headline*) later in this chapter. Many readers will decide whether to finish your ad after seeing the first few words. So make them as strong as you can!

4. ***Make every word in your ad work.*** Go over your ad again and again. Cut out every word that doesn't work. This will make your ad pull better, while reducing its cost. Why? Because you pay for classified ads on the basis of the number of words in the ad.

Let's take a typical classified ad and see how we can apply the principles given above. We'll use the product covered in Figure 5-1 as the subject of our ad. Features we'd like to include in the ad, from Figure 4-1, are:

- Make money quickly
- Work from home
- 2,500 loan sources
- Big fees possible
- Quick training

Using these features, we take a first pass at the ad thus:

MAKE MONEY QUICKLY from home in your own business using 2,500 loan sources to help you earn big fees as a financial broker. Quick training for all. Free details. Write ABC Co., 123 Main St. Anytown 00000.

This ad has 37 words. At $5.00 per word (a typical charge for large-circulation publications), your ad cost would be $5 x 37 + $185.00. That's a fairly high price, especially if you're not yet sure what response you'll get. So let's tighten up this ad to make it stronger and less costly. Here's our second pass:

FINANCIAL BROKERS MAKE MONEY QUICKLY at home. Big fees; quick training; 2,500 loan sources. Free information. ABC Co., 123 Main St, Anytown 00000.

Your ad now has 23 words. Yet it gives the same information as earlier. To save money, ask your Postmaster at your local post office if you can leave off your company name (you usually *can*) and the word "Street" from your address (you usually *can*). Your ad now becomes:

FINANCIAL BROKERS MAKE HOME MONEY QUICKLY. Big fees. Quick training. 2,500 loan sources. Free information. ABC, 123 Main, Anytown 00000.

Your ad is now just 20 words—a good length for this type of product. It's tight, factual, and easy to understand. And it will cost you much less—just $100.00 at $5.00 per word, compared to the $185.00 on your first version.

Note that the first few words of your ad are run in full capitals. Why? Because this highlights your message. Attention-getting first words that can pull in the inquiries for you include:

- MONEY FOR YOU NOW ...
- SECRETS OF ...
- HOW TO ...
- TODAY YOU CAN ...
- TEN LOANS FOR ...
- QUICK WAYS TO ...
- EASY WAYS TO ...
- CASHMAKING IDEAS FOR ...
- MONEYMAKING METHODS TO ...
- SURE-FIRE WAYS TO ...
- FREE REPORT SHOWING HOW TO ...
- BE YOUR OWN BOSS IN ...
- MAKE MAIL MILLIONS IN ...
- GET RICH IN ...
- MAKE EXPORT-IMPORT RICHES ...
- BE A LOAN BROKER ...
- GO FULLY FINANCED TO ...
- BEAT THE BANK ...
- CASH CREDIT RICHES TO ...
- ZERO-CASH WAYS TO ...
- GET A SELF-LIQUIDATING LOAN TO ...
- GET LOANS BY PHONE ...
- LOANS BY MAIL FOR ...

- GUARANTEED MONTHLY INCOME ...
- LOW-COST REAL-ESTATE FINANCING ...
- MAKE MONEY FROM MONEY ...
- GUARANTEED LOAN MONEY ...
- FREE MONEY GRANTS TO ...
- MAKE A FORECLOSURE FORTUNE ...
- OWN A MONEY MACHINE TO ...
- CAN YOU AFFORD NOT TO BE A MILLION-AIRE? ...
- HOW TO MAKE A FORTUNE ...
- HOW TO FIND MONEY TO ...
- HOW TO FIND VENTURE CAPITAL MIL-LIONS ...
- OWN YOUR OWN COLLECTION AGENCY ...
- MAKE MILLIONS IN AUTO/TRUCK LEASING ...
- Etc.

I'm sure you can come up with better attention-getters than these. But I've used a number of them and they really work! Thus, one classified ad I run that reads:

GET FAST LOANS NOW. Full info free. IWS POB 186 Merrick NY 11566.

regularly brings in thousands of dollars a year. Yet it costs me only a few hundreds a year to run!

And I don't have to change the ad. Why? Because it pulls so well as it is—just 12 words—that changing it would be risking disaster. That's what's so great about classified ads. If you write (or have someone write) a good ad, you can run it for 50 years and still make money from it!

Foxy-Smart Ways to Run Free Ads

But suppose you can't afford to run a classified ad for your product or service? What can you do to get started? There are a number of steps you can take, such as:

1. *Run commission ads* in publications of your choice having readers who are prospects for your product or service. Do the same on radio or TV.

2. **Run Per-Inquiry (PI) ads** in publications or on radio or TV programs. You have little up-front cost; you pay only for the actual inquries you get.

Let's look at each of these two ways to get free ads. They could put you on the road to your mailbox millions!

Commission Ads

With a *commission ad* you arrange with a publication to run either a full-page, half-page, quarter-page, etc., ad for free. Or you have a radio or TV station run a 30-second, 60-second, etc., commercial for free. With either media, you offer an item for sale.

Orders come to the publication or station. Most commission ads request payment with the order. So the organization running the ad knows exactly:

- How many orders were placed for the product or service
- How much money was paid for what was ordered

The publication or station deducts its commission— usually 33 1/3 percent from the money received and sends you the balance, along with copies of the orders. You then ship the product, keeping all the money sent to you. From this money you pay your expenses.

How do you set up commission ad deals? That's easy. You just:

1. **Decide** where you want to advertise. The pros and cons of various media are covered later in this book. We'll assume for the moment that you know—in a general way—the types of publications and stations that are read, listened to, or watched by your prospects.
2. **Contact** the media by telephone or mail. Ask about their commission ad policies. You'll find a number of publications *are* willing to consider carrying your ads on a commission basis. If you'd prefer to write publications or stations, use a letter like that in Figure 5-4. it covers the major points in any commission ad deal.

<u>YOUR LETTERHEAD</u>

Dear Publisher:

Are you interested in earning more money from the advertising pages of your excellent publication? If you are, we have a plan for you which is ideal for your readership. Here's how this plan works.

We publish reference books and other materials for the field your publication serves, namely---------------------(name of field). These books and other materials offer valuable information to your readers and do not compete with the data you publish in your publication.

What we do is supply you--at no charge--with camera-ready ads in a variety of sizes, full-page, half-page, two-thirds page, one-third page, and one-quarter-page, for your publication. All you need do is insert an ad when you have open space. The ads are written so your reader sends you a check for the publication he or she wants to buy.

You deposit the check and deduct your commission of one-third of the list price of the book or other material. Thus, if a book has a list price of $36, you receive a check for this amount, deduct your commission of 1/3, or $12, and send us the balance, or $24.

Once we receive your check we drop-ship the book to your customer at no cost to you. Since there are very few returns of these books, this completes the transaction. If a reader should return a book, we still allow you to keep the commission earned and make an adjustment on future sales of this or another book. Such adjustments are rarely needed.

To start this plan, just sign in the space provided below and we'll send you a supply of our camera-ready ads. Once you receive the ads all you need do is enter the name and address of the department you want to receive the orders. Then sit back and let your staff insert the ads on a space-available basis.

Every publisher we've worked with in the past has been happy with the results this program produces. We're sure you'll be happy with it too, particularly since it puts idle space to work earning money for you at no significant cost of any kind.

If you have any questions concerning this commission-ad plan, please call me. I'll be glad to answer them.

Meanwhile, we look forward to your signed agreement so we can send ads to you.

Very truly yours,

Your name and title

I hereby agree to the commission advertising plan detailed above. Please send me the camera-ready ads to start this plan.

_____   _____   _____
         Name   Title   Date

PS: Please sign and return to us one copy of this letter. Kindly keep the other copy for your files.

Figure 5-4

3. *Continue* expanding your commission ad offers to as many publications or stations as you can. Don't give up after placing a few ads! Why? Because in mail order, your ads *must* run month after month, if you want to build big riches. On-again, off-again ads seldom build the level of income you seek.

Commission ads will even be set in type by publications seeking to increase their cash flow. So all you really need supply is the copy—that is, the words that make up the ad. You should write your first few ads yourself. Why? You'll learn a lot about your offer and about ad writing! Once your income is high enough, you can hire a copywriter to write your ads for you. Such ads *may* pull better than your own. Then again, they may not! You won't know until you try.

Per-Inquiry (PI) Ads

With a PI ad you pay only for the inquiries the ad generates. Thus, if you run an ad in a magazine or a commercial on the air:

- You pay some agreed-on price—like 50¢—for each inquiry received by the media and sent to you
- The media does nothing more than deliver the inquiry to you. You must send additional ad material to the prospect; the media will *not* do that for you!

PI ads are attractive because you don't have to lay out any money up front. But you could be hit with a big bill, as a friend of mine was. Since it was a bit embarrassing to him, I won't mention his name. But:

A newsletter publisher took a PI classified ad space in a Sunday supplement. The circulation is in the many millions. But he didn't expect more than about 1,000 inquiries; at 25¢ each his cost would be only $250—an acceptable amount to him. But he was shocked to get 11,000 inquiries at a cost of $2,750! Fortunately, he could afford to pay the bill. And the inquiries converted at

an acceptable level. But he stayed away from PI ads until
he could work through the 11,000 names.

So pick your PI ad outlets carefully. Try to estimate how many inquiries you'll get. Then add at least 50 percent of this to get a possible maximum. Be sure you have enough money to pay for the inquiries you may get! No sense starting your business with a debt you can't pay!

In dealing with PI ad outlets, listen to the estimates the media person gives you. They're experienced in this field. Often they can tell you within a few hundred how many inquiries you'll get.

Steer Clear of Bargain Ads

As a BWB in mail order, you may be approached by leaflet mailers who offer to run 1-inch display ads for $1 each. Your first reaction is: "Gee, this is great. This person promises to mail 10,000 leaflets and my ad will cost me only one buck. And for another buck he'll even set the ad in type for me. I can't go wrong!

Sure, it sounds great. But there's only one catch: Such ads almost *never* even bring back the dollar you spent on them! Leaflet mailers send their poorly printed flyers to other leaflet mailers. So they're trying to sell to each other. Result? No one buys anything!

Other low-cost ad outlets will charge you $45 for a full-page ad. Again, it sounds great. The only trouble is that the ads don't pull. You're out $45 and don't have anything to show for it.

The basic mail-order principle at work here is this:

Cheap ads give you suspects, not *prospects*. Suspects rarely buy; prospects usually buy at a fairly predictable rate. To reach prospects, you must either pay the going ad cost, or use the low-cost methods given above. There are no "free lunches" in the field of mail-order ads! .

Now that we know how to get free publicity and ads,

let's move to "the king of the hill" in mail order—the full-page space ad. We'll show you how to make a fortune from well-written full-page ads that have great impact. And bring in enough for *your* mailbox millions!

CHAPTER 6

MOVE INTO
BIG-SALES SPACE ADS

CLASSIFIED ADS BRING in inquiries. You convert these into sales by a two-step process—(1) get the inquiry; (2) send data and make the sale.

Space ads, which typically run from one-sixth of a page to a full page, or more, make a sale directly. That is, you can ask the ad reader to send you money by mail, by one of the courier services, or by calling you directly (preferably on a toll-free 800 number) and ordering by credit card. Space ads have many advantages for you. They:

- Bring direct, measurable results within a short time span—one day, one week, one month
- Deliver cash to your bank account without the intermediate steps of sending ad material, waiting for a decision, receiving payment, etc.
- Allow the sale of high-priced items directly to the user, improving your annual sales

Offsetting these advantages are several considerations worth looking at, namely:

- Space-ad costs are many times that of classified ads' costs. Thus, a typical space ad in an "opportunity type" magazine may run $2,500, compared to $150 for a classified ad in the same publication.
- Space ads take time to write. While you can always have a copywriter do a space ad for you, it's best—in my view—

that you write the ad yourself. Not only do you save money—you quickly learn what brings in the big bucks from your readers.

- Space ads require more planning than classified ads. You have such a long message available in a space ad that you want to be sure that what you're saying ties in with your other marketing efforts for your mail-order company.

Still, space ads are the "king of the hill" in the mail-order business today. Let's see how *you* can use space ads to build your mailbox millions.

Pick Your Ad Outlets

Each space ad will cost you a bundle. But if it brings in two, three, four bundles in sales, it's cheap! So your main goal is:

1. *Choose* ad outlets—magazines, newspapers, newsletters, etc.—that will give you the largest sales possible from each ad you run.
2. *Get data* on the ad rate from each publication you choose. Just write or call the publication and they'll send you, free of charge, their latest "Rate Card" plus a few back issues of the publication.
3. *Decide* which publication is best for your product or service. Do this by taking the step in the next section— that is, study your competitors' ads to see if your offering would be attractive to the same market served by your competition.

Talk to ad professionals and you'll hear various expressions like "Cost per 'M,'" "quality of readership," etc. Don't let these throw you when you're picking ad outlets. True, the cost per M (cost per thousand readers) is important. But what's more important to you is whether your ad is in the right publication for what you're offering.

Suppose, for example, you're thinking of running a full-page ad in a publication that charges $2,500 per page and has a circulation of 250,000 copies. Your cost per M = $2,500/250 = $10. This means it will cost you $10 to reach 1,000 readers of this publication.

If another publication costs $3,600 per page and has 180,000 circulation, its cost per M = $3,600/180 = $20. So the first publication is the better buy because it costs you half as much to reach 1,000 readers. Right?

Perhaps. Perhaps not! The real key is how many dollars you bring in from each ad. If the first ad brings in $5,000 in sales and the second ad brings in $10,800, the second publication is much better for you, even though the ad is more costly! Here's a real-life example:

For years we've run the full-page ad in Figure 6-1 in a number of opportunity magazines. (If you want to know their names, call me and I'll tell you.) In one magazine we pay $2,200 for the full-page ad. In another we pay $1,800. Yet the higher priced publication brings in two to three times its cost, month after month. The lower priced ad brings in only one times its cost. We're no longer in the lower priced publication—for obvious reasons!

Now let's see how you can learn from your competition. You can use them to make yourself rich in mail order.

Study Your Competition

With your selected publications in front of you, take these easy and simple steps:

1. *Go through* each publication and note which full-page and part-page ads are run.
2. *Make a list* of the page numbers on which ads for items or services similar to yours appear.
3. *Record* the size of the ad (full- or part-page), price of the item offered, location of the ad (front inside cover, run of the book, back cover, etc.), whether color is used in the ad, etc.
4. *Try to get* back issues of the publication for the last 6 months. See if the same ad appears in the publication.

The Money Raiser's Directory of Bank Credit Card Programs
CREDIT CARD SUCCESS SECRETS
How would you like to know *before* you apply for a major bank credit card, just what that specific bank requires before they'll grant you the credit card you want? Well, now it's possible with credit card expert Louis R. Gorchoff's exciting new book, *The Money Raiser's Directory of Bank Credit Card Programs*.
Satisfy Your Credit Needs To The Maximum!
• For the first time ever in a new, easy-to-read and useful format, learn the inside secrets as to how a bank chooses who receives their VISA & MasterCards.
• Choose from nearly 1,000 financial card programs, of the 500 largest U.S. banks.
• Discover exactly what each of these banks require from you to receive their credit cards, so you can choose to apply to the one's that *won't turn you down*.
• Learn about interest rates that range from an amazingly low 8.0% to 22.2%, so you can decide which is right for you.
• Discover what banks have 'Gold' card requirements so *easy* you can qualify even if you've been turned down for a 'regular' bank credit card.
• Each bank's Regular and Gold VISA/MasterCard programs include the following information listed: Card holder fee, Interest rate, Minimum annual income for approval, Credit line range, Toll free number/address for application and much more.
• Have the realistic advantage of obtaining multiple credit cards, five, ten, twenty or more... all *legally* received!
• Some individuals have obtained cards giving them $50,000.00, $75,000.00, even over $100,000.00 *or more... all legally received!*
• Use your multiple cards to take advantage of investments, real estate, home downpayment, cars, start, expand or buy a business and many other opportunities you *used* to have to *pass up*.
• Use your credit cards for powerful investment leverage, learn where individual credit lines are offered from $5,000 to $25,000, and more! Unsecured, on your signature alone.
• Play the credit game to win and get the things you deserve in life.
• Whether you have credit cards or want your first credit card, our book will help you find the right bank credit card program for you.
• Everything done by mail, no long drawn-out red tape... just short applications.
• You'll learn what you need to know with credit card expert Louis R. Gorchoff's exciting new one of a kind book, "The Money Raiser's Directory of Bank Credit Card Programs."
• Why wait? These banks WANT you to have their cards. Everything you need to know to get YOURS is right here! Over 100 pages.
Here's Proof!
"So far it's been only 10 weeks from the time I received your book... I have obtained exactly 13 VISA and MasterCard 'Gold' charge cards. I expect to receive even more... undoubtedly, the greatest immediate access to sources of money. Thank you for your help." —S. Levin/Marne, MI
"Your exciting book is virtually THE shopping guide for Bank Credit Cards... brilliant. This has been the wisest decision, to easily, getting any additional BankCards." — E. Schoen/Houston, TX
"I imagined the thrill of going to my mailbox and finding it filled with BankCards I applied for. No, it wasn't a dream... I never expected to be approved on so many. The information in this one book is the most helpful I've ever purchased... what a breeze!" —Nicole G./Pacific Palisades, CA
An Exclusive Offer
Order from this ad and get a FREE copy of the 64-pg book HOW TO GET A MAJOR CREDIT CARD WITH NO CREDIT CHECK, plus a list of card issuers! Order NOW!
Special FREE Bonuses
IF YOU ORDER NOW!
1. "How To Make Money With Credit Cards." A $9.95 value. Your Cost: FREE!
2. SECRET BONUS - Little known "Secrets To Beating The Credit System In Obtaining Multiple Credit Cards." A $10.95 value. Your cost: FREE!
These bonuses alone are worth more than the price of this book.
© Copyright Louis R. Gorchoff
ORDER FORM
ONLY $19.95
TO IWS, Inc.,
24 Canterbury Rd.
Rockville Centre, NY 11570
☐YES I'm tired of waiting for the credit lines I deserve! RUSH ME your one of a kind, information-packed book "THE MONEY RAISER'S DIRECTORY OF BANK CREDIT CARD PROGRAMS." NOW! I understand that it will show me where I can apply and have a realistic advantage of obtaining multiple credit cards, five, ten, twenty or more, all legally. I further understand that it will show me where to take advantage of interest rates that range from an amazingly low 8.0% to 22.2%, so I can decide which is right for me. Please send me ___ copies. I've enclosed a check or money order for $19.95 for each directory.
☐I've enclosed an additional $3.00 for super rush 1st class delivery.
Name (please print) ______
Address ______
City ______ State ______ Zip ______

Figure 6-1

5. ***Continue doing this*** until you've listed all your competitors' ads.

Next, draw some conclusions from your study. Thus, in general, you'll find that:

- Ads for similar products bode well for you. If a number of firms are advertising the same, or similar, products, they must be making sales. You too can make sales!
- If a full-page (or partial-page) ad has been running six months or longer, it means that the ad *is* working for the advertiser. A similar ad would also work for *you!*
- Existence of competition isn't bad! The more people there are selling a given type of product or service, the larger—in general—the market and the sales. So you should welcome the competition. It keeps the public aware of the importance of what you're selling! So each sale *you* make is easier to do because you don't have to spend a lot of space on convincing the potential buyer that your product or service is important!
- It pays to pay attention to the price your competition is charging for its offer. Don't under-price your offer! You will only lose dollars that you might have otherwise made. For example: My firm advertised via a full-page ad an excellent book priced at $10 a copy. For years we sold about 200 copies from each ad, bringing in somewhat over $2,000 each month. Then we developed another, similar, book. But we priced it at $20 and ran full-page ads in the same publication. Result? We still sell somewhat over 200 copies from each full-page ad. But we bring in over $4,000 from each ad—twice as much as from the first ad. So, *never under-price your product or service.*

Once you've studied the competition, decide which outlets you'll advertise in. The best way to do this is to rank the outlets in a 1, 2, 3 fashion. No. 1 is the most desirable outlet; next is No. 2, etc.

Contact each outlet and get a price quote. Do this even though you already have the rate card from each publication. Why should you do this? Read on!

Negotiate the Best Price Possible

Never pay the rate-card rate for a page of advertising!
If you learn nothing else from this book, keep the above
principle in mind. Thus, in recent months I was able to
negotiate the following deals:

> A $4,400 rate-card price down to $2,200
> A $3,500 rate-card price down to $1,800
> A $4,000 rate-card price down to $2,200

Only fools pay full rate at any publication today! Don't
you be the fool that wastes money paying rate-card rate.

How do you negotiate a rate reduction? That's easy. You
just take these fun steps, *after* you've chosen an ad outlet:

1. *Call* the ad manager of the publication. Identify
   yourself, your firm, and your product or service.
2. *Tell* the ad manager you're thinking of taking a full-
   page (or lesser amount) space ad in the next issue of
   the publication.
3. *Ask* the rate for the amount of space you seek—even
   though you already know this from the Rate Card.
4. *When told,* say "Gee, that sounds rather high. I was
   hoping to get the space for a lot less." You'll be told
   that the publication is the best in its field, that it delivers
   all kinds of desirable buyers, etc. Listen politely to
   what you're told. Then say, "But your price still sounds
   very high to me. We're just a small firm starting out.
   We really don't have the kind of money you're charging
   for such an ad."
5. *Close out* the conversation by saying: "You have a
   great publication and we'd love to be in it. But the
   price you're asking is just too high for us at this time."
   Be polite; compliment the ad manager and the
   publication. But never pay the asking price!

Within a week or so, I'm almost certain that the ad
manager will call you back and say: "What would you
be willing to pay for a full-page ad?"

This is where your extraordinary negotiating skills come
into play. You answer: "I really don't want to tell you

what I'll pay because it might be an insult to you. You tell me what you'll charge me for a full page."

The reason I suggest that you answer this way is because you want the publication to set the price. Then you can react to it—either for or against. If you set the price you're locked into a number. And in most cases BWBs will give a number that's too high! I don't want *you* to do that.

The ad manager may do one of two things: (1) give you a price right then and there, or (2) say, "If you won't give us a price, we really can't do business." If he says that, say: "Thanks so much for calling. I really appreciate it. If you should change your mind, give me a ring."

Sure enough, a few days later the ad manger will probably call and say: "How about $1,900 for that page?" This price will probably be one-half the rate-card price. If you like it, take it! But *never* pay rate-card price!

Other Ways to Save on Space Ad Costs

You can use other ways to save on space-ad cost. Here are a few ways worth looking at:

1. Buy remnant space.
2. Swap names for space.
3. Run ads for space.
4. Run commission ads.

Let's look at each of these ways of saving money on space ads of all sizes.

Buy Remnant Space

Each month, many magazines have a few pages of ad space to fill because other advertisers canceled at the last moment, salespeople couldn't sell the space, etc. Yet—to make a publication having a certain number of pages— the publisher must sell this space. Such space is called *remnant space* because:

- You don't know in advance where it will be in the publication
- You *must* have an ad—ready to go—in the hands of the publication to be slipped in as the magazine goes to press
- Your cost will be only 20 to 30 percent of the regular space rate. Beggars can't be choosers!

But you *will* save 70 to 80 percent of the rate-card rate when you take remnant space. So if you know that you want to have your ad in a certain publication, call the ad manager and tell that person you'd like to be considered for remnant space. You'll probably be told that "We *never* have such space."

You will respond: "I understand. But I'd like to send you an ad to keep on hand, anyway. Then, in case you do have some remnant space, you can run my ad."

The ad manager will probably respond: "Well, if you insist on sending your ad in, we'll keep it on hand. But I don't think we'll have any remnant space. Our 'book' is always filled."

A few weeks later you'll probably get a call from the ad manager saying: "For the first time in years we had a page open up. So we're running your ad. Please send us $ _____ today!" You've made it!

Swap Names for Space

The opportunity magazines in which we advertise are constantly looking for new names. So they often come to us saying: "Do you have any recent buyer names? If you do, we'll be glad to swap them for space."

Today we get $200 worth of space for every 1,000 buyer names we supply a publication. So with 10,000 names we can "buy" a $2,000 full-page ad! *You* can do the same— once you build a list of buyers on your computer. Then all you need do is have someone press a button to spew out the thousands of names you want to swap for space.

Be sure *not* to pay rate-card rates on space you swap

for names! Instead, negotiate with the ad manager to get the lowest rock-bottom rate possible!

Run Ads for Space

If you have a newsletter, magazine, or other publication (books, kits, etc.) you can run ads in these and get credit for space in the publication for whom you're running ads. This is called *space swapping* and it's done every day of the week.

Set a nice high price for your space ads. Then you'll get more space when you swap with another publication.

Don't overlook running ads in books. It's allowed. And you *can* charge a much higher ad rate for a book since a book stays around longer than a monthly or weekly magazine.

When you swap space you can even do so with your competitors. Why? Well, most publishers regard space swapping as a neat, clean way of getting customers from the competition without running much of a risk. Further, the ad is going to people who are interested in your product or service. Hence, the ad might pull better here than anywhere else!

Run Commission Ads

We discussed these in Chapter 5. Remember: A commission ad is a low-cost way to get into a publication of your choice with no cash outlay for the space. So explore every possibility for commission ads in the ad outlets you've chosen.

Keep Your Eye on Ad Basics

Some BWBs get all excited when they hear about ad bargains—that is, low-cost ads in smaller publications.

Thus, I know of publications in which you can run a full-page ad for $45. This is cheaper than some classifieds.

But run such an ad and you're likely not to get even one response! Sure, the cost is low. But so is the response rate!

Remember that the key to any mail-order business is being able to make bank deposits every day! Low-cost ads are useless if they don't bring in the money!

So, a basic principle of mail-order advertising is:

> *Never select an ad outlet just because the cost of the space is low! You will seldom make money from ads chosen on the basis of low cost for the space. Run ads—and pay a negotiated space cost—in those publications which your analysis shows serve an audience that is a prospect for buying what you're offering in your ad!*

Keep your eye on ad basics and you're almost certain to make mailbox millions! How can I say that? Because I've done it myself, many times over. And *you* can do the same—starting right now!

In your effort to reduce ad space costs, keep in mind another basic principle. It is this:

> *Many publishers of magazines and newspapers offer a reduced space rate for Mail Order and Publisher's ads. So be certain to ask the ad manager what the ad rate is for these two types of ads if the item or service you're selling falls into either of the above categories.*

Design Space Ads that Pull Strongly

You advertise to make money! Once your company is large, you can spend big bucks on "image advertising"—that is, expensive ads that don't try to sell products or services. Instead, image ads just try to make a company look good to its buying, investing, and working public. For now, *you* must bring back at least $2—and preferably $3—for every $1 you spend on advertising. That's why you must design space ads that pull strongly.

Later in this book we talk about—and show you—how to write million-dollar ads. Here you'll see how to design ads that pull strongly.

Any ad that pulls strongly—that is, brings in the big bucks to your office every day of the week—must:

- Be arresting, that is, eye-catching
- Use type that conveys a message quickly
- Have a "grab-you-by-the-arm" headline
- Feature an ordering or response device of some kind

Let's look at each of these and see how you can use them to build your mailbox millions. Knowing how to design an ad for strongest results can put you on the fast-track to mail-order wealth. And I'm sure that would make you happy!

Be Arresting

Look through any publication and you'll see dozens of full-page ads for various products and services. How can you make your ad stand out above all the others? There's just one answer. Your ad must be eye-catching—that is, your ad must:

1. Stop the reader from turning the page before reading at least the headline in the ad
2. Compel the reader to read the body copy in your ad so your sales message gets across
3. Convince the reader to act—that is, call, write, or otherwise contact you to place an order.

Some ad experts believe an ad with an illustration is more arresting than one without. Yet there are plenty of all-type ads that are making millions for the firms running them. Thus, our Financial Broker Kit ad, Figure 6-2, generates enormous response every time we run it. It doesn't have any illustration at all, just selling copy! The headline— "Make Big Money from Money—Start Now"—stops the reader more quickly than any photo or drawing I've ever seen.

Loans for Health Professionals

BEAT THE BANK!

NOW YOU CAN COMPETE WITH THE LOCAL BANKS FOR THOSE DOCTOR LOANS AND MAKE GENEROUS COMMISSIONS FOR YOURSELF!

Here now for you are four loan programs for Physicians, Dentists, Chiropractors, Podiatrists, Optometrists, Veterinarians and others which are competitive with anything they can get from their local bank! Now you can turn these programs into cash for yourself!

* Average Commission Over $2000 Per Deal Paid By Lender (you never have to collect any fees from the client)!
* Available in all 50 States!
* Over 80% of Loan Submissions Funded!
* One Enrollment Entitles You to Market All Four Programs

HEALTH CARE PROFESSIONALS NEED MORE MONEY THAN EVER BEFORE for advertising, malpractice insurance, working capital and new technology equipment to compete in the rapidly growing health care market! This need can create many $1000's of dollars in commissions for you in the weeks and months ahead!

THE 20 YEAR AMORTIZATION PROGRAM! Yes, you can offer up to 20 year amortization under this program. 12% interest fixed for every 5 years at which time the interest is adjusted to prevailing rates but the loan cannot be called if it is current! Prepayment penalty of only 3 month's interest and up to 10% of the principal can be prepaid annually with no penalty at all! Amounts from $50,000.00 to $1,200,000 per borrower!

LOOK AT THESE PAYMENTS! $100,000.00 is only $1100 per month. $50,000.00 is only $550 per month. A bank loan for $100,000.00 would be $2000 per month at 7¾% (the current prime rate) for 60 months which is the very maximum that most banks will go without real estate as security.

LIBERAL COLLATERAL REQUIREMENT. Reasonable collateral such as practice equipment and receivables is required. Real estate can be used and collateral can be used from different states. This program is available in all states.

LIBERAL USE REQUIREMENT. Funds can be used for consolidation, new construction and improvements, working capital and investment. We'll finance those medical buildings that are too large for the Banks and too small for the Life Insurance Companies!

YOU MAKE LOTS OF YOU KNOW WHAT! The average loan is $300,000.00. We split our profit with you which means you make $3000 per loan. This program is so popular you should have no trouble making 2 or 3 of these per month. 7 to 10 day processing time.

SUPPORT YOU WON'T BELIEVE. Our loan consultants are available to you immediately by phone. The manual gives you everything you need to promote, package and submit the loans. We close and document for you. All you have to do is find the borrowers. We also have lead programs for you to use if you wish. You will have the doctors knocking your door down for this one — believe me!

UNSECURED LOANS WITH NO LOAN FEES! Up to $60,000.00 available with absolutely no loan fees. 7 over prime fixed for 5 to 6 years with no prepayment penalty. You make $1000.00 on a $60,000.00 loan.

SALE-LEASEBACK OF EQUIPMENT. We will buy and lease back your doctor's existing used office furniture and equipment. This program is also great for clients with tax liens or explainable bankruptcies. Those who cannot borrow from their bank can get funds under this program. Our manual will give you in depth details of how the sale-leaseback operates and how to offer it to your clients.

The average deal here is $50,000 and you make $2000!

ACCOUNTS RECEIVABLE LOANS. An entirely new concept for health professionals! This plan enables them to receive immediate payment for services rendered and still retain the convenience of personalized patient billing. The doctor patient relationship remains unchanged!

We will advance up to 85% of the existing accounts receivable and then 90-95% of current billings — all paid within five days! The Doctor continues to bill his/her patients in the usual manner while they continue to make payments as they have in the past. There is no minimum payment and there are no carrying charges or finance charges. You get 50% of our profit which will add up to $1000's of dollars of profit over a period of time.

YOU CAN DO THIS FULL OR PART TIME. You can do this while you hold down another job by simply having an answering machine or a service take your calls when you are at work. All of this can be done by phone or mail. You never need to meet your clients and you can advertise anywhere in the U.S.A. by using an "800" number or by making them write to you. These programs are so good they will draw your clients to you with very little effort.

YOU GET EVERYTHING YOU NEED IN OUR MANUAL TO BEGIN IMMEDIATELY. How and where to advertise. Sample direct mail letters and classified and display ads.

Scripts are provided telling you exactly what to say once you contact a prospect.

All the forms we use are shown so you know exactly how we work.

WE DO THE CLOSING DOCUMENTATION! All you have to do is find us the prospects and get some initial tax returns and we will take it from there!

PROSPECTS EVERYWHERE

■ 366,000 M.D.'s
■ 154,000 D.D.S.'s
■ 33,000 Veterinarians
■ 22,000 Optometrists
■ 18,200 Osteopaths

Call 516-766-5850 day or night to order by credit card. Act NOW!

Average Earnings

■ M.D.'s $126,000.00
■ D.D.S.'s $89,000.00

MAIL THIS COUPON.

MAIL YOUR ORDER WITH PAYMENT TO:
IWS, INC.
24 Canterbury Road
Rockville Center, NY 11570

I want to make money now! Rush me my copy of **THE FOUR DOCTOR LOAN PROGRAMS.** Enclosed is $150.00 — 30 day special offer.

Name _____
Address _____ Apt/Suite #
City _____ State _____ Zip _____
Phone _____

Figure 6-2

For years, photos of people leaning on the hood of an expensive auto were thought to be arresting. But so many of these photos have appeared that they've lost their ability to arrest the reader's attention. This means there's a wide-open opportunity for you to:

- Pick arresting illustrations for the space ads you run for your product or service
- Experiment with different types of illustrations to see which ones work best

When picking such illustrations, avoid sexual implications, unless your product or service is in the sex field. For almost all other products, using a sexual approach will produce fewer, and smaller, sales than a straight, factual ad describing the product or service. Look over a few back issues of the publication you plan to use and you'll see that use of sexual images is restricted to products and services in that field.

Be arresting with your ads. But be sure to tell as full a story about your product as you can. Why? Mail-order buyers *love* long copy—that is, full information about what they'll be getting when they place their order.

Use Quick-Reading Type in Your Ad

Today's mail-order buyers all seem to be in a hurry. They're in a hurry to order the product or service from which they'll benefit. Then they're in a hurry to receive delivery of what they ordered. Lastly, they're in a big hurry to get results with what they ordered.

You can serve this mad dash for results by today's customers by:

1. Using easy-to-read type in the headline of your ad. Your reader should not have to squint or strain to read your ad. If the reader must "work" at reading your ad, the reader might just give up and skip to the next ad. Result? You've lost a possible sale! So have your ad designed using fast-reading type.

2. Giving easy ordering information. Have a phone number for phone orders. Give a FAX number if your buyers are the type of people who might order by using the FAX machine in their office.
3. Including a coupon. Some ads no longer use a coupon for ordering. Why? Because this gives the advertiser more room in which the item or service can be promoted. Our findings in our mail-order activities—which are highly successful—is that readers enjoy filling out and sending a coupon for what they want. So we use an order coupon in all our full-page ads. You should see the number of coupons, along with checks and money orders, that pour into our offices every week of the year! We like our coupons. But if you like full-page ads without coupons, go ahead an use them!

By preparing hard-selling ads for magazines and other publications, you're really investing for the future. Why? Because:

> *Every full-page ad you run in a publication can later be re-run in your own catalog. And catalog ads can run for years—bringing mailbox millions into your bank every day!*

At my firm, IWS, Inc., we have a 48-page catalog which we issue twice a year. Priced at $5 (free to buyers of any of our products) it sells a full line of self-help financial books. This catalog uses a number of our full-page ads. And it keeps money flowing in to us every day of the year!

You can do the same. All you need is a few related products and you can start publishing your own catalog. I can guarantee that it will make money for you—if you send it to the right list!

Write a "Grab-You-By-The-Arm" Headline

The headline is the most important part of any full-page ad. Why? Because the headline:

1. Stops the reader, grabbing attention and inducing the reader to read the entire ad.

2. Sets your ad apart from the dozens of others in the same publication.
3. Gets the reader in the mood to send *you* money—which is the entire purpose of your ad!

Try to dream up as many headlines as you can for your product or service. Write down each headline as it occurs to you. I find that my best headlines seldom come whole— that is, I combine two or more and come up with the final headline.

To show you what I mean by "grab-you-by-the-arm" headlines, here are a few from recent full-page ads that are both effective and profitable. They come from both my own ads and those of others:

Write Your Own Commission Check
Credit Card Success Secrets
Use Our Money to Make Your Money
New Mortgage Cash-Out Program
There must be an easier way to real-estate riches ... and here it is!
Do You Want to Use Mega-Money Methods? Here's How:
Can You Afford Not to Be a Millionaire?
Beat the Bank!
How to Get Rich on Other People's Money
Guaranteed Monthly Income
Free Millions for the Asking
How to Become an Instant Millionaire
Free Grants & Low Interest Loans
Stay Home and Make Money
Free $10,000 Grant for One Phone Call
How to Make a Fortune Renovating Houses
Homeworkers Wanted!
Secrets to a Life of Luxury
Make $30,000 + Every Month Filling Out Simple 2-Minute Forms
From Bookkeeper to Millionairess
Self-Liquidating Loans
Get Millions in the Great Grant Give-Away
The World's Best Cheeses at the Lowest Prices

Fast Low-Cost Small-Business Accounting Services for
    You
Make Real Estate Millions Without a License
Get Rich in Export–Import Starting Today
There's a Time for Believing in Yourself ... That Time
    Is Now
$25,000 For a Few Hours' Work Doesn't Seem Fair
Instant Money Mailing Kit
How to Make $2,000 a Week Selling Information by Mail
$172 Billion from the Government Every Year!
Let Your Camera Make You $15,000

These actual headlines give you the feel of being grabbed
by the arm because you immediately:

- Want to know more
- So you read the full ad
- Which convinces you that you should send money to
  the advertiser for the item or service described

Aim at having such headlines in your full-page ads. If
you do, you'll barely be able to walk to the bank every
day because the load of checks and money orders arriving
at your mailbox will be so heavy!

Feature an Ordering or Response Device

The proven, millionaire-maker response device is the
order coupon. Millions of people regularly send billions
of dollars to mail-order companies with a coupon stapled,
glued, or taped to a check, a money order, or some carefully
wrapped cash. (When people send cash from overseas—
as they often do—they will wrap the cash in carbon paper
to prevent it being detected by machines or people).
    Most successful mail-order dealers swear by the coupon
as the best response device. A few experienced pros use
the noncoupon approach, saying "Why waste expensive
space? Make the response device part of the text of the ad!"
Thus, you'll see response devices that say:

To order this great wine cooler, get a pen and piece of
paper. Mark your name, address, and zip code on the paper.

*Then add, "I want the world's best wine cooler." Send
the paper, along with your check or money order for $25.00,
to Wine Coolers Unlimited, 123 Main St, Anytown 00000.
Or call 1-800-000-0000 to order by credit card.*

This response device is the very last paragraph in the
ad. So it is located where the coupon is normally placed.

Use—as we said earlier—the response device *you* believe
will pull best for you. Just be sure it brings the money
in every day!

Run Your Full-Page Ads with the Best Timing

Our full-page ads bring in many thousands of dollars
per month. Here's a schedule we find profitable for selling
products of several kinds:

1. Run at least one full-page ad in January of each year.
   Why? Because that's when most people are in a strong
   buying mood.
2. Follow up your January ad with either a March or
   April ad if your budget is tight. If you have excess
   funds, run your full-page ad *every* month until it stops
   making money. More about ad money making later.
3. Run your next ad in September, if your ad budget
   is still tight. Otherwise, run your full-page ad right
   through the summer. Response may fall off somewhat.
   But it won't be as bad as you think it will be because
   continuous running of any ad eventually convinces
   people to send money to you! And this—after all—
   is exactly what you want them to do.
4. Make your last ad of the year the December ad. Why?
   Some people will buy your product or services as a
   holiday gift for someone in the family. You might
   as well be the firm getting the money for the gift!

Whenever you run a full-page ad you'll get orders. Don't
disappoint your customers by not having inventory on
hand. Estimate—in advance—how many sales each ad will
bring in. Then have enough inventory to handle all orders

promptly and efficiently. You'll make friends and sell more to these friends!

Know the Numbers of Full-Page Ads

Mail order is a numbers business. These are easy numbers because the final number—or bottom line—is your profit. Or it may be your loss if you don't do things the way I advise!

The numbers you have in mail order using full-page ads are so simple a child could figure them out. Here they are for a product costing the buyer $20; your cost = $5.00. You run a full-page ad and here are your numbers:

Cost of full-page ad for one issue	=	$2,500.00
Sales price of item sold	=	20.00
Number of units sold through ad	=	250
Gross income from ad = 250 x $20	=	5,000.00
Unit cost = 250 x $5	=	1,250.00
Gross profit = sales - unit cost	=	3,750.00
Postage and handling @ $3/unit	=	750.00
Net before ad cost and overhead	=	3,000.00
Ad cost for one month	=	2,500.00
Net after ad cost	=	500.00

Now the $500 looks like profit. It covers all your direct costs—that is, the ad, the cost of the product, postage and handling, etc. But it does *not* cover your salary, your rent, etc. Since you are small—we assume you can apply salary and rent costs to the $500 in whatever way you may wish. If you're running your business from home, you don't have any rent. And if you're the only "executive" in the business, the $500 becomes your salary. Your profit will be whatever is left over after you take your salary.

While $500 may not seem like much from $5,000 in sales, you *do* have 250 new names of customers who've sent you money. And about 70 percent of these new customers will buy other items from you. So you're really building a list of paying customers who'll keep sending you money for years. When you make a sale after the first one, you're profiting from the *back-end* of your customer list. Many mail-order dealers make their largest profit from the back-end.

And don't forget—you can rent out the 250 new names you just obtained. (You need at least 1,000 names to rent). Today, good lists are renting in the $100 per 1,000 range. Rent your list three or four times a year and you can make as much from list rental as from product sales!

To make money from full-page ads, keep these basic ideas in mind:

1. Write, or have someone write, a powerful ad.
2. Use a response device of some kind in the ad.
3. Pick a suitable publication for your ad.
4. Time your ad so it runs when people are in a buying mood.
5. Price your product so it brings in a profit.
6. Work the back-end—some 70 percent of your customers will buy more items or services from you.
7. Keep running every profitable ad until it becomes unprofitable.

Now let's see how you can work the back-end without working! I do it every day of the week and it's great fun.

CHAPTER 7

USE MAIL-ORDER CATALOGS TO MAKE YOURSELF RICH

THIS IS THE era of the mail-order catalog. Just look in your mailbox between Labor Day and Thanksgiving and you'll see dozens of catalogs. And if you're a sports fan like I am, you'll see:

- Boating catalogs in spring and summer
- Skiing catalogs in fall and winter
- Gift catalogs almost year-round
- Home catalogs every month
- Etc.

Truly, the catalog era seems as though it will never end. Why is this? There are a number of good, valid reasons for the surge in catalog selling. These reasons include:

1. Greater confidence in mail-order houses of all kinds.
2. Less time in the lives of most people (especially working women) to spend on in-store shopping.
3. Speedy buying permitted by use of credit cards and the telephone and FAX.
4. Greater availability of toll-free 800 numbers which allow a buyer to place an order in a matter of moments at the expense of the seller.
5. More courier services to deliver overnight or next-day at a reasonable price.

Thus, all the elements of instant gratification seem to be in place for catalog mail-order selling. And who do *you* sell to? You sell to:

1. Customers who responded to, and sent money to, your full-page ad.
2. Customers who sent in inquiries *(called white-paper mail)* to your classified ads.
3. People who call and want info on what you have for sale.
4. Catalog collectors who respond to short classified ads telling about the availability of a catalog covering a certain type of product or service.
5. Customers who receive your catalog with their first purchase and want more of what you sell.

Why Catalog Sales "Is the Way to Go"

When you promote just one item or service in an ad or mailing, your prospect has an easy decision. He or she says: "Yes, I'll buy this item or service." Or, "No, I will not buy this item or service."

The decision time is just seconds. Why? Because there's only one item or service to choose from. So you're paying a relatively big price to get that "Yes" answer—which is what you want.

Send that same prospect a catalog listing dozens of items or services of interest to that person and you'll get many more "Yes" decisions, plus a lot more money. Why? Because you've spread a whole range of choices before your prospect. He or she browses through your catalog, checking off things to buy. So, with a catalog:

- Your average sale is higher in dollars than with the usual space ad or direct mail letter.
- You will usually get a stronger response for each dollar spent on a catalog than you will from the same amount spent on an ad or direct mail.
- Buyers become your friends and look forward to each new catalog to see what else they can buy!

For these reasons, catalogs are one of the best ways to get rich in mail order today. For instance, with a catalog to promote your products or services, you can:

1. Charge a profit-making price for your catalog. Thus, we charge $5.00 for our 48-page catalog and people are glad to send us their money for it.
2. Run space or classified ads from other mail-order sellers in your catalog and be paid for the space. Some full-page catalog ads go for $30,000, and up. Such a sale will really help you pay for your catalog!
3. Make your customers part of your family so they keep sending money to you week after week. And that, after all, is the whole idea of this business!

Catalogs tend to grow. Thus, with my firm, IWS, Inc., we started with a 12-page catalog. Next, we expanded to 24 pages. Now we're at 48 pages. Soon I hope to see a 72-page catalog that sells for us around the world.

And all of you have seen at one one time or another the hundreds of pages in the Sears and Ward catalogs. Yet these catalogs have sold to people for years and years. Do you need any more proof that catalog sales are the way to go?

How to Build a Million Dollar Catalog

To make money for you (the idea behind all this) your catalog should have certain proven features. These are:

1. Your catalog should be unique. It should be *you*, and the items or services you believe your prospects and customers need and want. You cannot make any large amounts of money from preprinted catalogs that you mail out, competing against thousands of others doing the same thing. Your catalog must reflect *you*—uniquely.
2. Your catalog must "hang together"—that is, it must present coverage of a certain area of interest (like home care), a certain hobby (like boating or electronics), a

certain area of business (like plumbing or electrical work), etc. Without a unified interest, your catalog won't rake in the big bucks which you want from your business.

3. Your catalog should have a response device—that is, a coupon for easy ordering. It should help the customer every step of the way to send you money! That's why you went to the expense and trouble of preparing your catalog—to have your prospects and customers send you money.

You want your catalog to work for you day and night. Most people don't throw catalogs away. Instead, they save them to be looked at when they have a few minutes' free time. When the person picks up *your* catalog, you want your offers to jump out at them and say "Order me now— you need me!"

To prepare your million dollar catalog, take these steps:

1. *Pick the products for your catalog.* I find the best products are those I develop myself, based on my view of what people want and need in my mail-order field— namely money. At the start you won't have enough products or services you've developed yourself. Don't worry. Take Step 2.

2. *Select related products* from reliable suppliers to include in your catalog. Choose these items or services so your catalog "hangs together," as we mentioned earlier. Don't pay more than 50 percent of your catalog list price for the item. And be sure to have the supplier drop-ship the item at *no* cost to you. Example: List price of an item in your catalog is $100. You pay your supplier $50 (50 percent of list price) for the item and the supplier sends it to your customer at *no* cost to you and the customer for shipping.

3. *Vary the list price of items on each page,* or on following pages. Thus, if you have several items on one page, try to have a low-priced item, a medium-priced item, and a high-priced item on the same page. Why? Because it makes it much more interesting to your reader to have several items of varying price on one page. If you use a full page for each item, vary

the price from page to page—that is, follow a high-priced item with a low-priced one, etc. Again, your reader will find your offerings more interesting and will send more money!

4. *Use at least 8 pages*—and preferably 12 pages—for your first catalog. Anything less than 8 pages really isn't a catalog. At 12 pages, people begin to think you're serious!

5. *Use two order coupons in your catalog.* (We use one on every page—almost) Why two (or more) order coupons? To increase the amount of money your good friends send you! Remember: People enjoy filling out coupons. And they'll send money with the coupon. So the more coupons, the *more* money your catalog will bring in! Makes sense, doesn't it?

6. *Make it easy for your prospect or customer to order* from your catalog. Allow the use of credit cards—it will increase your business by 25 to 40 percent. And use a toll-free 800 number for ordering. Sure, people will use the 800 number to call to ask questions. But at least they're calling *you*—not your competition!

7. *Offer a bonus item or items for quick orders.* Or for orders over a certain dollar amount. Such bonuses increase the cash flow (the name of this game) from your catalog. And they also can increase the average size of your orders.

8. *Promise fast delivery for credit-card orders,* payment by money order or certified check. This brings in more payments that don't bounce. Personal and even business checks may bounce and hurt you if you don't wait long enough for them to clear your bank. (One of the reasons why bounced checks take so long to be returned is the paying bank doesn't get around to returning the check to your bank. So protect yourself—wait at least 3 weeks for personal checks to clear). State your policy in your catalog and you'll get more payments that aren't rubber!

9. *Get as much information as you can on each customer who orders.* Thus, get the customer's phone number, whether he or she owns a home, type of auto, etc. This information will help you get a higher rental fee, should you decide to generate extra income by

renting out your buyer list. Remember: List rental income is pure money—you just drop it in the bank and enjoy it!

10. *Let your reader get in touch with you*—give them a phone number they can call if they have questions. This should *not* be an 800 number. Let your readers pay to make the call. They will be glad to do so—provided they know you'll answer their questions.

11. *Allow your buyer to send you the names and addresses* of friends who might want a copy of your catalog. This will increase the size of your mailing list and will get you new customers. But your new buyers will have to be trained to buy as strongly as your regular ones. How do you do this? Keep sending them a catalog—regularly.

12. *Include a copy of your catalog with every order you ship.* Why? Because your customer will be ready to buy again when he or she sees the excellent item you've sent. With the catalog handy, it's easy to order—right on the spot!

13. *Keep careful records* of how many people buy from your catalog. Do this by keying every coupon so you know which catalog it came from.

14. *Establish an estimated dollars-per-page* that you want to bring in from your catalog. If a page brings in much less than the average dollars-per-page you're seeking, remove its items and substitute others for the next printing of your catalog. Remember: The whole purpose of a catalog is to earn a profit for your business. Without a profit you won't be able to pay your bills. The whole idea of a catalog is to make you a mailbox millionaire—soon!

15. *Offer special services* to your catalog customers. Such services might include gift wrapping, enclosure cards for special remembrances, etc.

Keep in mind—at all times—that everything you do in your busiess ties back to marketing. So the more you can offer in your catalog, the better will be your sales.

Key *all* coupons in your catalog so you know the origin of the sale. This keying will tell you which ads and which products are selling best. And if you have some products that move slowly, you can either delete them or give them less space in future editions of your catalog. An important money-making technique for my 48-page catalog is this:

> *Never eliminate a product or service from your catalog because it isn't selling well. Instead, reduce the space given to the item in the catalog. This allows you to get the occasional sale that the item brings in—increasing your cash flow from the catalog without raising your costs too much.*

How to Get Your Catalog Around

The best catalog in the world is useless unless it's in the hands of prospective buyers. How can you get your catalog into the hands of these people? There are a number of ways, namely:

1. **Run space or classified ads** in appropriate publications and offer a free copy of your catalog. Send the catalog to people who respond. This is an excellent way to get names of people who will order from your catalog.
2. **Use the catalog-inquiry sections of magazines.** Most offer this space free of charge. By picking suitable magazines, you can get information on your catalog out to millions of prospects for little more than the cost of a printed catalog release plus one first-class stamp. Some firms even charge a nominal price for their catalog—like $1 or $2—and make a profit on the catalog before one item is sold from it! A typical catalog release writeup is given later in this chapter so you see how easy it is to get free publicity for your catalog.
3. **Rent mailing lists** and offer items or services for sale. Also include mention of the availability of your catalog—either free or for a nominal price. Be sure to rent lists of people who are interested in your products. Thus, you'll rent lists of boaters for boating products or services, skiers for ski items, etc. Such lists cost less to rent and will generally give you a stronger and more profitable response.

4. *Mail to special-interest groups,* like clubs, religious organizations, lodges, etc., composed of people who are interested in what's in your catalog. You can often do this at low cost by getting a membership list and putting up the names on multi-set labels yourself. One successful BWB mail-order millionaire I know boasted to me that when he started he could address, stuff, and seal 1,000 envelopes in 10 hours. These ads pulled strongly for him, as did the catalog he mailed to buyers and those requesting it. Today he has a whole bevy of people stuffing envelopes for him!

By now I'm sure you get the idea here. That is:

Get your catalog into the right hands and you're almost certain to bring in big money! A good catalog is a very strong sales tool. In the right hands it can make you a millionaire sooner than you think!

And one of the steps to getting your catalog into the right hands is to get free space in suitable publications. To do this, you just type up, double-spaced, a short description of your catalog. Here's one I wrote for our catalog. It really brings in the requests—and sales:

WEALTH BUILDERS 48-PAGE CATALOG shows Beginning Wealth Builders how to start their own business, make money in import-export, mail order, real estate, licensing, etc. Contains full product information on newsletters, books, and kits suitable for building wealth quickly in one's own, independent business. Gives phone numbers to call for advice on the product that would be most helpful to a Beginning Wealth Builder with certain business and career interests. Free from IWS, Inc. POB 186 Merrick NY 11566. Include $2 for postage and handling.

You can write just as good a description—probably even better! Try it and see. Here's a secret hint that most new mail-order wealth builders don't know. It is:

Write your own short catalog description before you put your catalog together. It will quickly show you if your catalog is needed and if it will sell. If you see that it's hard to describe your catalog, think it through again. Why? If you can't describe it, you really can't assemble it! A short description tells lots to you.

When to Get Your Catalog Out to Make Money

Copies of your catalog sitting in your garage or basement aren't making money for you. Instead, they're costing you money! Why? Because you paid to have the catalog printed. If the catalog isn't in the hands of prospects, the money you paid for printing is not working for you!

Get your catalog into the hands of your prospects. But be careful when you send your catalog. Some general, proven rules for consumer-type catalogs—that is, catalogs going to the general public—are:

1. Avoid sending your catalog when most of the others are being sent out—between Labor Day and Thanksgiving. If you send your catalog during those weeks you'll be competing with the giants—Land's End, Lillian Vernon, Sharper Image, etc. Their catalogs are so beautifully prepared that your thin black-and-white job will almost certainly be lost in the shuffle!
2. Time your mailing to coincide with the interests of your buyers. Thus, if your catalog features sports equipment or clothing, mail it *before* the start of the season for the sports you're serving.
3. Mail your catalog at least twice a year. With fewer than two mailings people forget that you exist. And if you can mail four times a year, do so. People will start to look for your catalog because it has info in it that interests them.

If the products or services you offer in your catalog are for special-interest groups, then you can use these rules for your mailings:

1. Mail your catalog year-round. Thus, in my business—money—seasonal aspects don't exist. Why? Because people are interested in money every day of the year. So we send our catalog out 12 months of the year.

You can do the same if your catalog covers a general topic like money.

2. Send your catalog to your customer's or prospect's business address. Then you won't be competing with the holiday clutter of the beautiful four-color catalogs aimed at garnering the holiday dollars from consumers.

3. Use a rubber stamp to imprint on the envelope in which you mail the catalog the words "You requested this information" when you send the catalog to people who asked for it. They're much more likely to open the envelope when they see these words than when the words are left off.

4. Mail your catalog when you know your competition is *not* mailing theirs. Then your catalog will get *all* the attention from your prospects and customers.

A good friend of mine, Dick Murcott, built a multi-million dollar mail-order business using a large catalog of several hundred pages which he mails to supermarkets, hotel kitchens, convenience stores, etc. He sells a wide range of products—from stamps for affixing price labels to cartons and cans to tote baskets, etc. His catalog is really a work of art and it brings back strong sales.

To keep his firm's name in front of his buying public, Dick also sends "mini-catalogs"—multi-page circulars—featuring special buys. His very interesting circulars extend the reach of his catalog. They also help reinforce his presence in his field of sales. While these circulars cost money to send out, Dick's business continues to grow every year!

Be Paid with the Order

You'll often see the expression *hard offer* or *soft offer*. In a hard offer, you require the buyer to send payment with his or her order. In a soft offer, the customer is allowed to order an item without sending a payment or giving a credit-card authorization.

At the start, the best way for you to sell is via a hard offer. Why? For a number of reasons, namely:

1. With a hard offer, you receive payment when you need it—that is, before you ship.
2. With a hard offer, you're saved from the complex accounts receivable accounting procedures.
3. Fewer people will rip you off when you have a hard offer. Why? Because you can wait for their checks to clear, for credit-card charges to be approved, etc. So you wind up with more good cash in your hands without having to go to a collection agency to collect, etc.

So set up your early catalogs with only hard offers. Once you're established you can switch to soft offers on some items or services. But at the start, use only the hard offer.

People who know just a little about mail order will tell you that hard offers reduce the response rate to your catalog. This may be true. But when you're just starting, you need money. So take this advice from a mail-order pro with many years of experience:

> Use only hard offers in your catalog. You will have a higher cash flow from each copy of your catalog. And the few orders you might lose because you demand payment with the order will hardly be noticed!

The only time you might consider using soft offers is when your catalog sells *business-to-business*. That is, when you're selling to other businesses by mail order and you can check your prospective customer's credit rating, soft offers are safe. You might even say they're required! Why?

Because almost every business buys on credit—30 days, 60 days, etc. For you to demand payment with the order can cause lost sales. So you'll extend credit to other businesses, after you run a suitable credit check on each business seeking credit from you.

But when selling to the general public, or to a specialized public (skiers, boaters, hikers, auto owners, home owners, etc.), you will demand—and get—payment with the order. People ordering from catalogs serving their interests or needs *do* expect to pay with their order. And you're entitled to such payments!

Seek New Sales Outlets with Your Catalog

A catalog gives you enormous opportunities to score new sales highs. Why? Because a catalog:

Creates interest of itself. People want to look at your catalog, to see what it offers. And the very existence of your catalog gives your firm greater credibility. So you're welcome and accepted in company that wouldn't look twice at your space ad! With such acceptance you can easily seek new sales outlets that can make you a mailbox millionaire.

New sales outlets you can seek with your catalog include these simple ones:

1. *Package stuffers:* Prepare a simple 3 × 5 inch order coupon for your catalog. Arrange to have this coupon stuffed in outgoing packages shipped to buyers of products or services similar to those offered in your catalog. The cost is much, much less than that of sending the same coupon by first class mail. And the results can be spectacular. People will order your catalog and then begin buying from it faster than you ever thought possible.

2. *Envelope stuffers:* You use the same request coupon as in (1) above and have it included with mailings being made by other mail-order dealers. Such envelopes are usually being mailed to prospects—*not* buyers. So the response rate may not be as high as with package stuffers, where your coupon is going to *buyers*—that is, people who paid money to obtain a product or service.

3. *Publication stuffers:* If your catalog is for a specialized audience — say, plumbers, electricians, carpet cleaners, window washers, etc. — you can offer to have it sent along with a publication such as a newsletter that serves your audience. The editor of the publication will usually welcome inclusion of your catalog with the publication because it is another service for the readers of the publication. And since they're your prime

Figure 7-1

Front of Double Postcard

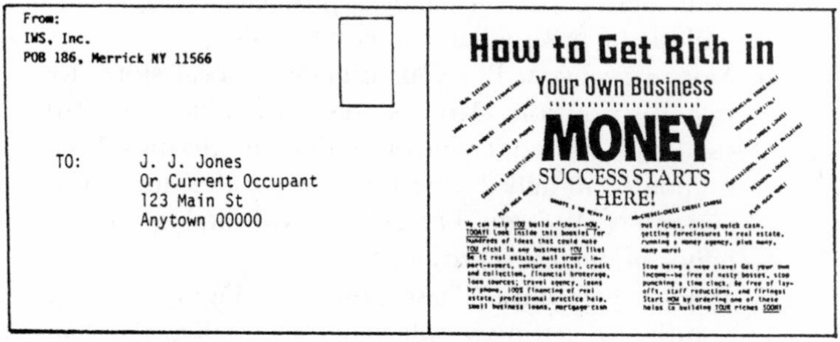

From:
IWS, Inc.
POB 186, Merrick NY 11566

TO: J. J. Jones
        Or Current Occupant
        123 Main St
        Anytown 00000

How to Get Rich in
Your Own Business
MONEY
SUCCESS STARTS
HERE!

Back of Double Postcard

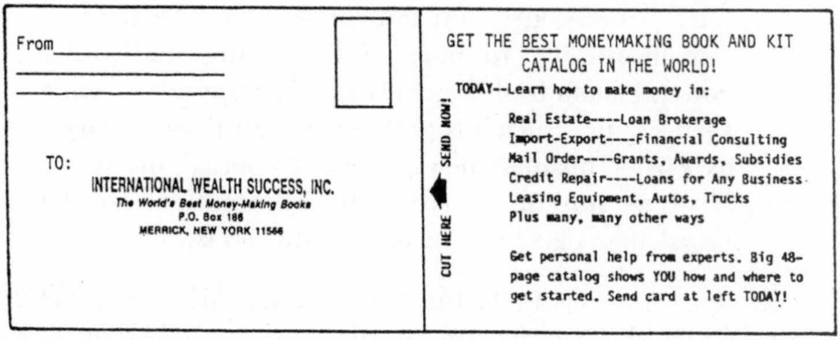

From_____

TO:
INTERNATIONAL WEALTH SUCCESS, INC.
The World's Best Money-Making Books
P.O. Box 186
MERRICK, NEW YORK 11566

GET THE BEST MONEYMAKING BOOK AND KIT
CATALOG IN THE WORLD!

TODAY--Learn how to make money in:

SEND NOW!

Real Estate----Loan Brokerage
Import-Export----Financial Consulting
Mail Order----Grants, Awards, Subsidies
Credit Repair----Loans for Any Business
Leasing Equipment, Autos, Trucks
Plus many, many other ways

CUT HERE

Get personal help from experts. Big 48-
page catalog shows YOU how and where to
get started. Send card at left TODAY!

prospects, the response rate can—as they say—"blow your socks off" with big, big orders!

4. **Trade show giveaways:** Arrange to have your catalog given away at booths at trade shows. All you need do is supply the catalogs. The staff on duty at the booth will hand out your catalog. Again, you're getting your catalog into the hands of prospects—people who will gladly order what you have for sale.

5. **Store giveaways:** Put your catalog in local stores for free distribution. Most stores will welcome your catalog, if it doesn't compete with their offerings. Your catalog is an added service offered by the store to its customers. And you'll be getting your catalog into the hands of interested prospects.

6. **Double postcards:** These postcards, Figure 7-1, are popular for getting people to order a catalog. One half of the card contains the mailing address and info about the catalog. The other half contains the return portion of the card with the address of yourself as publisher of the catalog, and the name and address of the person requesting a copy of it. If you use self-adhesive labels for the address of the postcard recipient, the label can be transferred to the second portion of the card to make requesting the catalog an easy task. Using this approach you can get lots of productive requests for your catalog.

7. **Free Advertising in the IWS newsletter:** As a one-year, or longer, subscriber to the *International Wealth Success* newsletter, you can run one free classified ad per month. A number of beginning mail-order entrepreneurs find these ads highly responsive. Some even say that such ads pull better than those in large, expensive business newspapers. To verify this you'll have to run an ad yourself. Information on the newsletter is given at the back of this book.

Catalog marketing is big today and will grow. Why? Because all the factors are in place to fuel this growth. So if you're in mail order—or want to be in it—you should consider catalog marketing. As a mail-order pro who has made millions with catalogs, I'm ready to help you do the same. Try me and see!

CHAPTER 8

DON'T OVERLOOK THE WEALTH IN ELECTRONIC MEDIA

NEW MAIL-ORDER operators must use every available way of selling products or services if they are to build wealth quickly. And the electronic media—radio and television— can bring you spectacular results. Why?

Because today's buyers are more likely to listen to radio or watch TV than they are to read a magazine. So you have to go where they are if you want to make a sale. And sales, after all, are what will make *you* rich!

Use Radio to Sell to Locals

One of our best lessons in the power of local radio was given us by a religious station in Texas. The station interviewed me on the phone and ran the interview a few days later. Within minutes we:

- Had dozens of phone calls asking for more info and data on our business loans
- Received calls from Texas and from nearby states the program had reached via the "sky wave" effect
- Made a number of sales to people who received our free 8-page catalog

- All at no cost other than the time on the telephone with the interviewer

This response quickly convinced us that radio is an excellent way to promote business products—in our case newsletters and books on making money in your own business.

Many other publishers use local radio to promote books, games, services, etc. Why? For a number of reasons, including these:

- Radio is low-cost, compared to some print ads.
- You can reach specific local markets with radio.
- A 30- or 60-second spot ad can give you instantaneous response—there's no need to wait weeks for a mail-in reaction to your ad.
- Production costs of a radio ad—i.e., the voice and any sound effects you may need—are very low.
- You can pick the best ad time—early morning, late evening, etc.—to reach your prospects.
- With a toll-free 800 number—such as we use—you'll know within minutes if your ad will "make it."
- When an ad isn't pulling well, you can quickly change it to build a stronger response—at little cost!
- You can take credit-card orders over your 800 line and speed your cash flow. Or you can use a WATS line service to take credit-card orders for you. The cost is really low, and getting lower all the time.

Why, then, you ask, don't more mail-order operators use radio ads? There are a number of reasons. Mostly, though, newer mail-order operators think only of dropping an envelope in the mail or running a small ad. As we've seen, both these methods *do* work and you *should* use them. But don't get left out of the big bucks available to you— use radio ads regularly!

Recognize What Works on the Radio

You can't do everything on the radio. Why? Because

you're limited to the spoken word, music, and certain sound effects. Thus, if you want to show a product or service in action, you'll have to use TV instead of radio.

Well, what does work on the radio? Here are a number of proven methods that do work on radio:

1. *Aim at local listeners.* If you're promoting a product or service to farmers, use radio stations serving the local agricultural community. Do *not* put your commercial on a station serving business listeners—it won't work!

2. *Make your message simple.* People often listen to the radio while doing something else—driving, working, gardening, etc. If your message is complicated, you'll lose the listener's attention. So keep your message simple and direct.

3. *Emphasize benefits to the listener.* We're all interested in ourselves. And today's "me generation" is strikingly interested in itself. When you point out benefits the listener will get from your product or service, you'll get immediate attention and—hopefully—sales.

4. *Profit from the cellular phone.* If you're selling to an executive audience, remember that many people have a cellular phone in their car. So they can easily call your 800 toll-free number to order your product or service using their credit card. Many executives know their credit-card number by heart—they don't even have to look it up!

5. *Listen to any advice the station ad manager offers.* This advice is free and it will reflect the experience of other advertisers in the area. While you need not accept this advice if it seems unsuitable for you, at least *listen!* You may learn something worthwhile.

6. *Stay with local stations at the start.* National radio advertising is much more expensive and competitive than local promotion. You will often make much more money from local ads than from national promotions.

7. *Try to work out free interviews with the station.* Often, a station will offer the businessperson a free interview as part of the ad package. Interviews can pull as strongly as ads. So it's worth seeking as many interviews as you can get for yourself or any others in your firm who are knowledgeable people.

8. *Be creative about your ads.* Don't just run a commercial asking for money! Offer useful information to your listener. Then ask for money! If the info you offer is interesting and helpful, your listener is much more likely to buy than when you just ask for a check or money order. Be helpful—it helps you sell!

9. *Try several stations in your area.* One station may out-pull all the others. But you won't know this until you try each station and compare the results.

10. *Use a post office box number for your ads* when you want the listener to write instead of calling. Why? Because it's easier for your listener to jot down a box number (or memorize it if a pencil isn't handy) than to do the same with a street address. But if you want *fast* results (and who doesn't), use a toll-free number with credit-card order taking. You will really see the magic results of radio when you do!

Where to Get the Lowest Cost Time

Radio time can be low in cost. Or it can go through the roof. And the most expensive time may not give you the best results. Our findings show that the cheapest time is often the most productive in terms of number of sales and the dollars brought in. So you'll find the lowest cost time:

- At religious stations serving a specific group. And just because you advertise on such a station does *not* mean that you're part of the religion or that you support its beliefs.
- At small-town local stations serving two or three nearby communities whose interests coincide with your products or services.
- At college and university stations which accept commercials. While the number of people served may be smaller than some commercial stations, you do have an active, intelligent, and interested audience.
- At stations that accept 800-number phone calls for which you pay only when one or more inquiries are generated

by the commercial. (But if you get thousands of inquiries, your cost may be higher!)

- At stations offering remnant time—that is, time another advertiser dropped for one reason or another. Your commercial must be ready and you will have to agree to pay the cost of the remnant time—usually about one-third the regular cost. Stations are willing to sell remnant time because once a minute passes without a sponsor using the time, the minute is gone forever—the station cannot re-sell the time. So a minute sold at one-third the usual price is much better than a minute on which no income is earned!

- At stations offering Per Inquiry (PI) deals. Here your only cost is for the inquiries—when they start arriving in your mailbox from the radio station. Just be sure you'll be getting the kinds of inquiries that will convert into sales. Is there any way to be sure of this conversion? No, there isn't. But if the audience of the station is interested in your type of product or service, then the inquiries you get could convert nicely into buyers—which is what you want!

Radio can be a valuable addition to your marketing efforts. It has many advantages and few disadvantages. So get started today! You'll never be sorry you did. But you *will* be sorry if you don't!

The radio sales of my firm, IWS, Inc., are steady, and climbing. You can do much the same. And the time you spend on doing radio commercials, interviews, and programs will be well repaid with strong sales. You really can't ask for much more in this great world of direct marketing!

Put Television to Work for Your Profits

You've all seen—I'm sure—the many TV commercials and "infomercials" on various real-estate seminars and courses. Most of these have a standard format. Thus, the program usually follows this sequence:

1. Introduction of the speaker and brief details of his success in business.
2. A look at some of the assets the speaker—usually an author or lecturer—acquired during his business career.
3. Brief descriptions of the business methods the speaker uses, along with examples of the deals closed and the amounts of money earned on each.
4. Brief interviews with people who're using the system recommended by the speaker, along with examples of their earnings while using the methods promoted by the speaker.
5. A pitch by the speaker to buy what's being offered—usually some books and tapes (audio and/or video)—along with the price and ordering terms. Most offers allow you to buy with a credit card over a toll-free number.
6. A final pitch by the speaker and by someone who's using the method.

These TV commercials can run at any time of the day or night. But they're very popular on late-night TV and off hours (afternoon) during the day. With so many people hawking products this way, you may ask: "Is there any room for me?" The answer is: "Yes, there's plenty of room for everyone!" Why? Because:

- TV commercials like those listed above have a certain expected life, after which their pull falls off.
- The public is attracted to new, fresh offers. So if you have a new—and different—offer, you're almost certain to be able to make money from it.
- The public tires of seeing the same—or similar—offers week after week. If you can come up with a new and different offer, you'll get the audience while others lose it.

Thus, we developed a TV commercial based on an interview with your author. But instead of covering just real estate, which has been done so often, we decided to cover:

- Mail order in all its many forms
- Financial brokerage and venture capital
- Real estate, starting with zero cash

With this varied format, the viewer can expect greater opportunities from the materials being offered. Priced in the $99 range, the materials are both effective and easy to use.

To give greater credibility to the offer, a number of actual users tell—on TV—of their experiences and the actual results achieved. These users were obtained by contacting people who wrote us letters about the usefulness of the items they bought from us.

Run on both cable and commercial stations, this TV promotion is doing well. We started marketing on the west coast of the United States and we're gradually expanding eastward. You can do the same!

What Makes Good TV Ads?

In TV you can take a 30-second time slot, or a 28-minute infomercial, as detailed above. Much depends on your product or service, who's behind it, and the best way to reach the market. Here are some general guidelines on what makes good TV ads:

- With a single product—like a book, a tool, etc.—a 30-second spot is usually best. Why? Because the price you can charge for the product or service is not high enough to pay for a longer commercial. Also, the information content of your ad is easily conveyed in the 30 seconds available to you. Going beyond this time limit won't—usually—increase your sales to a level where the extra income justifies the larger outlay for the additional time.
- For a multi-product package, a longer time on the air can usually be justified by these factors:
  1. Higher unit price provides more income from each sale.
  2. More information about the product and the benefits it provides must be given the prospect so a sale can be made.

3. Testimonials from satisfied users can increase sales significantly. It takes time to present such testimonials on the air.

- For these reasons you'll see more time given to infomercials which sell products in the $100 to $500 price range. Long experience shows that such products sell better with an extended coverage than with the typical 30-second commercial.

To summarize what makes a good TV ad from the time standpoint we can say:

- One-product offers—short commercials of less than one minute
- Multi-product offers—longer commercials with several testimonials by users

But there are other considerations you must recognize if you want to produce good TV ads. These are:

1. Your TV ad must be professionally produced. Viewers see so much TV (an average of 7 hours a day) that amateur productions are an immediate turnoff. Your commercial suffers by comparison with all the professionally produced ads the viewer sees day and night. So you must hire a professional to produce your ad. If you don't, you're wasting the money you pay for air time.

2. Your TV ad must provide answers to your viewers' needs. Think of why you buy from an ad—TV, radio, magazine, etc. The compelling reason to buy is the solution of some problem you have—such as starting a business, getting money for some stated use, finding a suitable job, etc. You buy because you believe the product or service will give you much more in benefits than you are paying for the product. So you must find out what needs your viewers are seeking to satisfy. Then, you must present your product or service in such a way that you show the viewer how his or her needs are answered by the item or service offered.

3. Your TV ad must offer solutions to viewers' needs at a reasonable price. That is, the price of your offering must be in line with the viewers' ability to pay and

the worth of the solution offered. For example: A book on Social Security benefits for senior citizens should not be priced at more than about $20. Why? Because the same information is available free from the government. Further, most of the potential customers are retirees whose income is limited. Pricing the book at too high a level will cause lost sales. But pricing the book at a level that most viewers can afford will get you a large volume of sales—large enough for you to show a high profit on each sale.

4. Your TV ad must give convincing evidence that high-priced products or services *do* work for the user. So if you're charging $100, or more, for your product or service, you *must* provide testimonials from real, live people who—in effect—say: "Look, folks, this deal works for me. I'm sure it will work for you, too!" The best testimonials are those that show ordinary people in their usual setting (home, office, etc.) talking about the great results they're obtaining from your wonderful product or service. If what they're doing also involves their spouse, then both husband and wife should be shown. Such a presentation improves the credibility of your commercial.

5. Your TV ad must have variety. It must *not* be dull or boring! Thus, if you want to present ten testimonials by featuring ten different people, consider dropping two or three people and showing closeups of actual testimonial letters you've received. This adds variety to your commercial and gives your viewer more to think about. Such an approach avoids letting the viewer know what comes next. Your variety makes the next scene unpredictable and sustains the viewer's interest in your message.

6. Your TV ad must make it easy—very, very easy—to order what you offer. So you must avoid complicated addresses, confusing price offers, convoluted ordering time limits, etc. The easiest ordering information for a viewer to understand is comprised of:

- A one-word company name. Leave off "Inc., Ltd." etc. Substitute, instead, just one word like "Books," "Records," "Tapes," etc.

- A simple address. Probably the simplest is "P.O. Box 123" followed by the city, state, and zip code. A person can write this down quickly, without having to think.
- A toll-free 800 number for fast ordering using a credit card. If you're into TV ads you might as well go the "whole mile" and accept credit-card orders via a toll-free line. Why? Because that's what today's customers expect! You might as well do what your potential customers expect—especially if it means more money in your pocket.

7. Your TV ad must show people as they are today. This means that you avoid actors in your commercial who all look like models for a fitness ad. Your cast should be young, old, fat, skinny, bushy-haired, bald, men, women, kids, pets, etc., if such types use your product or services. Don't make the mistake of having everyone in your commercial look like they just turned twenty-one and never had a setback in their lives. Your potential customers will be turned off because they'll think: "I used to look like that—but not now! I could never be a success with that item because I'm too fat (or too old, or too young, or too whatever). Remember: TV is a very powerful medium and it can bring up enormous numbers of images in the viewer's mind. You want these images to say—subconsciously—to the viewer: Look, these ordinary, run-of-the-mill people solved their problems with our product or service. Since you're just like them, you can do the same. And we'll show you how—for just a few dollars. Convince your viewer of how easy it is to use your ideas and you'll have the sale you seek—fast!

8. Your TV ad must appeal to the needs of today's consumers. These needs are:
   - *Speed*—everyone wants fast results.
   - *Ease of use*—people don't want theory; they just want to know what to do to get results.
   - *Full directions*—buyers want to be told exactly what they should do—they avoid thinking.
   - *Ready access to help*—a phone number or person they can call to get help when they need it.

- *Promise of large earnings*—people want to start fast, earn fast, and earn big! If you can help them do this, your TV ad will be a winner.

To show you the power of TV ads, let me tell you about a popular magazine that sells subscriptions via the tube. Here are some facts about this highly successful campaign:

- In one year, some 550,000 subscriptions were sold to viewers via direct-response TV.
- TV helped bring the total circulation of this consumer magazine to over 4 million subscribers.
- Both one-year ($18) and two-year ($28) subscriptions are sold via TV commercials.
- Both commercial and cable stations are used for the commercials for this magazine.
- More than 10 years' experience with TV commercials shows this to be a viable way to generate strong income for this consumer publication.
- Actual readers, editorial staff, and others on the magazine make more convincing people on commercials for this publication than talking-head actors who don't seem to have the credibility needed for strong sales on TV.

Yes, TV *can* be your source of big sales in the direct-response business. But you must have the types of products that sell well on TV. To decide if your products are the right type, talk to several TV commercial producers. They can quickly advise you as to the suitability of your product or service line.

Quick Ways to Make TV Ads

To make any TV ad you need the following items:

1. A script giving the words and scenes for the TV commercial you'll make.
2. A studio in which the commercial will be made, unless all the scenes will be outdoors in a street, field, ocean, lake, etc. Or all your scenes may be indoors in an office, building, etc. where a studio is not needed.

3. Filming equipment—cameras, lights, furniture, props, etc.
4. A producer who will direct the camera crew, actors, lighting experts, etc.
5. Actors who will convey the message you want to get across in your commercial.
6. Makeup consultants if your commercial will be competing on prime-time TV.

You don't have to run around looking for these people and equipment. Instead, you hire a studio which offers all these services as part of their overall price.

Typical prices studios charge range from $1,000 per minute of commercial time to as high as $3,000 per minute. Much depends on the services offered by the studio, the quality of its staff, and their previous work with commercials similar to the one you want. But don't let these prices scare you! We've seen plenty of excellent commercials produced for just 10 percent of the above costs by efficient, hard-working small studios.

For example, my first video commercial was made in my living room with just two portable cameras, five lights, a producer who doubled as my interviewer, and a camera crew of three. This 28-minute commercial looks as good and sounds as good as any studio-produced commercial I've ever seen. Yet it didn't cost me a penny because the producer knew he could make a bundle from this interview show. And the results prove the producer was right—sales are just booming.

The quickest way to make TV ads are:

1. Get a producer who wants to promote your product to produce both the script and show. Since the producer is using his or her time, things go faster!
2. Team up with a cable station seeking to raise its income. Offer the station 50 percent of your sales income if they'll produce your show and air it free of charge. With a good product, you'll have plenty of offers to do your show free of charge.
3. Work out a P.I. (Per-Inquiry) deal with a station. Offer *no* up-front money. Instead, pay a larger P.I. fee until

the cost of doing the show is recaptured. After that—known as the breakeven point—you keep your full 50 percent of the income from the show.

All these methods give you quick results. Why? Because the producer has his money and time tied up in the deal. Since the producer wants to earn an income from your show as soon as possible, the work is done quickly and efficiently.

Stay away from offers that come to you on the phone saying—in effect—we will produce your show and commercial from your script for just $15,000 up front. Then, if your show catches on, we'll arrange to run it on national stations and on cable. But if your show doesn't pull the response we're seeking, we'll have to cancel it.

The best TV producers—to my way of thinking—are those who come after you because they think they can make money on your product or service. Such producers *need* you to make their money. So they produce a good show quickly at *no* cost to you other than your time. And you make your money from the sale of your item or service on the show.

For example, right now we're working on a new TV commercial you'll see soon, which:

1. *Promotes* the business and real-estate loans my firm, IWS, Inc., offers to Beginning Wealth Builders in all parts of the world.
2. *Gives* full details on our newsletters and kits that help BWBs get started in their own business (see details at the back of this book).
3. *Presents* interviews with borrowers who've used our loans to build a new business or expand an existing one. Each borrower tells his or her story, showing how the low-interest loan helped in the business.
4. *Helps* viewers by giving them useful business tips from people who are actually in business today and making a profit today!

You know from watching TV yourself that plenty of real-life testimonials are strongly convincing. So when we bring on our borrowers and they tell viewers how easy it is to get a loan from IWS, Inc., once they become newsletter readers, the viewer is partly sold. As other borrowers join the first few, the message becomes crystal-clear: Here's a source of business and real-estate loans that's easy to work with, gives fast results, and charges low interest rates. That's the message we're trying to get across!

You need not take "forever" to make a TV ad. Just follow the suggestions above and you'll get better ads—faster!

Use Telemarketing as Your Third Profit Generator

Radio and TV are great for selling a variety of products. But if you want more direct contact with your customer, telemarketing is the answer. You or your salesperson talk directly with the customer. You quickly learn what your customer likes and dislikes.

Telemarketing is an excellent tool for selling a wide variety of products and services, such as:

- Books, records, tapes, films
- Food, blenders, kitchen equipment, outdoor cooking items
- Courses, educational materials, special tutoring
- Magazine subscriptions and renewals, fund raising
- Etc.

Now don't envision yourself sitting by the telephone making thousands of calls! It doesn't work this way. Instead, you:

- Employ a telemarketing agency experienced with your type of product or service
- To make phone calls throughout the day and evening to sell the item or service you have
- Calling people who've responded to ads, calling former customers, and calling prospects from lists you've rented or obtained by swapping names with another mail-order pro

Let me show you some of the rewards of telemarketing. One famous agency says "Out-going phone marketing is direct mail by another name." We found this to be so recently:

- We hired a professional telemarketing agency to call the expires (non-renewals) of our newsletter, *International Wealth Success* on a commission basis—i.e., no sale, no pay!
- Only about half had phone numbers available, meaning that the agency had to either call Information for the number or look it up in the phone book.
- With our annual subscription for 12 monthly issues at $24 per year, we thought that sales would typically be in the $24 to $48 range.
- But before starting the telemarketing campaign, the top person asked me: "Do you have any other items to offer to these expires?" "Sure, " I replied, "we have our books and kits." "Give me full info on them," the director said. We supplied our 48-page catalog, flyers, and a variety of other data.
- When the campaign started we figured it would bring in a few thousand dollars. Boy, were we wrong!
- After selling a renewal to our newsletter, the telemarketing people would sell a book or kit. So instead of billing $24 or $48, the telemarketing sale was $148, $248, $300, and up! Our income was a few thousand dollars a day, instead of the same amount over a period of weeks.
- This experience soon made us telemarketing converts. And we've used it every day since!

How can *you* get started in telemarketing? There are a few simple steps you can follow. These steps can put fast wealth into your pocket:

1. ***Decide what products or services*** you will sell via the telephone.
2. ***Contact a telemarketing service.*** You will find the names and phone numbers of such services in the *Mail Order Riches Success Kit* at the back of this book. Or look up the names in the "Yellow Pages" of your phone book.

3. *Ask the agency* if they'll take your product or service on. If the answer is yes, you know you have a saleable product.

4. *Negotiate—if you can—a commission arrangement.* Here you pay nothing up front. Instead, the telemarketing firm gets its profits from the commission it earns on each sale. It may take awhile but you can work out such a deal, if you try.

5. *Work only with a telemarketer* having a credit-card merchant account. Then your customers can charge their purchases to their credit card and the money will be remitted to your bank. This will save you a lot of time and energy and you'll get your money sooner. The phone agency may pass on their credit-card fees to you. But these are small—in the 1 to 2 percent range. The speed and ease of the service makes such charges well worth such a nominal fee.

6. *Up-sell your customers.* That is, with a basic item of $50, we'll say, offer related items at $150 and $250. Then have the telephone salesperson try to sell the $50 customer a $150 item after getting a yes on the $50 item. The overall effect is to make each phone call more profitable to you and your agency.

Don't use the computer-operated telemarketing machines! They often turn people off. And they can't generate the volume of sales an experienced salesperson can produce. Deal only with the living! It pays better.

What kinds of sales can you expect from telemarketing? Here are some numbers that are entirely possible with a needed product or service:

First Month	$10,000
Second Month	18,000
Third Month	32,000
Fourth Month	46,000
Fifth Month	58,000
Sixth Month	69,000
Total, Six Months	$233,000

And remember—this is just *one* way of selling!

Expand Your Telemarketing Results

Telemarketing and I stumbled together! I started telemarketing when I began publishing my newsletter in 1967. Little did I know that offering to answer questions free of charge during the day and evening was a major marketing step for my business.

Subscribers began calling me with many different kinds of questions. These questions gave me a cross-section of what readers wanted to know. So this helped me point the editorial content toward helping readers solve their problems. And almost all these problems revolve around just one five-letter word—namely *MONEY*! That's why my newsletter concentrates on helping people get the money they need for business or real estate deals.

Beyond this, though, telemarketing had many hidden advantages which I really didn't recognize at the time, namely:

- Direct contact with an expert just for being a subscriber for $24 a year, which includes the 12 regular issues of the *International Wealth Success* newsletter. (The price is still $24/year today!)
- Very low cost compared to the $395, $495, and $995 seminars being offered, at which the expert never even appeared. Instead, some underlings showed up and did a second-class job.
- Availability day and night. The night-time hours are especially important since many people want to call while at home so they don't alert people at their workplace that they're thinking of going into business for themselves.
- Instant access to a competent opinion without having to go through ten secretaries and five answering machines. People still call and say: "I never expected you to be answering your own phone. I expected to get a secretary and an assistant secretary before I could even get to you. Thanks for being available." My answer is: "I answer the phone better than anyone else around here. Besides, by answering directly, I save time."

Over the years my business has prospered beyond my wildest dreams. Meanwhile, some big-bucks seminar givers have gone bankrupt. As I say to people, we're so liquid we slosh. We even offer loans and grants to BWBs with good projects. And all of these benefits came from good telemarketing. But I really didn't know that when I started. Yet, over the years, it gradually began to dawn on me that telemarketing is an extremely powerful tool for every BWB in mail order.

To win the big bucks in telemarketing, take these easy steps:

1. *Be available* by phone to your customers. This will win thousands of friends for you. And these people will continue to send you money—which is what you want them to do!

2. *Be pleasant* on the phone. One mail-order pro I know well who's one of the most creative operators around is a horror on the phone. Call him and he's surly, short, sarcastic, and unhelpful. He makes lots of enemies and loses thousands of customers. Why he doesn't change his ways I don't know. Another mail-order pro who has great projects can never be reached by phone. He ignores messages left for him and never calls back. His business could be five times as great as it is now if he just used some telemarketing sense. Don't *you* be like either of these people. You'll only lose business and customers!

3. *Be at your phone at hours convenient to your customers.* When people know that you're available in the evening, for example, they'll be more likely to call. And you'll be more likely to make the sale. (If you abhor talking on the phone, hire someone who loves to talk on the phone, and teach them what they need to know. Then you'll be able to profit from telemarketing without being part of it.)

4. *Be true to your world.* If you promise to return a phone call, do so at the time you stated you would. And "earn points with your customer" by saying: "this is _____. I promised to call you back at two o'clock and I am doing so—right now." Then give the person

the answer he or she seeks. The reason why you should remind the person you're calling that you're keeping your word is that most people say: "I'll call you _____ ." And then never do. You show that you're a well-organized businessperson by calling when you promised you would. You make a friend and build a stronger bond with your customer.

5. *Be ready to take credit-card orders.* They will build your business enormously. And your business will have much greater credibility. This topic is so important that we discuss it at great length later in this book.

Yes, mail order *can* make you a millionaire! How do I know? Because it made me one. And it can do the same for *you.* Just use all the electronic media available to you—starting right *now!*

Tap into the 900 Number Market

With an 800 toll-free number *you* pay the entire cost of the phone call to order a product or service from your firm. An 800 number is a great convenience to your customer. And it *will* bring you more business. How can I say that? I've used an 800 number in my business for years. And it *does* bring in more orders. I can point to my firm's bank account as evidence that the 800 number *does* work!

With a 900 number the caller pays the phone bill. "What's so good about that?" you ask. Plenty, I say.

A 900 number shows your potential customers that you *do* welcome calls asking about your products or services. So even though the customer does pay for the call, there is an attraction about a company that *wants* calls. When you run your 900 number in an ad you'll find that the response is great. What's the secret to making a 900 number pay? Here it is:

- To make a 900 number caller feel they're getting their money's worth, you must offer something of value to the caller.
- Typical value-added offers include: (1) Your catalog; (2) Answers to questions about your product or service; (3) Products or services the callers can sell and earn a good commission, etc.

With a typical 900 number call, the person placing the call pays his or her telephone company $2.00 for the first minute, and $1.00 (or less) for each additional minute. You are paid about two-thirds of the amount billed. But if you use computer equipment to help the caller get answers to questions, the rental of this equipment (firms rarely buy it), plus the payment made to the equipment lessor for each call, brings your take down to about 50 percent of the amount billed for each call.

But the take per call really isn't that important! What *is* important is the product or service ordered by the caller using the 900 number. You're out to make *big* sales—not pennies on phone calls!

With a 900 number you can have menu-driven responses. This is where the voice answering the phone says, for a firm selling clothing by mail order:

- For information on children's clothing, press button Number 1
- For information on clothing for adults, press button Number 2
- For information on misses' clothing, press button Number 3

Yes, the 900 number can be a big lift for your business today. To get full information, call your local phone company. They'll be glad to get you started.

Didn't I tell you at the start of this book that the greatest business in the world is mail order? Aren't you beginning to believe me?

To show you how a creative mail-order pro can take a telephone company service and make money from it, let me tell you about a west coast friend of mine who started a money information exchange and network using a 900 number:

- To become part of the network, anyone looking for money can call the 900 number and record the need— i.e., how much, for how long, for what purpose, along with any interest-rate restrictions. There is *no* charge for this.
- Financial brokers, real estate brokers, etc., can also call the 900 number free of charge to get leads on people and firms seeking funds.
- My friend, the operator of the network, makes money on every phone call placed on the 900 number. But much more importantly, he'll get a piece of the action from the commissions earned for finding the loans. That's where the money really is!

Now that you know something about making money with electronic media, it's time to get started. I'm ready to help you every step of the way. Just call me— electronically—and I'm at your service!

CHAPTER 9

KEEP ADDING NEW PRODUCTS OR SERVICES

If you want to make millions in mail order you'll have to work at adding new products or services to the line you offer. Why? Because your customers want the *new*, the *exciting*, the *challenging*. And they expect all of this from *you*. To show their appreciation, they'll send you money every time you introduce something new. And that, after all, is why you're in this business—to make money!

New Offers Create Excitement

Once you get a few items that sell, you'll go back—again and again—to people who buy from you. Why? Because they're the easiest ones to sell!

Also, your line of products or services will put you in a certain type of business, such as:

- Home products, home services
- Business products, business services
- Financial publications or services
- Books for certain professionals—accountants, doctors, lawyers, etc.
- Sporting goods and sports wear
- Etc.

With your line defined by your first few products, you'll want to add more products or services to that line. Why? Because you can go back to your customers again and again with new items and they'll buy—again and again! Your "cost of sales"—that is, how much it costs to make each sale—will drop. This means you'll make more money on each sale. So your profits and income will be higher. Let me give you an example:

- Our first self-study kit was our *Financial Broker/Finder/ Business Broker/Business Consultant Kit* listed at the back of this book.
- The *Financial Broker Kit* was so well received that we decided to introduce other course kits on topics that interest people. The result is over a dozen kits catering to the needs and interests of a variety of people. These kits are listed at the back of this book under the product number starting with the letter "K" for kit.
- Kits were developed on real estate, mail order, mortgage finance, loans by phone, loans by mail, franchising, etc. After we covered the major basic topics, we turned to kits for specialized audiences. The results are under the letter "K" at the back of this book. As you'll see when you glance over the kit list, we have actively added new products and services as our business grew. *You* can do the same, no matter what line of products you sell.
- Today, this related line of kits generates many thousands of dollars in revenue for us each year. They're so popular that users come to us and say: "You ought to do a kit on _____." We listen and learn. And if the kit is—in our view—needed, we'll get it ready in just a few weeks. Sales will usually get off to a good start since we'll advertise the kit in our newsletter and other publications.

Treat your customers right and they'll become your loyal friends. So when you introduce a new product or service, your loyal customers will be among the first to buy. With enough loyal customers, your first offer of the new item may sell so strongly that you'll quickly reach your breakeven point. From then on you're making money!

Having a related line of products has many advantages
for you. For example, you'll find that:

- People will buy all the items in your line because they
  don't want to leave out or overlook any item that might
  help them live better, make more money, be accepted
  by a group, etc.
- Each item in a related line helps sell another one. Thus,
  if you're selling ski products by mail (a very good
  business, by the way), you'll often see an order for a
  ski jacket, hat, hand warmer, and beginner's book come
  in from the same customer. If you didn't have all these
  items in your offer, you might lose a sale of one or more
  of them. Or—worse yet—your customer might turn to
  another mail-order dealer to buy all the items on this
  list because your competitor carries everything the buyer
  wants!
- Having a complete line of products or services helps
  build your reputation in the field. How? A buyer—when
  talking to another prospective buyer—might say: "You
  see this beautiful jacket? I got it by mail from ABC Ski
  Supplies. That company has *everything* in its catalog.
  You ought to get a copy so you have it on hand when
  you want to order anything!" Result? You've picked up
  another customer because you've added new products
  regularly.

Your new offers create excitement because people like
to hear about the latest in their field. Remember: Most
people are bored with their lives and jobs. Bring them
something exciting and they'll welcome you with open
checkbooks.

To understand this better, think of any hobbies you may
have. Then recall receiving a flyer or catalog covering what's
new in your hobby. Remember how your hands almost
shook as you flipped through the material, trying to see
what's new? Your mail-order dealer "made your day" with
something that excites and intrigues you. Your next
reaction—probably—was to send off a check or money order
or call in a credit-card charge. This is what you want *your*
customers to do!

Extend Your Products or Services Profitably

Now when you add products or services you must do
so sensibly. Just throwing more products into a mailing
or a catalog won't do the job. You must extend your product
or service line profitably. How do you do this? Take these
easy steps:

1. *List the items you offer that are selling.* To do this,
   go to your records to see which items bring in the
   largest number of sales dollars. Every firm has some
   sales "leaders"—you want to determine exactly which
   of your items are your sales leaders.
2. *Find, or develop, similar products* that either go with
   or build on your sales leaders. It's best if you can develop
   your own "follow-on" products or services. Why?
   Because you can charge a higher price and have an
   exclusive source (yourself) of these products or services.
   So your competition doesn't stand a chance of beating
   you out unless they go through the long process of
   imitating what you offer. By that time you can have
   pocketed a million dollars or more because you have
   the market all to yourself. (David Buckley, an extremely
   creative young mail-order pro, told me he made more
   than one million dollars in the mailing-list rental
   business because he was the first on the market with
   a new approach to this business. His major sales were
   to those of his customers who had bought other, related
   products.)
3. *Offer your expanded product line* to every customer
   who bought one of your related products. Do this by
   a special mailing or offer to your customers. They'll
   be flattered that you thought of them. And they'll buy
   like crazy. We have as many as 60 percent of our regular
   customers buy a new, related offer within moments
   after they get the flyer or other ad material on it. I
   call such sales "happy money" because our customers
   are delighted to get another solid offer from us. And,
   good friend, we're happy to put the money into our
   business checking account!
4. *Keep offering your new items* until you replace them
   with others. But don't drop the previously new items—

keep selling them. Why? Because they're *new* to your newest customers! And if you keep attracting the same general types of customers (which most mail-order firms do), then your new customers will be turned on by the same offers as your earlier customers! The result? You build up a strong set of offers which your customers can hardly resist. So your business booms to the point where you wonder how you'll keep up with it. This is a delightful feeling!

5. *Follow the same steps* each time you introduce a new, related item. That is, start with what's selling and expand from there. This is a very powerful way to build mailbox millions. If you use this way, I can almost guarantee that you'll get rich in this great business. Why? Because when you expand your product line with related products, your cost of selling to your known customers is almost zero! This shoots your profits through the roof!

Mix and Shake for Best Results

Let's say you successfully sell a product line to your customers. When you consider expanding that line you think only of other, related *products*. Is this the right approach? *No!* Why?

Because if you "mix and shake" products and services you may get spectacular sales results. Let me give you a real-life, dollars-in-the-bank example:

> *As you know, I publish two monthly newsletters—* **International Wealth Success** *and* **Money Watch Bulletin**. *These are* **products**. *But we also offer several* **services**— *one of which is business and real-estate loans at low interest rates to subscribers of our newsletters.*
>
> *Recently, while analyzing how we might expand our product line I hit on the idea of adding another* **service** *offering to either of our newsletter* **products**. *This service? It is an expanded loan offer whereby we reduce the collateral requirements for a loan if we are given an interest in the*

> *profits of the business funded by a loan from my firm,
> IWS, Inc.*
>
> *Results of this offer both to non-subscribers and to
> subscribers were most encouraging. It seems that people
> are happy to share profits if they can get the funding which
> enables the profits to be earned.*
>
> *So we mixed and shook paper products (our newsletters)
> with a service (loans based on profit sharing) and came
> up with a winner. Why? Because our newsletter customers
> are almost all looking for business or real-estate loans. So
> the service offer of profit sharing loans "grabbed" our
> readers so they read every issue of the newsletter to gain
> data. And we'll earn more than just the interest on the
> loan since we'll be getting a share of the profits. This is
> a win-win situation—obtained by mixing and shaking
> well!*

Now I'm not the only mail-order pro doing some
profitable mixing and shaking. Other successes in the
business do much the same. Thus:

- Jim Straw, of *Business Opportunity Digest*, founded an
  offshore bank to meet his customers' needs.
- Donald Moore of "Business Opportunity Club" formed
  a cooperative to serve his customers' needs.
- Chase Revell founded a national magazine to serve his
  customers and to bring to the world the message of the
  benefits of having a business of your own.
- Robert Allen carried his real estate message to his
  thousands of staunch admirers by means of seminars at
  convenient locations around the country.

And there are thousands of other successful educators
and teachers who use similar ways to help their audiences.
You can do much the same. How? Just figure out a way
to mix and shake to give your customers better and more
valuable service in the area of business in which you operate.

Make "Service" Part of Your Offering

Until now we've been talking about you offering a
product or service for sale to customers via some form of

direct marketing. Now I want to talk about making *service* (what *you* do for your customers) a part of your offering. Talk to anyone who has bought by mail and you'll hear (except from *my* customers) the following complaints:

- It took forever for me to get what I ordered, even though I sent them a money order
- The item I bought was beaten up in the mail because they didn't take time to wrap it properly
- I tried to call them to trace my order but the phone was always busy
- When I finally did reach the company on the phone the person answering was surly and couldn't tell me anything about my order
- I asked to talk to the owner but they said he never talks to customers
- My overall impression of the company is that they really don't give a hoot about their customers
- Etc.

When your customer has any of these reactions to your firm, your future sales suffer. Why? Because the dissatisfied customer rarely re-orders. Instead, such a person goes elsewhere to get what he or she wants. Don't let this happen to *you*! Instead, take these easy steps:

1. Keep in mind—at all times—that *everything* you do in business is marketing! This means that you must be alert at all times to the image you and your employees project to your customers.
2. Send orders quickly—the same day, if possible—when a person pays by money order or credit card. You'll win a loyal customer who will order again and again.
3. Do what a customer asks when fast delivery is requested. That is, if the customer wants Express Mail delivery, send the item that way, if it can be done. (Some items may be too heavy or too bulky; the customer should be told this so Express Mail delivery is not expected.) And if a customer requests courier delivery (Federal Express, UPS 2-Day Air, DHL, etc.), deliver the item this way. (Two valuable from-the-trenches pointers on quick delivery methods: (a) Express Mail from your

Post Office delivers seven days a week at *no* extra charge. Courier services have a very high charge for Saturday or Sunday delivery. (b) When a customer tells you to use his or her courier account number to charge the cost back to the customer, use the customer's name and address as the sender *and* as the recipient. Then you avoid your being charged the delivery cost by the courier service. Using this approach you can avoid a lot of arguments over who should be paying the cost of delivery. It's billed to the customer—who will remember that he or she instructed you to charge the delivery cost to him or her.)

4. Wrap all products carefully before shipping them. If you use "Jiffy Bags" to ship items, wrap the product in a separate covering to prevent the interior of the bag from spewing on the product if the bag is ripped. Such thoughtfulness makes a highly positive impression on your customer when he or she opens the package. Your very wrapping makes the sale a more positive one. As I said earlier, everything in this business is marketing!

5. Be available to your customers when they call. In my business I'm available to my customers from 8:00 A.M. to 10:00 P.M. seven days a week. I tell people this in my books and newsletters. Yet when they call and I answer the phone people are amazed. But, as I said, I regard my answering of the phone as marketing. I'm there to answer questions, take orders, give an opinion, etc. Meanwhile, my business booms.

6. Be polite at all times when answering the phone, writing a letter, or sending a FAX. Honey gets more affection than vinegar. Sure, you may be annoyed by a demanding customer. But your goal is to sell more of the expanded products or services you've introduced. You *can* do this if you're polite and courteous!

7. Talk to your customers—you'll learn from them. They'll tell you what new products or services you should add to your line. Even if they don't tell you directly, they may say: "Did you ever think of offering a _____ ?" This question gives you a direct clue as to what the customer would like to have available to buy—from you! Or the customer might

say: "If you only had a _____ , I'd buy it right now!" Again, you have a key suggestion as to what to add to your product line. Many of our products are the result of a customer saying, "You ought to have this or that." And most of them were right!

Expand Your Line with Other People's Help

There are many creative people in this world. While I like to think that I'm one of the most creative blokes in town, I often run into other people who are almost as creative as myself. Some are even more creative! This realization is one of the best I ever had. Why?

Because it got me to look at what other people in my field of business (which is financing and publishing) are doing. And do you know what? There are a lot of smart folks in this business! Some are even smarter than I ever thought of being!

And the products these people develop! They're just great. So what do I do? I take these simple steps to expand my product line:

1. I get on the phone and tell this creative person who I am. A few have heard of me.

2. Next, I tell the person that I think their new book, kit, course, or other offer is just great. "I'd like to see a copy of it. And I'll pay you full price—I'm not trying to get a free ride."

3. Once I see the item, I decide if I can sell it to my customers. If I can, I call back and arrange a deal. I offer the seller 50 percent (one-half) of the list price. Everyone so far has accepted this offer.

4. Next, I order a number of copies so I can inventory the product. Why? For a number of key reasons. These are:

   a. Drop shipping, where the seller sends the item to your customer, can be fraught with all sorts of hidden problems. You may wind up with the customer screaming at you that he hasn't yet received the great product that's supposed to expand your line. So you get on the phone to the seller (if he or she can be reached) and try to find out what went wrong. You can spend hours on a simple one-item offer. And it's not worth the time and energy because it can easily be avoided.

b. Drop shippers *never* seem to love your customers as much as you do! So they usually (but not always) treat them like second-rate citizens.

c. When you ship an item, you know the full details—when, how, where, etc. Having your sales items in hand gives *you* full control. So you don't make enemies of your customers because you treat them right at all times!

5. I request—and get—advertising material from the seller. Why? Because then I don't have to spend time writing ads, checking copy, etc. We just put our name and address at the end of the ad so our customers can order from us. Another advantage of using ad material from the seller is that such ads are often much better written than the person promoting the product could write himself or herself. Yes—strange as it may seem—there *are* good ad writers around!

6. Try to get an exclusive on the item you're buying. If you're the only one promoting a saleable item you stand to make much more money than if 50 others are also selling it. The exclusive means that you have the sole and only right to sell the item. If the seller is unwilling to give you an exclusive, try getting one for six months, a year, etc. Sometimes the seller will be more willing to give you an exclusive when there's a known cutoff date. Be sure to include a clause which allows you to renew the exclusive arrangement if you reach, or exceed, a stated sales level. This clause will spur you on to reach a profitable sales level for both yourself and your supplier.

One word of caution about expanding your line using other people's help. This is:

Don't pay your supplier such a high price for the item or service that you'll have to charge a higher than expected price for the offer in your market! Why? Because it's difficult for both your supplier and yourself to make a high profit on any item if it is priced too high for the market. Many a good product or service is killed by greedy businesspeople seeking to squeeze the last penny out of a sale. It's better to make a little less but to get the sale!

How to Build Riches with Products from Others

One of the most exciting mail-order businesses is a great example of using products from other people to build *your* riches. That business? It's selling food by mail.

Food by mail is a $1 billion a year business in the United States alone. And with the rest of the world catching on to the delightful kinds of foods available by mail, this market is certain to expand enormously.

What kinds of food might you sell by mail? There's almost no limit to the foods you can sell. Typical foods available today by mail include:

- Cheeses of all kinds—sharp to mild
- Candies—from gourmet chocolates to salt water taffy
- Fruits—apples, oranges, grapefruit, berries, etc.
- Meats—hams, steaks, diet cuts, etc.
- Seafood—lobsters, shrimp, salmon, etc.
- Baked goods—cakes, biscuits, breads, etc.
- Etc.

Such foods are promoted by catalogs, direct-mail letters, radio, TV, etc. You can start with one type of food you enjoy preparing—such as gourmet soup—and take on other, related foods. Thus, with soup you'd think of selling a line of fine crackers, biscuits, and breads. With these items you might also consider butters of various types, even cheeses. Before you know it you're a "soup to nuts" mail-order marketer of gourmet foods!

The key, of course, is that you start with one or two good foods and expand your line with excellent foods from other people. And the beauty of selling food by mail is that it's consumed and people have to reorder to satisfy their urge for good food!

Returned merchandise in the food mail-order business is infrequent—just 1 to 2 percent. Almost all your buyers will repeat their orders—as many as 85 percent of your buyers will reorder. Some mail-order food sellers report sales of over $8,000 for every 1,000 catalogs mailed. This is a very high amount for catalog sales. Orders can average $40 to $100 each, depending on what you charge for your food.

You can even start a *continuity club* or *continuity program*. With either approach, you send food automatically to your members at stated intervals—say every four or six weeks. When your member receives the food, he or she sends you a check or money order for the amount owed. Or you can automatically charge the amount to your member's credit card if you have written authorization to do so.

Such continuity programs can give you a solid base for your business. Why? Because you can be certain of a known dollar amount of sales for each continuity period. So you can easily plan ahead for a year and know what your business income will be.

If you have a *negative option* feature in your continuity club, your member has the right to refuse a shipment in any cycle. But few members will refuse any shipment. Yet having the negative option feature makes it easier for a prospective member to justify joining your continuity program.

With a negative option, you mail your members an advance notice of what's in your next shipment. The member then has a stated time interval—10 or 15 days— to respond if he or she does not want the shipment. If you don't hear from a member, you automatically go ahead and ship the food.

How can you get started with just one food product?

Use a *magalog*, which is a catalog that carries paid ads. Your ad cost will be low. And if you pick your magalog carefully, you should have strong sales.

As your sales increase you can look for other products. Once you have about a dozen, it will be easy for you to issue your own catalog. With the right food products, you can easily expand using other people's creative output to fatten your bank account!

Grow Big and Strong with New Products

You can't get big in this business with just one product. To grow you *must* introduce new products or services. But there are a number of ways you can make this easier for yourself. Here are a few ways that work well in any mail-order business:

1. Change your ad headline for fast moving products. Thus, if you have a sales leader that's starting to show signs of tapering off, write a new ad headline. This is quick, easy, and can attract customers who turned away when they saw your first ad. Figures 9-1 through 9-4 show new headlines.
2. Rewrite the body copy of your ad if the headline change does not give you the increased sales you seek. A new ad can work wonders for increasing the sales of your product or service.
3. Vary the ad size. If you've run full-page ads, switch to half-page or quarter-page ads. The difference in ad size may attract buyers you missed before. Why? Because some people turn away from full-page ads and read only smaller ads. Don't ask me why. It's just one of the crazy aspects of this business I've observed!
4. Get a professional copywriter to write a sales letter for you. We more than tripled the sales of our International Financial Management Program after having our sales letter redone by a professional copywriter. With a $100 program, tripling your sales can put a lot of extra fuel in the tanks of your yacht!

How to Get Rich in
MAIL ORDER
CA$H LOAN DOLLARS.

°Overcome BAD CREDIT for yourself and others!

°Get CASH in a flash--maybe one day, or less!

°Find an "Angel" for your cash needs!

°Develop signature-loan MONEY POWER!

°Rate YOUR loan chances in minutes!

°Wipe out ALL DEBTS with just one loan!

°Deal by mail--NO interviews; NO pain!

°Get liquid assets for any personal need!

°Get INTEREST-ONLY mail-order loans!

°Be the "fastest loan broker" around!

°Get DOZENS of different kinds of loans!

°Be a MAIL-ORDER UNSECURED SIGNATURE LOAN wheeler-dealer!

°Make friends with money lenders forever!

°Get MAIL-ORDER LOAN convenience, speed, efficiency, confidentialty!

°Earn BIG FEES helping others get quick unsecured signature loans!

°Know who's lending for what use!

°Laugh "all the way to the bank" NOW!

°Deal by mail and avoid face-to-face hassles and arguments!

GET UNSECURED PERSONAL SIGNATURE LOANS FOR YOUR CLIENTS OR YOURSELF using the IWS MAIL-ORDER LOAN SUCCESS SYSTEM--the fastest way to get a signature loan today! Learn how to deal with lenders--prepare winning loan applications--help yourself or others to the BILLIONS available for unsecured loans! Build your own, or your client's loan rating fast! It's ALL here--plus much, much more in this NEW powerful SYSTEM!

Written by Ty Hicks, a man who has supervised the lending of some $50-million in all types of unsecured signature loans, this SYSTEM is just what's needed to get people the money they seek! And YOU can use the SYSTEM for your clients, or for yourself. It works, works, works for YOU! And it works for anyone you're helping get a loan. The SYSTEM gives you thousands of lenders to contact--shows YOU how to build your own list of willing and interested lenders! Send your check or money order for your SYSTEM today! Get loans SOON!

THIS IS THE ORDER BLANK

$$$

$ Here's $100. Send me my MAIL-ORDER LOAN SUCCESS SYSTEM. If you wish, you can call Ty $
$ Hicks with your credit-card (Master or Visa) order at 516-766-5850 9am to 10 pm. Have $
$ your credit card ready? Ask Ty any questions you may have! $

$ NAME_____Apt/Suite #_____ $

$ ADDRESS_____CITY_____STATE_____ZIP_____ $

$ Send check or money order to: IWS, Inc., 24 Canterbury Rd, Rockville Centre NY 11570 $

Figure 9-1

GET THE SYSTEM FOR FAST MAIL-ORDER LOANS

°<u>Overcome</u> BAD CREDIT for yourself and others!

°<u>Get CASH in a flash</u>--maybe one day, or less!

°"Find an "Angel" for your cash needs!

°Develop signature-loan MONEY POWER!

°Rate <u>YOUR</u> loan chances in minutes!

°Wipe out <u>ALL DEBTS</u> with just one loan!

°Deal by mail--<u>NO</u> interviews; <u>NO</u> pain!

°Get liquid assets for any personal need!

°Get <u>INTEREST-ONLY</u> mail-order loans!

°Be the "fastest loan broker" around!

°Get <u>DOZENS</u> of different kinds of loans!

°Be a <u>MAIL-ORDER UNSECURED SIGNATURE LOAN</u> wheeler-dealer!

°Make friends with money lenders forever!

°Get <u>MAIL-ORDER LOAN</u> convenience, speed, efficiency, confidentialty!

°Earn <u>BIG FEES</u> helping others get quick unsecured signature loans!

°Know who's lending for what use!

°Laugh "all the way to the bank" <u>NOW</u>!

°Deal by mail and avoid face-to-face hassles and arguments!

<u>GET UNSECURED PERSONAL SIGNATURE LOANS FOR YOUR CLIENTS OR YOURSELF</u> using the IWS MAIL-ORDER LOAN SUCCESS SYSTEM--the fastest way to get a signature loan today! Learn how to deal with lenders--prepare winning loan applications--help yourself or others to the <u>BILLIONS</u> available for unsecured loans! Build your own, or your client's loan rating fast! It's <u>ALL</u> here--plus much, much more in this <u>NEW</u> powerful <u>SYSTEM</u>!

Written by Ty Hicks, a man who has supervised the lending of some $50-million in all types of unsecured signature loans, this <u>SYSTEM</u> is just what's needed to get people the money they seek! And <u>YOU</u> can use the <u>SYSTEM</u> for your clients, or for yourself. It works, works, works for <u>YOU</u>! And it works for anyone you're helping get a loan. The <u>SYSTEM</u> gives you thousands of lenders to contact--shows <u>YOU</u> how to build your own list of willing and interested lenders! Send your check or money order for your <u>SYSTEM</u> today! Get loans <u>SOON</u>!

THIS IS THE ORDER BLANK

$$$

$ Here's $100. Send me my MAIL-ORDER LOAN SUCCESS SYSTEM. If you wish, you can call Ty
$ Hicks with your credit-card (Master or Visa) order at 516-766-5850 9am to 10 pm. Have
$ your credit card ready? Ask Ty any questions you may have!

$ NAME_____ Apt/Suite #____

$ ADDRESS_____CITY_____STATE_____ZIP_____

$ Send check or money order to: IWS, Inc., 24 Canterbury Rd, Rockville Centre NY 11570

Figure 9-2

There's a better way to MORE
LOW-COST
REAL ESTATE
FINANCING

100% Financing!
110% Financing!
120% Financing!

GET ALL KINDS OF REAL-ESTATE LOANS FASTER!
Take the hassle and delay out of getting a
real-estate loan! How? By using the IWS
REAL-ESTATE LOAN GETTERS SERVICE! This NEW
service from Ty Hicks gives you:
- **Proven ways to get loans
- **Forms for fast loan approval
- **Names & addresses of lenders
- **Step-by-step tips for borrowers
- **Keys to getting ANY type of
  real-estate loan today
- **A turn-key business for you in any
  state, city, or county
- **Ways to earn BIG commissions
  from the easiest loan ever
- **Speedy decisions--sometimes in
  just an hour
- **Built-in collateral--no credit
  check hassles
- **Sources of the unusual and hard-
  to-get real estate loan

100% Financing!
110% Financing!
120% Financing!

YOU CAN USE THIS SERVICE to get loans for

your own real-estate deals, or for deals
that other people have! Ty Hicks gives YOU
complete support in this service--giving
you the forms you need, the lenders you can
work with, and advice over his hotline!

GET REAL-ESTATE LOANS for any type of deal,
from single-family homes to office-complex
developments, etc. If it's real estate, this
service can help YOU--with 1st, 2nd, 3rd--
even 8th mortgages! Get money for raw land,
air rights, shopping centers, garden/senior
citizen apartments, marinas!

MEGA-MORTGAGES INTO THE MULTI-MILLIONS are
there--just for the asking! Don't let them
go to waste! Get in on the real estate boom.
Be part of the lending spree that's putting
billions into new and used real estate every
year! Know who's lending for what use!

TO START USING THIS SERVICE send $100 TODAY
to IWS, or call in your credit card order!
MAIL THIS COUPON NOW OR CALL IN YOUR
CREDIT CARD ORDER! DON'T WASTE TIME!

SUCCESS STARTS
HERE!

Send your check or money order for $100 to
IWS, Inc. at the address at the right. Or
call Ty Hicks at 212-512-6528 from 9am to
4pm New York time or from 8 to 10 pm at
516-766-5850 with your VISA or MASTERCARD
order. If ordering by mail, give card no.,
expiration date, and your phone number.

Send me the REAL-ESTATE LOAN GETTERS SERVICE.
Here's $100. Or charge my credit card at left.

NAME_____ PHONE NO._____

ADDRESS_____ Apt/Suite #____

CITY_____STATE___ZIP_____

Send to: IWS, Inc. 24 Canterbury Rd
          Rockville Centre NY 11570

To order by Credit Card, call Ty Hicks at
516-766-5850, day or night. Have card ready!

OVER **OVER** **OVER** **OVER**

Figure 9-3

HOW TO GET 100% FINANCING FOR ANY REAL-ESTATE DEAL

Run your own real-estate business from home with only a telephone and a few scraps of paper.

GET ALL KINDS OF REAL-ESTATE LOANS FASTER! Take the hassle and delay out of getting a real-estate loan! How? By using the IWS **REAL-ESTATE LOAN GETTERS SERVICE!** This **NEW** service from Ty Hicks gives you:

- **Proven ways to get loans
- **Forms for fast loan approval
- **Names & addresses of lenders
- **Step-by-step tips for borrowers
- **Keys to getting **ANY** type of real-estate loan today
- **A turn-key business for you in any state, city, or county
- **Ways to earn **BIG** commissions from the easiest loan ever
- **Speedy decisions--sometimes in just an hour
- **Built-in collateral--no credit check hassles
- **Sources of the unusual and hard-to-get real estate loan

100% Financing!
110% Financing!
120% Financing!

YOU CAN USE THIS SERVICE to get loans for

your own real-estate deals, or for deals that other people have! Ty Hicks gives **YOU** complete support in this service--giving you the forms you need, the lenders you can work with, and advice over his hotline!

GET REAL-ESTATE LOANS for any type of deal, from single-family homes to office-complex developments, etc. If it's real estate, this service can help **YOU**--with 1st, 2nd, 3rd-- even 8th mortgages! Get money for raw land, air rights, shopping centers, garden/senior citizen apartments, marinas!

MEGA-MORTGAGES INTO THE MULTI-MILLIONS are there--just for the asking! Don't let them go to waste! Get in on the real estate boom. Be part of the lending spree that's putting billions into new and used real estate every year! Know who's lending for what use!

TO START USING THIS SERVICE send $100 **TODAY** to IWS, or call in your credit card order!

SUCCESS STARTS HERE!

Send your check or money order for $100 to IWS, Inc. at the address at the right. Or call Ty Hicks at 212-512-6528 from 9am to 4pm New York time or from 8 to 10 pm at 516-766-5850 with your VISA or MASTERCARD order. If ordering by mail, give card no., expiration date, and your phone number.

MAIL THIS COUPON NOW OR CALL IN YOUR CREDIT CARD ORDER! DON'T WASTE TIME!

Send me the REAL-ESTATE LOAN GETTERS SERVICE. Here's $100. Or charge my credit card at left.

NAME_____ PHONE NO._____

ADDRESS_____ Apt/Suite #___

CITY_____ STATE___ ZIP_____

Send to: IWS, Inc. 24 Canterbury Rd
Rockville Centre NY 11570

To order by Credit Card, call Ty Hicks at
516-766-5850, day or night. Have card ready!

OVER **OVER** **OVER** **OVER**

Figure 9-4

5. Team up with another friendly mail-order pro and cross-sell products. We do this by allowing people to use pages from our 48-page catalog in their mailings with their name and address on the page. Orders come to our mail-order dealer. He or she deducts their commission and sends the order on to us. We drop ship at *no* cost to the dealer or customer. This works well because we both get some new products which sell nicely to our lists.
6. Try new and different ways to promote sales. Thus, if you've used only magazine ads, try:
   • Direct mail
   • Radio ads
   • TV ads
   • Card deck mailings
   • Weekly newspaper ads
   The whole key is to get your products or services out to people who haven't seen them before. To them your "old" product or service is "new" because they haven't read any earlier ads about it.

But I can't urge you too strongly to develop and introduce new products or services on a regular basis. It's the life-blood of mail order. And, as your product list grows, you become more respected in your field. You and your firm become known as leaders in your field. People come to you to buy what you offer because your name is one of the best in the business.

Thus, in my field, that of helping new businesses find financing, we are well-known because we have such a wide product line. We pick up orders just because people don't want to be without items from the leader in the field! Such business keeps us growing every year. You can do the same— just by being certain to introduce new products on a regular basis.

Sure, it's work! But it can keep you in yachts (like myself), fancy cars, mansions, sun-drenched vacations in winter, great schools for your kids, and a big bundle when the day comes to hang up your track shoes!

CHAPTER 10

SELL TO BIG BUYERS
TO MAKE MEGA-BUCKS

THERE WAS A time when mail-order businesspeople dreamed of selling thousands of items at $10 each to make millions. But the day of the $10 item is nearly gone. What with higher postage, increased package costs, and big labor costs, the $10 sale is almost ancient history.

You can still of course make a $10 sale as a loss leader. But if you do this, you *must* upgrade your customer via the back end to a larger dollar sale. While this is an approved approach, I find that going for the big runs in the early innings wins more ball games than waiting until the ninth inning to score! Why? Because you may not score with only three outs to go. So I recommend finding the big buyers and selling to them. You win more games that way!

Locate the Big Buyers for Your Business

Every business has a group of *big* buyers. While such buyers may be only 20 percent of your customers, they can account for 80 percent of your sales dollars. So you cannot—and should not—overlook such an important segment of your business!

To show you how to locate the big buyers for your business, let me show you the big ones in my business—that of selling financial information. Our big buyers are:

149

- Large chains of bookstores
- Book wholesalers
- Libraries, both public and university
- Financial clubs and groups
- Our own sales reps
- Multi-kit buyers
- Other newsletters selling our products

How do we find out who our big buyers are? We watch the orders. Over a period of time we're able to identify the big hitters.

"But," you say, "I'm not even in business yet. How can I spot the big hitters?" You have to take a number of logical steps which are both fun and useful to come up with *your* big hitters. These steps are:

1. Write down a word picture of your typical customer. Is that person:
   - A businessperson
   - A hobbyist
   - A leisure seeker
   - An interested consumer?
2. Figure out who might be major suppliers of your typical customer's needs. Thus, if your typical customer is a businessperson, the major suppliers might be:
   - Office supply stores
   - Price-club outlets
   - Discount chain stores
   - Other outlets—like mail-order suppliers
3. Once you know the major suppliers to your customers you must ask them to buy from you if you want to make big sales to earn mega-bucks. But don't rush out with your order book in hand! It takes planning to sell the big buyers. Here's what you can do.
4. Develop a discount schedule for big buyers. Why? Because if you go in—either in person or by mail— seeking an order you must have an offer that attracts attention. In making such sales myself I always noticed that the big buyer complained about the small discount being offered by most suppliers. In my case the standard discount offered was 40 percent. So I upped my discount to 50 percent. Result: The big buyers order like crazy!

And when some of the competition upped their discount to 45 percent I countered by agreeing to pay the shipping cost. This further increased our orders!

Finding the big buyers will vary from business to business. Thus, the big buyers in the bowling business will certainly be different from those in the garden furniture business. So each business must be approached separately. And if you're not familiar with a business that interests you:

1. Talk to people in the business. Ask who are the big buyers. Get info on the location of such buyers.
2. Find out what publications (magazines and newspapers) serve the business. Look through back issues and current copies to get the names and addresses of such buyers. This is part of your market research.
3. Get—from people in the business—the typical size of an order placed by the big buyers. Knowing the dollar amount and/or quantity for a typical order will quickly tell you if it's worth your time and energy to push a high discount and freight-paid policy. If the orders *are* typically large then it's worth going all out to get them. Why? Because you can get a big bucks cash flow into your business quickly and easily. And that, after all, is why you want to get into the mail-order business!
4. Read books and reports covering the business. Such items will often identify the types of big buyers to look for. In a matter of hours you can become a mini-expert on a specific business that interests you.

Make an Offer to Big Buyers

Knowing the big buyers won't do you much good if you don't try to sell them. Knowledge without action is not too effective. You can approach your big buyers in any of three ways:

1. By mail—an effective but slow way
2. By telephone—quick and modern
3. In person—takes direct-selling skill

Our experience shows that the first two ways are the most effective. Why? For a number of reasons, namely:

- People are busy; many don't like to give up the time needed for a personal sales call on them.
- Mail and telephone solicitations give both a record (mail) and personal contact (phone) and allow a fast and correct decision by an experienced person. Any questions can be answered quickly by a simple phone call.
- Big buyers are set up to handle sales via form letters and other time-saving methods. So they really *like* to do business by mail. And remember this: What might seem like a large sale to you could be a routine small sale to your big buyer!

So to make that first *big* sale to a major buyer, take these easy steps:

1. Decide on the offer you'll make. That is, figure out what discount you'll offer. When you're doing this, keep in mind what I said earlier about beating your competition's discount. Don't be one of the crowd— offer a little more so your big buyer can make a larger profit selling your products or services. Then the big buyer will buy more and you'll earn more!

2. Prepare your offer in an attractive way. That is, have it typed on your letterhead in a clear and easy-to-read typeface. Don't try to sell to big buyers using a handwritten or printed offer. It won't work! Your offer will be tossed out with no response of any kind. You *must* be professional in your presentation.

3. Send your offer to the buyer. Get the name and address of the chief buyer by either calling or writing and asking to whom you should address your offer. Use a short letter to tell the buyer why you're sending the offer. One such letter is shown in Figure 10-1; the offer is shown in Figure 10-2.

4. Be ready to answer any questions about your offer. These will seldom come by phone; instead they will be in a form letter with certain questions checked off. Send your answer immediately. Then your first order will reach you sooner and you'll be able to deposit

```
                          YOUR LETTERHEAD


Chief Buyer
Big Buying Company
123 Main St
Anytown 00000-0000

Dear Mr. or Ms. _____:

Enclosed is one of the best profit-making offers you've ever seen. It
will make big money for your firm--quickly.

We're sending you this offer because your firm is so well-known and so
highly respected in the retailing field throughout the world. Further,
this offer matches your product line ideally.

As you'll see from the enclosed offer, you'll receive very generous
discounts which will allow you to show high profits on every product
you handle from us.

Further, we stand behind every product we produce. You'll find that they
are the highest quality. Your customers will be delighted with them.
Many will say that they're a bargain at almost any price.

We look forward to your order soon. Meanwhile, if I can help in any way,
please call me at the above number.

Very truly yours,


Your name,
Your Title

Secretary: Your Initials
```

Figure 10-1

SPECIAL NEW PRODUCTS OFFER

XYZ Corporation (your company) offers the following new products (which have had many successful market tests) on the following terms:

60% discount for purchase of 100, or more, units.

Free delivery anywhere in the United States.

One FREE unit for each 25 purchased.

The products offered under this big moneymaking plan are:

1. Product "A" _____ Name the product here _____

2. Product "B" _____ Name the product here _____

3. Product "C" _____ Name the product here _____

On every order you place there is a full overhaul   guarantee for your customers who return the products to you in renewable condition within three days. NO REFUNDS OF ANY KIND ARE MADE TO YOU OR YOUR CUSTOMERS AT THIS DISCOUNT. That is, ALL SALES ARE FINAL. For further information, or to have any questions answered, please call _____ Your Name _____ at _____ Your Phone Number _____.

Figure 10-2

your check earlier! *Never* delay getting money into your firm—a dollar today is better than a dollar tomorrow!

5. Process your first order yourself! Don't allow any errors. You want your big buyer to be impressed with the speed and accuracy with which you fill orders. So don't be ashamed to wrap and pack that first order. It will pay off in more orders in the future.

Develop Related Product or Service Lines

There are other ways to develop large orders. One such way that works well for us is based on our product line. Thus:

> With a series of related products or services, there's a good chance that your customers will buy several of your offers instead of just one. You thereby turn what might have been a $20 offer into a $100 sale; or you turn a $100 offer into a $1,200 sale. This "magic" quickly builds your income and profits while making your customers happier and bonding them more securely to your company.

To help sell related products, be sure to use a toll-free 800 number, a FAX number, and to accept major credit-card charges. By offering such ordering facilities you:

- Bring your firm into the modern age of mail order
- Satisfy the urge for speed that infests people today
- Give your firm a strong image in its field
- Take advantage of the major new marketing tools available today
- Use a FAX number to give your customers another way to order your products or services

There are other steps you can take to boost the sale of related products so your income from each customer is larger. These steps are:

1. Offer a *FREE* bonus item with the purchase of two or more related items. In mail order the word *FREE* is the most powerful one you can use in connection with any product or service. Use the word *FREE*

liberally and really give away something valuable. No word in your sales pitch is more powerful than *FREE!*

2. Use testimonials from satisifed customers who've bought related items from you. To avoid having to get written permission to use a testimonial, just give the location (the state or country is enough) of the person supplying the testimonial. People really don't care who wrote the testimonial; they just want to know what the user said about your product or service. And your testimonial need not be long. Look at this one, which says: "Thank you for writing *How to Make a Quick Fortune.* I followed your method for taking over a 'sick business.' It worked! I am now *owner* of a buyer's guide paper." NC.

3. Take the "one source" approach to your customers. That is, set your firm up as the one and only source your customer needs to get the products or services you sell. With this strategy your customer won't even think of going elsewhere to get help. It may burden you with phone calls. But the money that flows in will keep you in fancy yachts and big cars for as long as you want!

4. Advertise where people need the most help. Thus, we find that the military newspapers—*Army Times, Navy Times,* etc.—give excellent results. Why? Because the readership is large and is comprised of people seeking information on a variety of topics which we cover— namely loans, credit cards, grants, small business, real estate, mail order, etc. Buyers obtained from such ads are likely to buy more than $1,000 worth of products to be sure they have all the information they need.

5. Position your product or service so it fills a gap where there's no—or very little—competition. Thus, my firm, International Wealth Success, Inc., is positioned as a major player in the financial information field. But to separate us from the crowd of other, similar firms (many of which sprang up by imitating us), we position ourselves as the *only* firm that offers low-cost business and real estate loans to its customers and other needy people. By lending out some of our corporate profits we make our firm unique in its field. Some businesses

which are successful today got their start using one of our low-interest rate loans as seed capital.

6. Sell products or services that—by their very nature— need regular updating. Thus, my good friend, Tom Azzara, who founded and publishes *The Tax Haven Reporter*, a monthly newsletter, also publishes an excellent book which we at IWS sell, titled *Tax Havens of the World*. If you buy Tom's book, you'll want to keep it updated. How? By subscribing to Tom's newsletter! So he makes a bigger sale by having related products than he would if he had only one. You can do much the same in your own field.

7. Use a merchant account to take credit-card orders. When people use their credit card to buy from you they will usually order more. Why? Because they have 12 or 24 months in which to pay off their purchase debt. Knowing this, most folks will buy 20 to 30 percent more than if they're ordering by check or buying across the counter. Not only will your orders be larger, you'll also rank higher in the eyes of your customer. Why? Because having a merchant account means that you're a fully responsible dealer! People will be happy to buy related products from you. Some of your credit-card orders will be in the hundreds—and even thousands— of dollars.

Get Other Mail-Order Dealers to Sell for You

You can have the best—and biggest—mail-order business in your field. But I can tell you one thing—and I do this for your benefit (and mine!)—you will *never* have the name of every buyer in your field! Why?

Because people buy out of habit, out of emotional bias, or based on an image a company projects. Your company will never (nor will mine) appeal to everyone. This is just a simple business fact.

So how do you latch onto those potential customers who haven't yet bought from you for any of the above reasons? That's simple. You:

Get other mail-order dealers to promote your product or service. You drop ship at no cost to your dealer or its customer. Result? You sell to people who were not on your mailing list. And if you treat them well, these customers will buy and buy from you!

Now you may think: "Why should I give away one-half of my sales dollar (you will normally be paid 50 percent of the list price by your dealers) when I can sell the same item myself and keep *all* the money? There are plenty of good reasons to get other mail-order dealers to sell for you. Some of these reasons are:

1. Other mail-order dealers can enormously expand your customer list at almost *no* cost to you! This way of selling can beat space ads, classified ads, radio, and TV.
2. All you need supply a mail-order dealer is camera-ready copies of your space ads. The dealer will include these ads with mailings to his or her regular customer list. So your ads get good exposure to other mail-order *buyers.* That word buyers is important because people who buy by mail will buy again and again. And if they see your ads they'll eventually buy from you!
3. The credibility of your mail-order dealers "rubs off" on your products or services. So if you pick your dealers carefully, your products or services will be promoted by some of the best mail-order dealers in the country. The image of your firm will improve—producing more sales for you.
4. By working with a large number of mail-order dealers you can get coverage in virtually every market in which your products or services might sell. This can double, triple, or quadruple the size of your firm—quickly and easily!
5. Once you get a customer with the help of another dealer, that customer is yours for life! You can sell and sell to that customer and make big money from him or her.

Our products—newsletters, books, and courses—are sold by hundreds of mail-order dealers around the country. And we treat the checks from these dealers as money orders—shipping the *same* day we get the order. Some dealers don't even send us a check for their orders. Instead, they use their credit card. The result? Fast service to the customer. And today *every* customer wants speed.

Mail-order dealers will send you *big* orders. While you may be selling things one at a time a mail-order dealer may order 50 at a time. So your sales volume jumps. Sometimes you'll have more trouble getting the items to sell than you will have selling them!

To find mail-order dealers to sell your products or services, take these easy steps:

1. Decide what types of dealers you want to work with. Thus, with us, when we decided to pick mail-order dealers, we looked for newsletters and magazines serving what we call the Beginning Wealth Builder or Opportunity Seeker. We found lists of them in directories listing publishers.

2. Contact each dealer by mail. Or, if you wish, call the dealer on the phone. Offer your products or services on a 50 percent discount basis. (Some services may not be able to stand such a high discount. So adjust the discount to suit.) We use a letter (Figure 10-3) to sell mail-order dealers on working with us. It has been very effective and brings in thousands of dollars each month.

3. Work with the dealer to offer the best service you can. Remember: The dealer must be able to make money. If you press the dealer too much neither of you may be able to make a profit. Better to make a few dollars less per sale than nothing at all!

4. Offer a sliding scale discount to reluctant dealers to entice them into working with you. That is, pay a higher discount after the dealer reaches a certain sales level. Thus, with our Publisher's Executive Representatives, we give them a 40 percent discount for the first $2,000 in sales. After that, the discount goes to 50 percent for life. New dealers are thereby motivated to reach the $2,000 sales level because on every sale thereafter they get 10 percent more commission!

INTERNATIONAL WEALTH SUCCESS.
Inc.

P. O. Box 186, Merrick, N. Y. 11566

Office: 24 Canterbury Rd, Rockville Centre NY 11570   516-766-5850

Dear Rep:

Thank you for your 5-year subscription to the IWS Newsletter. Here are the discounts available ONLY to you and other 5-year subscriber rep-dealers:

Dealer Data--Discounts, Delivery, Returns, Etc.

Book and Kit Availability: Immediate; we do not have out-of-stock situations.

Discount: 50% off list price on all titles and Kits.

Payment: Please send check with your order for 50% of the list price.

Payment for Shipping: We pay all shipping charges to send books to either you or your customer, depending on where you tell us to send the items ordered.

Date of Shipment: Same day as order is received. We treat your check as a money order and don't delay shipment for check clearance.

Method of Shipment: We use U.S. Postal System, United Parcel Service, Federal Express, depending on your wishes. For Federal Express there is a $25.00 charge to you for overnight service anywhere in the United States.

Returns: With the 50% discount, freight paid by us, we cannot--and will not--accept returns. So if you have any question about your customer possibly wanting to return the product, we suggest you order with a 20% discount and pay the freight both ways.

Our experience over the last twenty years with this 50% discount policy is that booksellers and dealers like it, especially with us paying the freight. We insure all shipments to all buyers. Explain to your customer--NO RETURNS!

Ad mats: We can furnish camera-ready ads mats for our books and Kits.

Ordering address: Send orders to the Office address, above--i.e., 24 Canterbury Rd Rockville Centre NY 11570. We ship quickly and efficiently.

Book lists: You'll find us in BOOKS IN PRINT and in other standard reference works.

Figure 10-3

5. Don't look on your dealers as competitors. They're your partner! Viewing each dealer as a partner expands your business enormously. Result? More dollars flow into *your* bank account. And that's where you want them— not in someone else's bank.
6. Urge your dealers to push your products or services as strongly as they can. You will get more, and larger, sales as a result. And it's the *big* sales that will increase your daily and weekly bank deposits.

What kinds of products and services might you promote for big sales with other mail-order dealers? Here are just a few—cookbooks, newsletters, travel clubs, overseas tours, collector plates, cakes of all types, flower bulbs, books, courses, etc. You can say that if there are two or more firms promoting a product or service, the two can get together to make more money for each!

If you can't interest other mail-order dealers in your products or services, consider contacting the leading mail-order houses. The top 300 mail-order houses account for more than a billion dollars in sales. While it may take you longer to sell a product to a large mail-order house, your orders can be in the thousands of units. My friend Melvin Powers, probably the most creative book publisher in business today, regularly sells large quantities of his excellent books to large distributors. And his orders are often in the thousands of copies!

Don't Overlook Clubs and Other Large Groups

BWB mail-order dealers sometimes overlook the obvious large groups to whom they might make a sale. Why is this? Because they start with the thought that:

To make large sales I must discover a hidden market that no one ever thought of before this. Then I'll make millions long before the other dealers find the same market.

This isn't so! Some of your biggest markets have been

around for more than 50 years. They need—and want—good items or services to sell. Markets like:

- Book clubs—they often buy many thousands of copies of a book, which they sell widely.
- Hobby groups like antique car buffs, model airplane builders, boaters, etc., will likewise buy large quantities of a product or service to market to their members.
- Collector groups—limited-edition plates, coins, paintings, expensive statues, etc.—also buy in large numbers to service their membership.

You can approach large groups by mail or phone. In almost every case you'll have to supply a free sample of your product or service for evaluation by the group. But this is a worthwhile expense. Don't expect a decision unless you do supply such a sample!

Find Retail Outlets for Your Products

Will your item sell to the general public? Or will it sell to a special-interest group like health-food faddists, sports-car buffs, boaters, telescope owners, etc.? If so, you may be able to sell it to retail outlets—by mail order! So you're really not getting out of the mail-order business. You're just finding ways to earn more money from your products or services. And that, after all, is why you're in this business—to make money—tons of it!

Retail outlets include your corner store, gas stations, boatyards, horse stables, hotel and motel lobbies, etc. Any place where people gather to do something can be a retail outlet for you if your product or service ties in with the reason people are at that spot.

If you have a specialty product—for example, one for sports people—you'll find that:

- There are trade shows for most sports, which are attended by retail people looking for new products or services.
- Attending such a show and exhibiting your wares can lead to large orders for your item or service.

- Retail dealers will often suggest ways in which you can improve your product or service. And they may also give you ideas for new products or services which they can sell strongly.

Our firm markets more than a dozen products for boaters. We attend the annual Motorboat Show in a number of cities to get feedback from retail boat dealers and marine stores. They tell us what the boaters visiting their stores seek. We tailor our products to more nearly meet the needs of these boaters. Result? More units sold, every year!

So don't be afraid to branch out from your mail-order business to build larger sales. Mail order is one way to move a product to market. If you can achieve larger sales by using a different way to reach the public, go for it! You'll deposit more money in your bank—every day!

Jump on Proven Sales Paths

In the mail-order business you can make millions in many different ways. But the two most distinct ways are:

1. Develop an original product idea and market it to everyone who might be a prospect for the item or service. This can be a sure road to millions when your idea catches on.
2. Expand an existing product or service idea to bring out a new and improved offer that will seem like a "natural" in proven sales outlets.

You don't have to look far to find examples of these two basic approaches. Thus, the Hula Hoop and Pet Rock were original product ideas that caught on and sold like wildfire. Creative people came up with these items and profited enormously from them.

In the service area you'll find "products" like mail-order life insurance and credit-card protection plans which received widespread acceptance. Again, you have original thinkers who blazed a path to riches using their minds.

For many people—especially those just starting out—expanding an existing idea into proven sales paths is the easiest and best way to get started. Let me give you two examples from my own mail-order money-making which resulted in sales of millions of dollars.

I first went into mail-order sales because I was working for a large corporation and became fearful that I would be laid off without warning. Why? Because I saw friends of mine "cut off at the knees" for the slightest error. I decided that I wouldn't be caught without an income if this should happen to me. So I looked around for a low-cost business that I could start from home. Mail order was the answer.

At the time a brokerage house was advertising its services with the line "Get a Second Income." This, I realized, was what I wanted. A second income I could tap into if my boss decided I should be "excessed" as they say in corporate lingo. Being a writer of technical (engineering) books at the time, I suddenly said to myself, "Why not write a book on developing a second income? I know a little about it and I'll certainly learn more as I do the book."

Thus was born my first money book, titled *How to Build a Second-Income Fortune in Your Spare Time*. It was published and sold some 300,000 copies in its first year—almost all by mail order! I was one happy guy because the royalties gave me the second income I wanted and made me less afraid of my big-company boss. Yet the book idea expanded on the brokerage ad!

Letters began to pour in from readers of the second-income book. And, as I read the letters I noticed:

- Almost every letter writer had *good* business ideas. There were few crackpots among the letter writers.
- But *every* letter writer asked "Where can I find the money to start my business? Or to buy a great business that's for sale down the street?"
- Some letters told long, sad stories of trying to get money for a business. Almost none of the beginners were able to get the money they needed.

These letters suggested that I expand on a proven sales

path and do another book. That—my third money book
(the second, *Smart Money Shortcuts for Becoming Rich*,
was suggested by the publisher and sold better than the
first. It also brought in thousands of letters talking about
getting money.)—is titled *How to Borrow Your Way to
a Great Fortune.*

Sales of the borrowing book quickly reached one million
copies in its various editions. Why? Because it sold into
proven sales paths—that is, the almost-universal need for
money by small business operators. And the book spawned
nearly one hundred other, related products selling into the
same proven sales paths, namely:

- The monthly newsletter, *International Wealth Success,*
  which I edit and write
- Some 70 books, courses, and kits, many of which are
  listed at the back of this book
- A loan and grant service to subscribers and all readers
  today of the International Wealth Success newsletter.
  This service offers loans up to $500,000 for business and
  real-estate use (with most loans being in the $5,000 to
  $50,000 range because these are the most common
  amounts requested). Grants in the same ranges are
  available to the readers when the money will be used
  for a productive and beneficial purpose with a large
  number of people getting benefits from the money.
- Personal consultation with BWBs by myself and other
  staff members to answer questions that our newsletter
  subscribers may have.
- Raising money for subscribers with *no* fee of any kind.
  Over the years we've helped subscribers raise millions
  of dollars for good, solid business and real-estate projects
  and we've *never* requested, accepted nor been paid a fee
  of any kind for getting the funds for the BWB.
- Plus a variety of other services available on demand from
  any BWB or EWB (Experienced Wealth Builder) when
  requested of us.

So you see, selling into proven sales channels spawned—
and continues to spawn—a number of valuable products
and services for BWBs. These have also increased our mail-

order business enormously. We've achieved larger sales while helping more people. Can you ask for anything more?

You can do much the same in *your* mail-order business. Just look for the big buyers who will put *you* in the mega-buck class. Just be sure not to overlook obvious markets—they're all around you!

CHAPTER 11

DO OVERSEAS
MAIL ORDER FOR
A BIGGER INCOME

Overseas mail order—where you sell your products or services to buyers in foreign countries—is booming. In my own mail-order business we sell in every country in the free world. We've even had requests from Communist countries for free information on the capitalistic products we publish! As a capitalist's capitalist I've declined to spend my hard-earned money to provide *free* books or kits. If they want to pay for them, fine!

Doing overseas mail order is much like domestic sales. But there are certain procedures you must observe if you want to make really big money. I give you these methods in this chapter so you can build your mail-order millions sooner!

Internationalize Your Offerings

You can make your products or services more acceptable in the international market if you take a few simple steps when creating your offerings. Such steps might include:

• Using international monetary and measurement systems in your product or service. Sometimes this means nothing more than including a simple conversion table or scale for the user.

- Including key addresses of international organizations for your customers so they know where to get help locally, if they need it.
- Reflecting—in instructional materials—the differences between your laws and those of international countries. Such differences are easy to obtain if you just check with the consulates of the various countries in which you'll be selling. You can get loads of free information by just calling, or writing, the various consulates.

The way you internationalize your offering varies with what you're selling by mail overseas. In the next section of this chapter we show you what you might do to internationalize various types of offerings.

What Can You Sell Overseas?

Almost any item or service you sell at home can be sold overseas. Thus, you can sell overseas typical mail-order products and services such as:

- Books, courses, kits
- Newsletters, newspapers, journals
- Mechanical and electrical equipment of many types
- Games, videos, audio tapes
- Instruction manuals of many types
- Clothing, bathing suits, accessories
- Boats, aircraft, autos, tractors
- Etc.

In my business—which is book and newsletter publishing—we have an expression which says "It travels well" when a product or service is easily sold overseas. To make your products or services travel well, follow the hints given above. For specific products, take these steps:

- Mechanical and electrical equipment—be sure the items meet the governing standards for the countries into which they will be sold. Thus, there may be voltage and frequency differences. You *must* meet these if you are to make an overseas sale!

- Publications like books, newsletters, courses—be certain to include suitable international sources, names, addresses, telephone numbers, etc. Where you have a bibliography in a book, be certain to refer to international books and journals. This gives your book greater relevance to its international readers. You'll even sell more books when you include such bibliographic references! Enough said.
- Clothing, bathing suits, accessories—give the overseas size equivalents. These may be different from the domestic sizes. There's no point in your having to ship the same type garment twice if it would have "stuck" the first time if the person buying it had the right size chart!
- Instruction manuals—give both the United States Customary System (USCS) measurements and the System International (SI)—often referred to as "metric"—in the manual. Thus, when giving speed in miles per hour, be sure to also give it in kilometers per hour for European and Asian buyers of your manual!

I think you get the idea on how to alter domestic products or services so they sell well overseas. Often you don't even have to alter the item—just include information that permits use overseas.

There are some products or services that will take extra work to sell overseas. Typical of these are:

- Data on the laws, regulations, and rules of one portion of a country. For example, a book on Iowa State Law on Cattle Raising might not travel well because it is pertinent to just one of the 50 states in the United States.
- License-plate frames made for one country's autos might not fit another's because of differences in plate dimensions.
- Children's toys using unique characters known in just one country will not—in general—sell worldwide.

You can name other items or services that won't travel well. One well-known service that has an excellent domestic market but a poor foreign one is Income Tax Preparation.

Tax laws vary so widely from one country to another that a course based on United States Tax Law would not have much of a market in England, France, Germany, etc.

So—to sell overseas—pick your products carefully and thoughtfully. While you may stumble on an item that has instant worldwide acceptance, it won't happen often. You must think your way through product and service selection if you want to get rich from overseas sales.

How to Crack Overseas Markets

You can take easy, proven steps to start selling overseas. If you do take such steps you'll almost always receive a courteous and profitable welcome by overseas customers. To crack overseas markets, take these easy steps now:

1. Decide what you will sell overseas. See the earlier tips on product choice.
2. Figure what overseas countries might need, or want, the product or service you've chosen to sell. But try not to make the common mistake of thinking—as some BWBs do—that "everyone in Germany needs, and wants, this product." You may find that almost no one wants what you have to offer!
3. Explore ways to reach the market in the countries you believe will buy your offering. Do this by looking for places in which you might advertise your offer. Most countries have newspapers, magazines, and journals in which you might advertise.
4. Contact possible ad outlets and get their advertising rate quotations. You can contact such outlets by mail. Or if they have local reps you can contact them by phone. Consulates will give you free publication info.
5. Examine several recent copies of the publications you're considering. See if they carry ads for products or services like those you plan to promote. While a lack of such ads does not show that the publication is a poor choice, be sure to get data on the readership so you can see if the readers are prospects—not suspects.
6. Try to negotiate a reduced rate for your advertising.

Some publications offer lower rates for certain types of advertising—such as books, medicines, sporting goods, etc. Be sure to ask—either in writing or by phone. The most that can happen is that you're refused a lower rate. Then again you will often be given the lower rate you request!

7. Run your first ad. Keep careful track of the response. Try to make sales of at least three times your ad cost. Thus, a $100 ad cost should bring in $300 in sales. If you bring in more—great! Less, try other publications unless you feel your ad wasn't suitable for the market you're trying to reach.

8. Keep expanding your ads as long as you're making money, or breaking even. If you want to develop an overseas market you must keep pushing.

What kinds of results can you expect from overseas ads? Much depends on your offer. My own experience in selling newsletters, books, and courses overseas is:

• Our overseas ads pull better than at home. We get a stronger return per dollar spent overseas than per dollar spent at home.

• Unqiue products or services are gobbled up by overseas customers because similar offerings in their own country are often poorly made and lack competent preparation or manufacture.

• Overseas customers will recommend your products or services to others, if they're satisfied with them. This leads to more business for you without any extra ad cost. So it's wise to make your offering as perfect as possible.

• Consulates of foreign countries (listed in your telephone book) will gladly give you much free info about your customers if they are companies, about addresses that might not be clear on a customer's envelope, customs rules (if any for your product or service), etc. Once you have an order from a country you'll be amazed at the extent to which a consulate employee will go to help you. And even before you have that first order you'll find that you can get all sorts of free help and advice— just for the asking!

In cracking overseas markets, you must decide if you'll

shoot for the individual customer or the company customer. This decision is often automatic—that is, your product decides for you.

Thus, if you're selling books on personal success, as we are, the individual is your most likely customer. Yet we do sell some of these same books to public libraries and universities. But the major sale is to individuals seeking to earn large sums of money.

Were we selling cleaning fluids for industrial machinery, our major customers would be companies. We'd saturate such firms with our ads and mailings. Sales methods we'd use would be much the same as in our domestic market at home.

Overseas Mailings for Big Profits

In the United States you can rent a mailing list for almost any category of customer. Overseas the story is somewhat different.

While overseas countries do have mailing lists available for rent, there are more restrictions on their use than in the United States. And you'll find that mailing lists of individuals are fewer in number and have smaller counts of names on them. For this reason, direct mail to overseas individuals is more difficult to make money on than in the United States. This is why we stick to space and classified ads when selling to individuals.

Selling to companies is different. There *are* well-prepared mailing lists for sale. And there are almost no restrictions on their use. So you can make mailings in much the same way as you do at home.

To save money on overseas direct mail, consider using the Air Lift Method offered by certain airlines. With this method you:

- Prepare your mailing in the normal way—that is, you print your ad and letter, insert it into the envelope and seal it.

- Deliver your mail to the airline in sacks provided to you. Mail for each country is put into an individual sack. *No* postage is put on any of the envelopes.
- Your mail is transported overseas by the airline. Then postage is affixed to each envelope and the mail is entered into the mail stream in each country for which it is destined.
- Result? Faster delivery, at lower cost! Check with an airline serving the area of the world into which you want to sell. They'll give you plenty of free info and money-saving tips.

But before you rush out to send your ads by airline, check the U.S. Postal Service offerings. The Post Office has a number of excellent plans for overseas delivery of mail at low cost. And the offers are constantly under study with frequent money-saving revisions. So be certain to check in with your Postmaster—it could save you big bucks!

One way we've built our overseas business to a level where it brings in sizeable profits is this:

- We offer overseas people the opportunity to sell our products and earn a commission on each sale, and on all future sales.
- We drop ship the product via surface mail at no cost to the customer or dealer.
- Each dealer, whom we call an Executive Representative, earns a 40 percent commission on each sale for the first $2,000 in sales. After a total sale of $2,000 is once reached, the commission goes to 50 percent for life. Some of our dealers sell $2,500 worth of products from our line each week.

Why do we use reps? For a number of good, proven reasons. These are:

1. Reps know their own country better than we do. So they can take our advertising materials and slant them to the interests and beliefs of their potential customers.
2. Our reps mail the ad material for us. So it saves us the local postage cost and gets the mail into the hands of people who are most likely to buy. It's much more

efficient to have reps do the mailing than having us do it.

3. When a sale is made, the money goes to the rep first. The rep deposits the money in a local bank. So we don't have to concern ourselves with currency fluctuations or other changes in the money market.

4. To pay us, the rep sends an international money order in U.S. dollars. We treat this as cash and ship instantly. The customer gets his or her order sooner and is more likely to re-order. If so, the rep automatically gets the same commission percentage on all future orders. The rep's record is kept on our computer so it can be checked at any time by the rep to see if the correct amounts have been paid. This system assures the rep that the full amount due him or her is paid in a timely manner— in our case, once a month.

5. Once reps begin earning big money they become great promoters of our products. They not only sell by mail— they sell face-to-face to their friends, business associates, and others. The result? Stronger sales than we could ever hope to make ourselves.

6. Reps do all their printing locally. So we're saved the time and work needed to get materials printed for each rep. Further, the rep can make any language changes that may be needed. The translation the rep does will be better than any we might arrange.

So if you want to sell overseas, consider getting reps to do the work for you. You'll be delighted to see the amount of work the rep will do for you and the cash flow this work gives you. You can easily find reps by running short classified ads in newspapers and magazines in the countries in which you'd like to sell items or services. Such ads can read:

REPS WANTED to sell money-making products in <u>Name of Country or Colony</u>. Write for full info to ABC Co., 123 Main St., Anytown 00000.

SELL VALUABLE SUCCESS PRODUCTS. Full info from ABC Co., 123 Main St., Anytown 00000.

> MAKE A FORTUNE selling fortune-building new books and kits. Write ABC Co., 123 Main St., Anytown 00000.

Using the rep approach we sell our newsletters, kits, books, and courses all over the free world. And with the Communist countries learning that their system really doesn't work, the entire behind-the-Iron-Curtain world will soon want our capitalistic success materials. Can you imagine the size of the yacht I'll buy when we start making sales to the millions hungering for success in Eastern Europe and Russia!

Score Big with Unusual Products for Overseas Customers

I have hundreds of mail-order friends who are pros in this business. And I have millions of customers who bought products and services from me. Let me show you how some of my mail-order pro friends use unusual products to earn a bundle in the overseas market.

Time Shares Boom by Mail

Carl C. is an experienced time-share salesperson. The time shares he sells are in vacation resort areas like Florida, North Carolina, California, etc. A time share—as you know—is one, two, three, four, etc. weeks which you buy and own in a popular vacation area. Thus, you might buy two weeks in March in a Florida luxury building. Each year you can use these two weeks. Or you can swap them with other people in the building for different weeks. Or you can swap for the same weeks in other areas—for example, in California.

Time sharing is one of the most creative ideas in real estate. But, like any other business, it has its problems with:

- Unsold units which plague a developer
- Foreclosed units resulting from non-payment of the unit's price by the buyer
- Unpopular weeks for which the seller can't find buyers
- Etc.

Carl likes mail order. One day, when trying to create some new items to sell by mail order in his spare time, Carl suddenly had a brainstorm:

- Why not, Carl thought, combine his time-share sales business with his mail-order business (which he was just starting)
- Selling time shares by mail order. To keep his "product" cost low, Carl decided to sell "remnant" time shares— the ones we listed above
- And since he knew that Europeans from the cold countries love the tropical parts of the United States in the winter, Carl decided to aim his sales at the overseas markets

To get his products lined up, Carl took these easy steps. He:

1. Contacted banks who financed time-share buildings and asked if they had any foreclosed time-share weeks they'd like to sell off cheaply. He got dozens of enthusiastic offers—so many that he had to stop calling banks. (Many people buy a time share while they're on vacation. This violates Hicks' first rule of investing, namely: Never buying anything large while you're on vacation. Your critical judgement is influenced by the beautiful weather, which probably won't last!)
2. To get a greater variety of time-share weeks, Carl also called developers and government agencies. The response was much like that of the banks—Carl was flooded with offers. So Carl became selective. Why? He had so many weeks available to sell he could pick those weeks that would sell best by mail, based on price, location, timing, etc.

With his products lined up, Carl planned his sales efforts. From friends in the resort business he was able to get lists of names and addresses of overseas tourists who visited the Florida area. These were his prime prospects for mail sales of time-share weeks. To sell his weeks Carl took these steps. He:

1. Prepared a strong letter giving the many advantages of time-share ownership in the Florida area. The letter included photos of typical time-share buildings and units.

2. Priced his weeks so they were affordable to the tourists he was mailing to. Thus, the pricing of a typical unit was worked up thus:

Price of 2 weeks to Carl	=	$3,000.00
Estimated sales and marketing cost	=	1,000.00
Price customer will be charged	=	4,995.00
Gross profit to Carl	=	995.00
Overhead at 10% of sales, rounded	=	500.00
Net profit to Carl	=	495.00

3. For his first mailing, Carl used the names he obtained from friends and mailed from the United States. Results were strong and profitable. From a mailing of 200 names Carl sold 5 time-share packages of two weeks each. From this mailing Carl concluded:

   - There *is* a mail-order market for time-share weeks among overseas customers.
   - Prices in the $3,000 to $5,000 range *are* acceptable to overseas buyers in the right projects.
   - Names of tourists and other visitors to the area make good prospects for these sales.

Today Carl has an active business selling remnant time-share weeks via mail order in both the overseas and domestic markets. With no shortage of product, Carl sees a bright future for himself and his staff selling time-share weeks by mail order and in person to those prospects who want to visit the area before buying.

Business Opportunities Sell Well

A good friend who subscribes to my newsletter, *International Wealth Success,* wanted to get started in mail order. Searching around, he decided that business opportunities are wanted by everyone. So he started the Business Opportunity Club.

Immediate acceptance of his idea in the United States led him to think about the overseas market. Taking ads in newspapers and magazines in remote areas of the world again brought quick acceptance of his offer.

Today, Donald Moore and I talk about once a month. Donald's business continues to grow as he introduces new products. But his basic idea of the business opportunity goes right on. Neither he nor the world will run out of interest in business opportunities. So his business will grow and grow. Fully 99 percent of his sales are by mail or telephone—he does little face-to-face selling. This is another great example of the power of an idea in mail order.

Products for Boaters Are Popular

Our firm has some 15 boating products that sell strongly by mail all over the world. Why? Because boating is booming in almost every country where people can afford to get out on the water in their own craft. To make these products more saleable overseas we:

- Use commonly understood measures and terms in our descriptions so they "travel well."
- Have a colorful design with universal appeal.
- Keep promoting the products in overseas and domestic markets because we find that ads in U.S. publications are often seen by overseas prospects who order directly or write for more information. Every overseas and domestic inquiry—whether on a postcard or in a formal letter—is answered instantly. Why? Because that's how you make sales—a fast response is part of your marketing effort to make more sales!
- Carefully watch the competition to see if they have any new products which might displace our own. If we find any such items, we immediately order them to see if they are truly competitive. So far none have been. And we're happy to see that no overseas firms have yet

introduced products directly competitive with our own. So we really have the market to ourselves. Again—unique and unusual products sell well to overseas customers!

Money "Sells" Anywhere in the World

As you know, my firm offers business and real-estate loans to two-year subscribers (and non-subscribers) to *International Wealth Success*. Since the newsletter is international in scope, we get a few applications from overseas.

These applications are generated by mail-order offerings to overseas buyers. What we do when making such loans is:

- Lend out accumulated profits from our business to needy borrowers for good projects
- At low interest rates, compared to rates charged in overseas countries
- With *no* points, *no* fees, *no* front money charges of any kind to the borrower

Such loans are popular with overseas borrowers because it gives them the opportunity to start, or to buy, a business of their own. The reason why we ask that the loan be only for active business or income real-estate use is because our mission in life is to help such projects. We do *not* lend money for personal items like clothing, autos, residences, etc.

We get our overseas subscribers using direct mail and mail order. So the loans are an outgrowth of those activities. And I can tell you this—money "sells" easily via mail order! Try it yourself and see.

Use Agents to Sell for You Worldwide

If you have products (and some services) to sell overseas you may find that agents can bring big sales into your business. How? By finding customers for you overseas.

Here's how it works:

1. You contact—by mail or FAX—overseas agents wanting to sell products of certain kinds in their country.

2. After you get enough information from the agent to satisfy yourself that he or she will do a good job for your firm, you supply info on your products, plus a few samples. All this is done by mail.

3. The agent then takes your catalogs and information sheets and alters them to suit local market conditions. Mailings are made to local prospects. Sales will almost always result from such mailings. You either drop ship the items directly to the customer or you have your agent do the shipping. Much depends on what you worked out with your agent.

4. You and the agent continue making sales to expand your market to the level you seek.

Where can you find such overseas agents? The Department of Commerce in Washington D.C. can help. Also, your local Business Development Company (BDC) can help. And sometimes airlines and steamship companies can provide you with the names of agents seeking products.

Should you drop ship or have your agent carry an inventory? There's no one answer to this question other than "It depends"! At the start of working with an agent you probably won't have enough money to buy lots of inventory. So you'll probably find it better to drop ship in the early days of your business.

Once you have a cash reserve, it may be cheaper, and more efficient, to have your agent inventory your products. Then they can be shipped fast and at lower cost.

The key is to do what's best for your customers so they'll buy from you again! Each business is different and requires a separate analysis as to what's best for it.

You *can* build a million-dollar-a-year mail-order business selling to overseas customers. To get started, use the hints in this and other chapters in this book. And if you have any questions, or need financing help, I'm as near to you as your telephone! Just give me a ring and see.

CHAPTER 12

RUN YOUR MAIL-ORDER BUSINESS FOR HIGH PROFITS

YOU GO INTO any business to make money. In the mail-order business you can gross $1 million a year sooner than you think—if you use the right methods. This chapter gives you tips on the right methods to use to bring in big money in your own successful mail-order business selling products or services of your choice.

Run Your Business from This Key Idea

In mail order everything is marketing! What do I mean by this statement? I mean that everything you do has an effect on your customer's image of you and your firm. So you *must* plan your activities carefully. Thus, simple decisions are important:

- Your company name conveys an image to your customer
- Your letterhead creates a favorable or unfavorable image
- Your ads—small or large—lead to sales or rejections
- The way your employees answer the telephone makes friends of your customers—or loses them

Until you realize the truth of the above your business won't reach its maximum potential. Let's see how you can run your business so you get the maximum sales every day of the year.

Deliver Your Products Colorfully

Take time to pick colorful address labels for your products, catalogs, and ad materials. Why? Because your very package is marketing!

Put yourself in the place of your customer. He or she ordered your product or service with the hope that it would solve a problem. When the "problem solver" arrives, its wrappings, address label, and condition all transmit a message to your customer. That's when:

- A colorful, neatly typed label gives an instant message to the customer that says
- This company cares about *you*. It took time and care to wrap your "problem solver" so it arrives safely in your hands!
- What's inside is more than worth what I paid for it. I'll be glad to buy from them again!

There are dozens of label supply houses that will print your labels quickly using colors of your choice. At IWS, Inc., my firm, we use brilliant reds which are distinctive and eye-catching. This is one reason why our return rate is far below one-tenth of one percent—the lowest in the industry!

Make Safe Delivery Your Daily Goal

Use self-adhesive labels for your packages. But do *not* depend on the glue on the back of the label. In high-humidity conditions, and in extreme heat this glue can fail. So be certain that every label is taped to the package using clear 4-inch wide adhesive tape. Then your package will arrive safely because the tape prevents label smearing and loss.

Your customer, on seeing the tape covering the label with a clear, shiny surface, says to himself or herself: Gee, these people really care! They truly want me to get what I ordered.

If you use padded bags to deliver your products, take one extra step to ensure that your customer gets a clean, unmarred product. Buy clear plastic bags that are large enough to hold what you ship. Wrap the product in the bag and tape it shut *before* inserting it into the padded bag.

Why? Because padded bags often tear on the inside during shipping. The dust which is released can make any product unattractive. But when wrapped in a clear plastic bag inside the padded bag, the dust doesn't get on the product. And it's easily blown off before the plastic bag is opened.

We love our customers so much we even use the plastic bag inside cardboard cartons. Why? A little extra protection never hurts. And its cost is less than a penny per package.

Where you must fill out a carton to prevent damage to what you're sending, think of your customer. (In fact, I recommend that you think of your customer day and night!) Don't use packing materials that adhere to the product or that make a mess of the customer's home. Thus:

- Newspaper stuffing (using outdated papers) is effective, cheap, and non-littering for the customer. Use it whenever you can.
- Plastic "peanut" packings tend to stick to a product. The "donut" plastic packing material adheres much less to the product. So consider using it.
- Save discarded cardboard boxes. You can often use parts of these as cheap, effective packing materials. And the cardboard can be used creatively when you have different size products to wrap.
- Try to have all your products the same overall size. Then your wrapping and shipping will be much easier.
- When you send more than one package to a customer, use a "There's-more-to-come" label (Figure 12-1) on the outside. Again, this tells your customer that you know he or she will be thinking, when they get your first

THERE'S MORE!
THIS IS CARTON NO. ☐
OF ☐ TOTAL CARTONS

INTERNATIONAL
WEALTH SUCCESS, INC.
The World's Best Money-Making Books
P.O. Box 186   Merrick, NY 11566

INTERNATIONAL
WEALTH SUCCESS, INC.
The World's Best Money-Making Books
P.O. Box 186
MERRICK, NEW YORK 11566

TO

RETURN POSTAGE GUARANTEED

BUSINESS REPLY MAIL
NO POSTAGE STAMP NECESSARY IF MAILED IN THE UNITED STATES

INTERNATIONAL WEALTH SUCCESS INC.
P.O. BOX 186
MERRICK, N. Y. 11566

Figure 12-1

package, "Is this all there is? I know I ordered more!" The label says "This is the first of three packages; there are two more on the way." Besides, the label saves you from irate phone calls saying: "I sent you $400 for my purchase. But you only delivered $200 worth of products. How come?" You can get such labels for just pennies from one of the many label houses serving the mail-order world. Figure 12-1 shows some of the labels we regularly use in our highly successful mail-order business. Each label is printed in one or more colors.

You can, of course, use regular self-adhesive labels from your personal computer printer. But—in my view—these labels are small, look cheap, and convey a negative image to your customer. Yet I could be wrong, as my teenage son likes to tell me. You make your decision. Before you do, please attach one label like the large one in Figure 12-1 to a package and a computer label to another package. Compare the difference!

Computer self-adhesive labels are excellent for advertising mailings. People expect such labels on a No. 10 business envelope. If you use a fancier label they might suspect you of "gussying up" the mailing. The usual reaction is to turn away from such a mailing and not even open the envelope!

Keep Mailing to New Prospects

You'll never sit still in the world's greatest business! Why? Because you'll always be happily looking for another way to make a buck in the mail. The key to making sales is to mail to *new* prospects *every* day. We even mail Christmas Day!

Where do you find new prospects? Your classified and space ads will bring in hundreds to thousands, depending on how many ads you run. Other new prospects can come from mailing lists you rent, or from swapping with other mail-order pros. Let's look at these two ways of getting new prospects.

Rented Lists Can Pay Off

There are dozens of *List Brokers* who rent mailing lists to mail-order pros. These list brokers can be extremely helpful to you because they can:

- Tell you which lists are pulling (making sales) for firms with products similar to yours
- Advise you on how many pieces to mail to get a return that will show if you should "roll out"—that is, mail to every name on the list
- Indicate—in a general way—what your competition is doing and what kinds of results they're getting

To get this kind of help from a list broker you need do little more than supply him or her with a sample of your mailing piece. You have to do this before a broker will rent you a list, anyway.

With your mailing piece in hand a good list broker can give you a wealth of information in just a few minutes. So take time to consult a list broker. There is *no* fee for the advice and information you get. And as long as you keep your mouth shut and *listen*, I guarantee that you'll learn plenty!

Once the list broker recommends some lists for your mailing, ask him or her for the List Data Card for each of the recommended lists. When you get these, study them carefully. Why? Because you can get much valuable info from each card, such as the one in Figure 12-2:

- How the list was obtained—i.e., where the list owner advertised to make the sales. (You might wish to consider advertising in the same places.)
- The dollar value of the average sale made, plus the high and low dollar values of the sales. This is extremely useful info. For example, if your product sells at $100 per unit, you will probably not want to use a list in which the people paid $10 for what they bought!
- The number of sales made. Thus, if the card says "8,000 buyer names for January through June," you know that this number of mail sales was made for the first six months of the year using the ads mentioned above.

INTERNATIONAL IMPORT SOURCES NEWSLETTER INQUIRIES, SUBSCRIBERS, AND BOOK BUYERS

Quantity	Year	Description	Per M	Arranged/Addressing
150,000	--/--	Inquiries	$90	In zip order; 4 or 5 across Cheshire
		Subscribers	$125	or 9-track 800/16008PI. $50 deposit
		Book buyers	$100	for magnetic tape. Gummed labels
		Expires	$95	$4.50M extra. Pressure sensitive
				$10 extra/M. Minimum rental 5M names.

PROFILE: People who subscribe to the monthly "International Import Sources" newsletter ($84 to $820); buy financial, real-estate,import-export, and other small business books and kits ($15 to $2,500). Average order $100+.

Most buyers purchase multiple units over a period of time. Payment is by check, money order, or credit-card charge. Bad debt ratio is much lower than for usual opportunity seekers. Inquiries are from people seeking a business opportunity of some type in which they can invest their excess cash to earn a good income. Expires are former subscribers who did not renew their subscription to the newsletter. Over a period of several months, most expires eventually renew unless they are no longer alive. All lists are cleaned monthly. Buyers are both import and export oriented.

AVERAGE AGE: 41.   SEX: 50% male; 50% female.

SOURCES: Full-page space ads in a variety of opportunity magazines; spot ads on radio shows appealing to the upwardly mobile; occasional TV spot commercials and interviews with the principal of the business, Edward M. Muldoon.

WHERE EXCEPTIONAL RESPONSE CAN BE EXPECTED: Promotions for books, business courses, cassette tapes on success, franchises, import-export trainees, mail-order students, business opportunity seekers, real-estate wealth-builders, videos on business, etc. SAMPLE OF MAILING PIECE MUST ACCOMPANY EACH ORDER.

SELECTS AVAILABLE: State ($5./M); Section Center and Zip Code ($5./M). This data card is effective May 1, ----. Minimum order: 5,000 names.

Figure 12-2

- The total response to the ads, if the inquiries (non-buyers) are also available for rent—and they usually are. Between buyers and inquirers for the same period, you can build an accurate picture of the business covered by the card. And the use of such data is completely legal because you are given the info in the hope that you'll rent the list after reviewing the facts on the card.

Using such data we have built competitive products to challenge others that sold well. There's nothing wrong with doing this. The technique is called *innovative imitation*. What you do is:

1. Find a product that sells successfully in your field of business.
2. See how you can develop a similar—but better— product that can sell in the same market.
3. Use the same—or similar—ad outlets for your product so you can reach a like group of buyers.

Another step you can take to make rented lists pay off better for you is to:

Send for the ad material covered by the List Data Card. See if your ad material appeals to the same needs and offers similar benefits to your buyers. You may even want to make your ads look similar to those of the successful firm. People will mentally associate you with the successful firm and buy because they have a good image of the company!

When renting lists, take these money-saving steps:

1. Wheel and deal to get the lowest price-per-thousand names. Just because a broker quotes a price doesn't mean you have to pay it! Tell him how poor you are and how bad business is. He may drop the price for you and you'll make more money. I guarantee you that the broker and list renter won't go broke because you negotiated a somewhat lower price!
2. Rent the smallest number of names you can. This will usually be 3,000 or 5,000 names. Why the smallest number? There's no sense wasting money; the list may not pull well for your product or service.
3. Insist on hotline names—that is, the names of buyers

who bought in the last 30 days. Stay away from inquirers—they seldom pull well. Most are just curiosity seekers without a dime in their pockets.

4. Test 1,000 names if you rented 3,000; 2,000 names if you rented 5,000. You don't have to mail to every name you rent! You have the choice of mailing, or not mailing, to every name you rent.

5. Keep careful records of your sales. If the names pull well, mail to the balance of your list. If the remaining names make money for you, talk to the broker about renting more of the same names. Just be sure the new names you rent are the same kind as you first rented. If the new names aren't the same, you may find the results are way off! Don't let this happen to you.

Now let me say a word about "nixies"—ads returned to you from your list mailing marked "Not Deliverable As Addressed," or "Moved—Forwarding Order Expired."

Some list brokers will furnish one, two, or three new names for each nixie you return. Why? Because your nixies help the broker clean the list—that is, remove the names of people to whom mail can't be delivered for one reason or another.

Nixies will—I guarantee—annoy you! Why? Because you're distressed by the postage you wasted, plus the sale you didn't make. But consider this:

We rented the list of an opportunity magazine to promote our newsletter. The nixie count was enormous—we seemed to get back more letters than we mailed. But the number of sales we made was also enormous. This list gives us the best return of any rented list we use. So we ignore the nixies and just rake in the big bucks. And every time I mention this to other newsletter publishers they tell me they've had similar experiences—the list with the highest nixie count will often pull the best in terms of orders and dollar income!

So don't let nixies get you down! Just watch the sales you make from every list by keeping a careful record. If sales are profitable, forget the nixies, other than getting replacement names, if your broker offers them.

List brokers can help you in other ways. They can get you special selections for each list. Thus, your list broker can get:

- State selections—i.e., western states, eastern states, etc. Or you can choose just two or three states to which you want to mail.
- Zip code selections. If you want to mail only to certain zips, your names can be run that way for you.
- Nth name selection. Some mailers don't want every name on a list. Instead, they want a random selection, called the Nth name. Such a choice gives you a true cross-section of a list.
- Specific types of labels. You can get self-adhesive labels— pressure-sensitive. Or you can get labels that require moistening before being attached to the envelope.

There are other selections you can get. Just ask your broker and he or she will gladly tell you what's available. Working with a list broker can be one of the best forms of help you can get for your company. Just be sure to pick the best list broker you can find!

List Swapping Can Get You Many New Names

A low-cost way to get new names is to swap or trade your names of customers and inquirers for similar names from another company selling by mail. The only cost to you is that of running off the names on your office computer. This will be just pennies in most offices.

By swapping names with other companies having mail-order buyers with similar interests you save as much as one-third of your mailing cost. Why? Because you're not paying for the names. So your cost becomes only printing and postage—you don't have any name rental expense. With top-quality names the cost of renting them can be almost one-third your in-the-mail total expense.

Now don't be afraid of swapping names. Many BWB mail-order operators worry that "my names will be used too much." Not so! Any number of studies show:

- The more you mail to your customer names, the more money they'll spend.
- Good customers enjoy getting mail on new and improved items that can solve their problems.
- Not mailing to names can be much worse than over-filling their mailboxes with good offers.
- Many times your offers will star when compared to offers from similar firms.

To arrange a swap of names you must have your names in an easily reproducible form. The best form today is on computer tape or disk. Then you can run your names off on any type of label needed by the firm using your names. And that firm can run its names on any type of label you specify for your mailing.

Get on Computer as Soon as You Can

When you first start your mail-order business you'll do a lot of typing of individual labels and envelopes. But as your business expands you'll have to stop using such antiquated methods and get a computer.

Today there are personal computers that fit on a desktop that have more power than some of the older computers taking up 100 times the space of a PC. So you'll find that your PC can be one of your best moneymakers.

We have five PCs in our mail-order business. I call them "my dumb typists" because they run off a mailing list faster than any typist ever could! I just love to hear the printer clicking away, knowing that it is spitting out names that will make money for me!

What kind of computer should you buy? I really can't answer that question beyond saying that your computer should be able to quickly handle:

- Mailing lists of all kinds
- Customer data files (Name, address, telephone number, what was bought, amount spent, how paid, source of name, etc.)

- Business financial records

You'll use all these capabilities of your computer as your business grows. Since you'll be installing additional computers as time passes, be sure your first is compatible with future models. You don't want to be stuck with a computer that can't talk to other computers!

You can get plenty of free advice and useful demonstrations from your local computer store handling business computers. And computer manufacturers often run free seminars on using computers in different types of businesses. Attend a few of these free seminars to learn as much as you can about computers *before* you make your final purchase decision.

Recognize here and now:

> *You will* have to go on computer as your business grows. So it's *not* a question of "Will we go on computer?" Instead, ask yourself "When will we be big enough to justify buying, or leasing, a computer for our business?" As a general guide, when you have 5,000 customer names it's about time to get one PC for your mailing list. Then you can use it for your customer data base and financial records. If computers turn you off, get a young computer student to run it for you. Your computer buff will have loads of fun and you'll have low labor costs!

Rent Your Mailing List for Extra Income

Once your customer and inquiry lists (keep them separate) are on computer you can consider renting these lists for extra income. Every time you rent one of your lists you get pure income that requires *no* work other than dropping the check in the bank! And I'm sure you can find the energy to do that.

To get maximum rental income from your list, get a list broker to take it on. The list broker will find customers for your list. The usual commission the list broker will charge you is 20 percent of the list rental fee.

Thus, if your list rents for $100 per 1,000 names, the broker keeps $20 and you get $80. For this you do nothing but put the names up on computer when the person first becomes a customer. In our business:

> *We have our lists with a highly competent list broker. This broker gets our lists rented several times a year. And the income is significant because this broker gets rentals of 50,000 and 100,000 names at a time. Figure out what 100,000 names at $80 net per 1,000 will give. (It's $8,000— for just taking one phone call and agreeing to the rental!)*

And if you're worried that the competition will rent your list, forget it. You have full control over *your* list! And your broker will demand a sample mailing piece *before* your list is rented out. If you or the broker feel that your competition would be given an unfair advantage, then the rental will be declined.

What amazes me about our list broker is that the organizations renting our lists are far removed from what we do. Thus, political parties, travel clubs, and insurance companies seem to like our lists. Why, I don't know. But their checks don't bounce and a buck is a buck!

Note that renting your names is much different from swapping names. When your names are rented you're paid. And the firm renting the names can use them only *once*.

When you swap names you're *not* paid. Instead, you're given an equal number of names for your own mailings. So your income will be derived from sales of your products or services to the new names you got in the swap. You may be able to use the names only once, if that's what you agree to with the firm doing the swapping. Or you can use the names more often, if your swapper agrees to this usage.

The usual list broker will put your names up on computer for a nominal charge—$10 to $20 per thousand names. And the names will be maintained—that is *cleaned* (undeliverables deleted, new addresses inserted when people move)—for another few dollars per thousand. So you really have little to do except put the money in the bank!

Your list broker will be able to copy your names from tape or disk. So you're not wasting your time when you put the names up on your office computer. The ususal way list rental works is this:

1. You start your mail-order business and begin making sales to your new customers.
2. As each sale is made the customer's name is put up on computer. And—if you wish—you can start a data base for each customer.
3. As your company grows, so too does your mailing list of satisfied customers. You can also have a list of inquiries—people who asked for information but never bought what you offer. You won't be paid as much by renters of this list as for customers. But what you're paid is still money that you can drop into your business checking account!
4. While your company is growing you'll be introducing new products or services. You'll use your *in-house* mailing list (that is, your customers) to mail information on your new products. And you'll make sales to them. These sales will help pay the cost of keeping the mailing list clean—that is, removal of undeliverables, address changes, etc. So the work you do putting up your list is repaid by the extra profits your firm earns from the list.
5. When your list reaches 5,000 names list brokers will suddenly become interested in it. Take your time in selecting a broker. Why? Because you want a broker who will actively push your list, instead of just sitting on it and waiting for someone to express interest in it. Get written pledges from each broker as to how, and where, they'll market your list. Compare the plans; then make your decision.

Remember that it's important to have an aggressive list broker. Some mail-order firms get more than $100,000 a year in list rental income. That's pure money that goes directly into your bottom profit line.

Other mail-order firms just about break even on their product or service sales. Their real income is derived from their list rentals—beautiful unattached money that's straight profit—all the way! So be sure to take the steps outlined here to make some of this money yours. You deserve list rental income if you do the work to make the sales and then put the names up on computer! Start now—it really pays.

Be Easy to Work With

In mail order many of your orders today will still arrive by U.S. mail (the best in the world!), Federal Express, DHL, United Parcel Service, etc. You will, of course, get credit card orders if you have a Merchant Account. But for most mail-order businesses, about 75 percent of your orders will be by mail.

So you should make it as easy as possible for your customers and prospects to order from you. One way to do this is to use a Business Return Envelope (BRE) for which *you* pay the postage. Why? Because with a BRE:

- Your customer doesn't have to hunt for a stamp
- Your address is already printed on the envelope (see Figure 12-1)
- All your customer need do is insert a check or money order in the envelope, along with an order coupon, seal and drop in the mail
- The whole process is so simple for your customers that they will—in general—(a) order more, (b) be less resistant to ordering from you

The result—of course—is more money flowing into your mailbox every day of the week. And that, goood friend, is why we're all in this business!

True, you do pay the post office an annual fee for your BRE. But it's not that high. Also, you pay a per-piece postage charge for each BRE that you receive. You can open an account at the post office to keep funds there so you don't have to pay for the BREs every time you pick them up. You'll be given a regular statement of how much is "in the till" and when you must make another "contribution."

But the cost of all of this is small compared to how easy you make it for your customer to order. And that, after all, is what you're trying to accomplish.

Another way to make it easier for your customer is with a business card (see Figure 12-1). Use such a card whenever you write to a customer, call on a supplier, or deal with others in your business. With the card in hand it's easier for someone to call you, order something, or even complain!

There are plenty of low-cost sources of business cards. Just get a simple black-and-white card giving the key information. No need to go to multi-color cards with fancy printing that's so small or so curly that people can't read the names or numbers on the card! Just use straightforward lettering that's legible and accurate.

Give Refunds or Get Out of Business

In every mail-order business you'll have customers who want a refund of their money because they don't like what they received. In my business our refunds are under one-half of one percent! Why? Because we try to give top value for what people order.

If a customer asks for a refund, make it instantly! Don't mope and groan saying "Why does this so-and-so want his (or her) money back?" Stop wasting time—just make an instant refund. Then go out and make twice what you refunded. Use the refund as a spur to earn more for yourself.

Be sure, however, to have rules for your refunds. Thus, you might say that:

- Items must be returned within 10 days after receiving them
- All items must be in resaleable condition
- Return postage or shipping must be paid by the customer
- The customer should insure the item so everyone is certain it *was* returned and received safely

Are there any other reasons than motivating yourself why you should make instant refunds? Yes, there are. And they're very good reasons, namely:

1. The United States Postal Inspection Service supports a full, unquestioned refund policy and action by all mail-order dealers. You are, of course, permitted to have fair and sensible refund guidelines. But you must follow them at all times. My personal recommendation is: *Even if the customer does not follow your guidelines exactly, make the refund.* People will respect your business more and you'll have fewer hassles.
2. The Better Business Bureau supports a full refund policy by mail-order dealers when the customer abides by your guidelines. And since we recommend that you join the BBB, you'll be making refunds like all its other members.
3. The Federal Trade Commission (FTC) supports a full refund policy by mail-order dealers when the customer abides by your guidelines.
4. The various state Attorneys General support a full refund policy by mail-order dealers when the customer abides by your guidelines.

I hope you get the point by now. You should make refunds when the customer requests one. And the refund should be made quickly in the form of a check to the ordering customer, unless it was a credit-card order. When the customer orders by credit card you should make a refund through your Merchant Account, if the Account rules require it—which they usually do.

Some mail-order dealers make their refunds by just enclosing the check or credit slip in an envelope and sending it out. Others write a short letter thanking the customer for the order and expressing disappointment that the customer didn't like what was ordered. Others include a catalog or flyer with the letter, hoping the customer will order something else. Some will!

We've made refunds the same day the person returned the product in good condition. The customer was so impressed with the speed of the refund that he returned our refund check saying: "You guys are so nice that I want to order a different Kit. So I'm enclosing a check for another $100 to cover the cost! Thanks." To which we say the same—thanks!

The key to eliminating refunds is to give such high value to each customer that the thought of a refund never occurs. We've followed this policy every year in our business. Our refunds are so few I can almost remember every one of them. And many of those getting the refund order something else. You should make this a goal in your mail-order business if you want to gross one million a year—starting right now!

Guarantee What You Sell

You'll make many more sales if you guarantee what you sell. Why? Because people feel safer in ordering when they know you guarantee what you sell.

But you must word your guarantee *very* carefully. And you should have an attorney experienced in mail order review the wording of every one of your guarantees. Watch these points in preparing your guarantee:

- Never make a guarantee that you can't fulfill. Thus, *never* advertise: "Read this book. It's guaranteed to make you a millionaire!" You can't control such a guarantee because it's the reader of the book who must do the work—not you!
- Never say: "Make $10,000 a month—guaranteed." Again, *you* can't guarantee that your customer will earn money in this amount! He'll probably earn less. But he might make more!

The kinds of guarantees you *can* make relate to what you can control. Thus, you might say:

- Full refund *guaranteed* if you're not satisfied with this _____ and return it in good condition within 10 days. (You *can* fulfill this guarantee yourself.)

- We will refund your money in full if the _____ advertised is not exactly as described in this ad. (Again, you can control the refund if the person asks for it).
- We want you to be completely satisfied. If you're not, return the _____ in good condition within 15 days and we will make a complete and exact refund— no questions asked! (As in the earlier guarantees you control the action.)

To sum up, *never* guarantee an action over which you have no control! Why? Because such a guarantee can get you into a heap of trouble. You're liable to have all sorts of regulators demanding that you prove your claims.

While most mail-order pros claim that an unconditional guarantee increases sales, others think differently. They believe that calling attention to a full money-back guarantee only encourages people to return items! So these mail-order operators—who are highly successful—follow this policy:

> *They never state a guarantee in their sales literature or ads. But if requested to make a refund based on a "guarantee" the customer claims he or she saw, or thought they saw, the refund is made instantly. Thus, the firm complies with the obligation to make a refund to a dissatisifed customer. But the firm does not put the idea of a refund in the customer's mind!*

Now that you know the different ways to tell (or not tell) customers about your guarantee policy, take your pick. You know your customers better than anyone else. So you should decide which policy is best for you!

Make Your Order Form Fun to Use

If you're selling just one product, you can use a simple order form like that in Figure 12-3a. But where you have dozens of offerings, a larger form, Figure 12-3b, is needed.

In designing your order form, leave plenty of space for entering the needed info. If your customer has to squint

Order Form

Here's my $17.50. Please send me one copy of E June Mall's great book GETTING WEALTHY PUBLISHING A NEWSLETTER! Send to IWS, INC, 24 Canterbury Road, Rockville Centre NY 11570. Act NOW—start sooner!

Name: _____ Apt/Suite #_____

Address: _____

City: _____ State: _____ Zip: _____

No Risk Request Form   This is the best book we've ever seen on newsletters! Get it!

Figure 12-3a

HOW TO ORDER
List the books, kits, or other items you want by title and price. We pay postage and handling—there's no added charge to you. Total everything up. Send the order form with your check or money order to: International Wealth Success Inc. 24 Canterbury Rd., Rockville Ctr., NY 11570.

IWS ORDER FORM

NAME _____ APT/SUITE NO. ____

ADDRESS _____

CITY _____ STATE ____

ZIP CODE _____ DATE ____

Telephone Number: _____   C-3

Send check or money order for total amount shown below.*

QUANTITY	TITLE/DESCRIPTION	PRICE	TOTAL
	Total Amount Enclosed		

*Or use your credit card for the total amount shown. We ship the same day your order arrives!   ☐ Please charge my ☐ Visa ☐ MasterCard credit card account

Print Name
For credit-card orders, call 1-800-323-0548 day/night.

C-3   IWS, Inc., 24 Canterbury Rd, Rockville Ctr, NY 11570
To order by phone call 516-766-5850 day/night!

INTERNATIONAL WEALTH SUCCESS, INC.
Credit Reference: Irving Trust Company, New York, NY 10019, Member: Better Business Bureau (this is not an endorsement). Founded 1967 and in business constantly since.

Figure 12-3b

Here's my $99.50. Send me my FAST FINANCING OF YOUR REAL-ESTATE FORTUNE SUCCESS KIT. I understand that I can consult free of any charge with Ty Hicks as a bonus for my buying this great KIT.

NAME _____ Apt/Suite #____

ADDRESS _____

CITY _____ STATE _____ ZIP ____

Note: Your KIT will be sent by Special Handling Insured Mail. Overseas Air Mail Registered $20 extra. Send check or   IWS, Inc., 24 Canterbury Rd money order to: Rockville Centre NY 11570·

Figure 12-3c

and squeeze info onto the form, he or she may give up and say, "Why bother?" So you lose an order.

If you can't design your own order form (it's really easy), get a graphic designer to do it for you. Your cost won't be too great. And you'll get an eye-catching form which will encourage orders—not discourage them!

If you want to carry your money-back guarantee in a place where it will convince people to order, put it on your order form. Then people will be encouraged to send you money to help you create a million-dollar business— starting from scratch! Figure 12-3c shows one such order form.

Handle Inquiries Quickly

Once your business starts you'll get inquiries by mail, phone, FAX, and courier services. Follow these money-making rules for *all* inquiries:

1. Answer every inquiry immediately. People want information about your products or services so they can make a buying decision. The longer they have to wait for this info, the less likely they are to buy!
2. Send your response by First Class Mail, or other speedy delivery method. Your potential customer may be turned off it you use Third Class Mail (which is usually much slower) to respond to his or her request. The small additional cost of First Class Mail is well worth the favorable impression you make on your potential customer. If the potential customer went to the trouble to request info from you, the least you can do is to get it to him or her as quickly as possible!
3. Respond to inquiries before you do any other work! Why? Because inquiries represent *future business*. And if you want to build a million-dollar business you must do it by building toward your future *each day* of the year. So send out responses to inquiries the first thing every day. Then your mail-order future will be secure. (In our office we have a written policy which says: Do your inquiries—even before you start

counting the day's money! This policy really works because we grow each year in sales and profits.)

4. Use a special envelope teaser for each inquiry. The teaser we use is rubber-stamped in black on the outside of the envelope. It says: *You requested this information.* So the person who receives our mailing knows that the material is not being sent to them unsolicited. As a result they're much more likely to open the envelope and read what's inside. That's when a sale is made!

5. Send at least five responses to each inquiry over a period of time. We send four follow-up responses over a period of about six months. You need not follow this timing. A more frequent schedule might be better for what you're selling. The only way to determine the best schedule for your follow-ups is to keep records. Compare sales when using a quick, closely spaced follow-up with one at more extended intervals. The key to the number and frequency of follow-ups is sales. In mail-order, everything comes down to the numbers!

6. Experiment with different prices in your follow-up mailings. But keep careful records! Some mail-order pros reduce the price of their offer as each follow-up is made. When you do this you must be careful not to anger earlier customers who might have paid a higher price for the same product or service. Other mail-order operators say: "Never sell anything at a reduced price! Stand your ground and they'll eventually buy—at *your* price." The choice is yours. But the only way you can tell if you earn more with gradual price reductions is to test such an offer against one in which you don't reduce the price. Again, you *must* keep accurate records so you know which offer pulls better. (As an aside, we never reduce the prices of our offers. And it seems to work well—people eventually buy!)

Some mail-order pros sell their inquiry names to noncompeting firms. The price? It ranges from 10¢ to 50¢ a name, depending on the business. Of course, if you can negotiate $1.00 a name—or more—great!

Why would other firms be willing to pay such high prices for inquiry names? Because they're "hot"—that is, recent and ready to buy. So it's much easier to make a sale to such names than to tired names that have been around for months.

Selling your inquiry names is another way of building your income. In this business you have to be resourceful—even if you're the smartest operator around! To find buyers of your inquiry names, just call or write to noncompeting firms. You'll be amazed at how quickly they'll snap up your names for a good price. You can, of course, go on using your names if you've put them up on computer so they can be run off any time you want to make a mailing.

Keep in Touch with Your Customers

If you're a cold-fish type you'll have to change if you want to build a million-dollar business in mail order! Why? For a number of good reasons, namely:

- Customers *like* dealing with a warm, interested, and concerned company. Think of firms like L. L. Bean, Lillian Vernon, Sharper Image, etc., that *care* for their customers and show it. Their business booms. So will yours if you show your customer that he or she *is* important to you and your business. You can learn a lot from the major players in the mail-order game. They're successful because they *do* care and they *do* show their customers that they care!
- Customers often turn away from a firm that slights them by not answering letters or phone calls. So if a customer or prospect takes time to get in touch with you, give that person a fast answer. When you have thousands of customers, you may have to use a form letter to respond. But you *must* respond—you must *not* ignore a customer if you expect continued business from that person. One of the form letters we use profitably is that in Figure 12-4. We check off the desired message in red. The customer gets a fast answer and knows that he or she has not been ignored.

Pick an interesting letterhead for your firm. At the start you can go to one of the mail-order printers having a variety of letterheads in many different designs and colors. Prices are reasonable and delivery fast. *Just be sure to use your letterhead when you write a customer!*

Why? Because some customers are so disorganized that they won't remember they wrote you unless you respond on your letterhead! Further, if you have an attractive letterhead, as recommended above, your customer will be impressed. Not only have you responded—you did so with class! A typical letterhead is shown in Figure 12-4.

As I said earlier—Everything is marketing! Keep in touch with your customers and they'll keep sending you money.

Today your most frequently asked question will be: When was my order shipped? To answer this quickly, keep your shipping record close to your telephone. Then you can give an instantaneous answer to this familiar question. Once your customer knows his or her order was shipped they'll be happy.

A good friend of mine, who's a highly successful mail-order businessman, is George Wein, who owns and operates Select Information Exchange. This organization provides sample issues of newletters to its customers.

George uses correspondence with his newsletter publishers in a highly effective way. Each year he issues a comprehensive catalog of the newsletters he represents. Before a newsletter is listed in the catalog, George asks for a copy of the most recent two issues. A form letter, which is very personal in its tone, asks the publisher to send these copies in to George. We respond each year because the form letter is right on target.

Also, George's letterhead and catalog are highly attractive. Using such designs enables George to do an excellent job for his customers and for the newsletters he lists in his catalog. As a result, his business continues to grow.

INTERNATIONAL WEALTH SUCCESS.
Inc.

P. O. Box 186, Merrick, N. Y. 11566

Dear Reader:

Thank you for contacting IWS. We were delighted to hear from you. To speed our service to you, we've checked one or more items below so that you'll have a FASTER REPLY.

_____Your IWS PROGRAM was mailed by SPECIAL DELIVERY to YOU on_____. You should get it soon. Thanks for your order.

_____Yes, YOU CAN RUN FREE ADS IN IWS, if you're a 1-year, or longer, subscriber to IWS.

_____Please send a NEW AD EVERY MONTH--they will PULL BETTER FOR YOU when you do!

_____Why not run the item you mention as a FREE AD in IWS? Just send us the EXACT wording.

_____To run a FREE AD, just send it in. Please TYPE or PRINT CLEARLY! Thank you.

_____Please send us YOUR phone number and we'll call YOU FREE to answer your questions.

_____Are you a NEW subscriber (NO ISSUES RECEIVED YET)_____, or a RENEWAL (YOU HAVE BEEN GETTING ISSUES)_____? Please check the correct box and return to us. If YOU are a RENEWAL, please include your MEMBER NO._____. (See the large white envelope).

_____Please send the NAME and ACCOUNT NUMBER OF THE BANK in which your check or money order was deposited. These appear in the endorsement on the back of the check. Thank you!

_____YOU can obtain the following Ty Hicks books from Parker Publishing Co Inc, West Nyack NY 10994 for $7.95 each: "How to Build a Second Income Fortune in Your Spare Time;" "Smart Money Shortcuts to Becoming Rich;" "How to Start Your Own Business on a Shoestring and Make Up to $100,000 Per Year;" "How To Borrow Your Way to a Great Fortune;" "Magic Mind Secrets for Building Great Riches Fast;" "How to Make a Quick Fortune."

_____YOU can call Ty Hicks at   any evening between 8 and 10 PM New York time to discuss your questions and get Ty's ideas on your situation.

_____Ty Hicks is glad to call readers FREE OF CHARGE when they renew their subscription for one year beyond the present ending date.

_____Please USE the Loan Application Form sent YOU. It is suitable for your loan. Thanks.

_____YOU can order THOMAS' REGISTER from Thomas Pub Co 1 Penn Center, New York NY 10001

_____YOU can order COMMERCIAL CORRESPONDENCE IN 4 LANGUAGES from IWS INC POB 186 Merrick NY 11566 for $25.

_____Please send $_____for AIR MAIL postage of your materials. Thank you.

_____It takes at least 4 to 6 weeks to hear on the VCS, PIR, and SL applications.

_____Other:_____

_____

_____

_____   Cordially yours in GREAT SUCCESS,
                                             INTERNATIONAL WEALTH SUCCESS, INC.

_____

                                             Steven C. Crane
SCC:st   Steven C. Crane, Vice-President

Figure 12-4

Don't Give Discounts Too Easily

Once your business is doing well, people will ask you for discounts on their purchases. In general, avoid giving any kind of discount.

Now and then a person will buy everything we publish—about $2,000 worth of materials. If they ask for a discount I will give them up to 20 percent off. But the only reason I agree to such a discount is because the order is large. On such large orders you make a friend when you offer a modest discount.

Our Executive Reps—people who sell our products—get a 40 percent discount at the start of their sales efforts. But they've earned their Rep place before being appointed. So the earnings raise 40 percent discount they get on items they buy for themselves.

But the 40 percent they earn when they sell our products to other people is worth it to us. Why? Because the Rep has found customers for us that we might never have found ourselves. They're entitled to be rewarded for their work.

Yet the price the regular customer pays for his book, Kit, or newsletter is the same as everyone else pays. We just do not offer discounts to the buyer of one or two items. Follow the same policy and you'll earn more and your customers will have greater respect for you! Our reps are allowed to sell every item we publish. This gives them a really unique line of products to sell—a line not equalled by any competitor.

Use Your Testimonials to Sell More

No matter what producr or service you sell, you'll eventually (I hope) get some complementary letters from your customers. Be sure to take these steps with these letters:

1. Put each letter in a safe place. The safest place is your company safe deposit box in a bank.

Your FREE ADS are helping me very much in this
brokerage business and I am very thankful to you at
IWS for this very wonderful favor....OHIO

I truly believe that your ideas in this great magazine
can and will bring success to those who believe and
act on them.....UTAH

Thank you for the help you have given me in the
past. I treasure your monthly magazine and have been
a long time subscriber.....TEXAS

I cannot express how much I appreciate the wonderful
job your Newsletter is doing.....GEORGIA

I appreciate your service and your outstanding Newsletter.
Keep up the good work.....ARIZONA

...because of the...loans....I was able to obtain from
venture capital investors only through the writeup you
gave me in your excellent publication...I was able to
"climb back out of financial debt with the mail order
businesses"... and have now started to show a profit...
and with 2 partners (just young fellows of 79 yrs
young and 63 yrs young)...purchased a smoke shop.
.....WASHINGTON

...thanks to you, I'm on my way. I firmly believe
this will be a very prosperous year....ILLINOIS

...your books and other writings present ideas and
methods that ordinary persons in a 'rut' can use
to help them work out of their particular rut.....
MARYLAND

Have been well pleased with the monthly Newsletter;
it beats the other similar publications I used to get
.....VIRGINIA

Since taking your Financial Broker, Finder, Business Broker,
Consultant Kit........I have had very good success...As of this
date I have placed 85% of loans...Also in the Import-Export
am doing real fine.....NEW YORK

As a subscriber and avid reader of your Newsletter, I find
it very helpful in my business as a financial broker. I appreciate the value of your Newsletter immeasurably.....KY

Firstly congratulations on your excellent publications. I cannot
explain how my thinking has changed for the positive since
receiving IWS.....NEW ZEALAND

It is a pleasure to compliment you on your publication...
I have been a subscriber for several years, and it has been a
valuable source on business information for me.....VIRGINIA

You'll be pleased to know that I helped my small business
clients raise almost exactly $2-million in loans and investments
in the last 12 months. Methods I learned from your books
and Kits....... were responsible for most of that success...My
gross income for the month was $3200. That may not be
much to some people, but it is 4 times what I was making
in 1973....TEXAS

Not long ago I was working my head off at two jobs and
not enjoying either one...I make more money now and work
at home when I feel like it.....OKLAHOMA

I raised $50,000 from your idea.....FLORIDA

Thank you for the warm reception you accorded me during
my short stay.....NIGERIA

I again thank you for your time on the phone with me. I
am under way and doing quite well. I have completed one
merger deal and placed 2 loans totalling $78,000.....MASS

Figure 12-5

2. Make copies of each letter before you put it away for safekeeping. The copy of the letter will give you the exact wording your customer used.

3. Highlight your testimonials in your promotion material. Figure 12-5 shows how we use a few of our thousands of testimonials in our promotional material. Read a few of these and see if they get you charged up!

4. If you want to use the name and location of the person writing the testimonial, you *must* get *written* permission *before* you print the testimonial. But if you use only the location of the person you do *not* have to obtain written permission to do so. Some purists think that a testimonial giving the writer's name and address is stronger. They are probably right. My view, though, is that a testimonial is just as strong with just the location of the sender. And I might add, I notice that I drive a much bigger yacht and a much better American auto than these know-it-all purists. So you decide who you think is right and do as you please. A typical release for use of a testimonial is given in Figure 12-6. Use it if you want to include the name and address of the testimonial writer.

5. Don't date your testimonials unless dating is a part of your sales pitch. You can use a testimonial for years if you don't date it. But if you put a date on it, people will soon turn away, saying "That no longer works today; it might have been true years ago. But things are not the same now." Result? You lose a sale!

6. Consider using a "blockbuster" testimonial approach to hard-sell prospects who've resisted all your previous mailings. To do this, assemble as many testimonials as you can on several pages and send them to your hard-sell prospects with a letter saying:

   We've been trying to sell you something for the last six months. But you haven't bought and we're really puzzled because we know that our products (or services) are far better than any you can get elsewhere.

TESTIMONIAL RELEASE

DATE_____

PUBLISHER OR USER_____

ADDRESS_____

For valuable consideration, I hereby irrevocably consent to and
authorize the use, publication, and copyright by you, or anyone
authorized by you, of any and all testimonials which I have
written and sent to you, without further compensation to me. I
am over 18 years of age.

Testimonial Writer_____

Address_____

Witnessed By:_____

Figure 12-6

To prove how good our products are for your needs, we've assembled a number of recent testimonials from our customers. Take a few moments to read these and I'm sure you'll be convinced that you'll benefit from using our products. We're also including for you helpful data on a number of our products.

Mine the Gold in Deadbeats

In the world of mail order you'll run into a variety of people who try to rip you off. Their techniques vary. But the most popular ones are:

- Payment by check on a closed account
- Writing a check against insufficient funds
- Claiming they sent you cash through the mail
- Use of an expired credit card
- Unauthorized use of someone else's credit card
- Etc.

While these people *are* trying to "beat" you, many are not hardened criminals. They're almost playing a game— seeing if they can get something for nothing. So you can play two games with them—and make money from one of the games. Here are your two games.

Game 1: Don't Get Taken

You can avoid almost every loss caused by these deadbeats by simply having a sensible policy with respect to check and credit-card orders. This policy is:

1. Wait up to *3 weeks* for *all* personal and business checks to clear before shipping any product or starting a service.
2. Save every order that comes into your business for at least five years. Why? Because the greatest business in the world is also the simplest business that can

make you a millionaire today. With every order saved you can easily reconstruct any sequence of events in your ordering and shipping cycle.

3. Stamp every order with the date (month, day, year, and time if you wish) received. Then mark on the outside of the envelope the following information:

   • Type of check or payment. For a "regular" check, that is a personal or business check we mark "R." For a money order we mark "MO."

   • Next to the above information we mark the date of the deposit thus: 3/26/YR for a check deposited on March 26, 19 _____ The year is entered in the usual two-digit form.

   • The product is not sent until at least three weeks after the deposit date, if the bank is a distant one. For local banks we wait at least one week. (As an aside, banks are sometimes slow in returning "Account Closed" and "Not Sufficient Funds" checks. So you have to protect yourself and your business against such delays.) And, good friend of mine, please note that the FTC "30-day Rule" which says you must ship within 30 days or offer a refund, starts the clock ticking from the time you receive payment in the form of *good funds* (as the banks say). This is *not* the deposit date, *not* the date you received the check, *not* the date the customer mailed the check! Instead, it *is* the date your business checking account was credited with good funds, meaning that the check didn't bounce and you received payment in full.

4. For credit-card orders, either verbal or electronic approval of each charge is required *before* an item is shipped. If the response is "decline", we inform the customer of this. Often, they'll say: "Oh, I guess I'm maxed out on that card. Here's another one that still has some credit on it." You're then given a second number and when it is put through it will usually clear. Only then is the merchandize shipped to the customer.

5. Our staff stays completely alert to people who might

be trying to commit fraud by using a stolen or expired credit card. Typical indicators of attempted fraud are:

- A lack of concern over the amount to be charged. An honest person spends his or her money carefully. So they're really concerned about the total amount that will be charged to the card.
- Confusion over the customer's home address or telephone number. Most people know their home address and telephone number almost as well as they know their own name. So any hesitation in giving either is often a tip that fraud is being attempted.
- Using phone numbers that aren't normally assigned to home phones. Thus, a number like 123-4000 is seldom assigned to a residence. Such numbers are saved for a business—and usually a big one at that. The easiest way to check this out is to accept the number as given and then call back later to determine if the customer is there. Usually the person answering the phone will say: "No such person works or resides here."
- A hurried order with demands for overnight delivery at a high price that is to be charged to the card is often a key to possible fraud. Most people are proud of their credit card and the bank that issued it. So they'll say, "This is a _____ Bank _____ Card that I've had for five years." Then they launch into the number, expiration date, etc.

5. To avoid being taken—which is our Game 1—get the following information from every customer ordering by credit card:
   - Name, address, telephone numbers (home/business)
   - Card number, expiration date, name of cardholder—do *not* accept orders from people other than the named card holder unless you can get verbal or written authorization that the order is acceptable to the cardholder.
   - Once you have the above information, tell the person ordering that the charge will be $_____, billed by _____ (give the

> name of your merchant account billing; this will
> sometimes be a shortened version of your
> company name
> • Process the order; then send the customer a copy
> of the charge slip with their name, address,
> telephone number, and amount billed shown
> clearly. Be sure to include the approval code given
> by the credit-card center

You can win at Game 1—it just takes an unending attention to every aspect of your business. Avoid getting burned and you'll be ready for Game 2.

Game 2: Get Paid Every Time

Most deadbeats want what you're selling. They'd just like to get it without having to pay for it. You *can* beat almost every deadbeat by taking steps to see that they pay for those great items or services you offer. To get paid:

1. Insist on payment with the order. Then wait long enough for the payment to be credited to your business checking account. Observe the 30-Day Rule, remembering that the 30 days begins with the day you receive good funds in your bank account.
2. Go after deadbeats who send you a bad check. Do this by outlining to them the penalties of not making good on a bad check. Figure 12-7 shows a typical letter and reminder used by one mail-order operator who states that he collects 60 percent of his bad debts with these.
3. Get your attorney (you *must* have one in this business) to write a letter telling deadbeats what's in store for them if they don't pay up. You can even include with this letter a summary of the law of the state in which the deadbeat resides, citing the penalties the person might incur. This can be quite effective with certain types of deadbeats.
4. Send information on the deadbeat and the check to one or more of the mail-order protection groups that publicize such information. Some of these organi-

Dear _____:

We regret that we must tell you that your check Number_____, for $_____,
dated_____, was returned by your bank_____times marked:

_____Insufficient or Not Sufficient Funds

_____Account Closed

_____Refer to Maker

_____Uncollected Funds

_____Other

No doubt this is an oversight on your part which we're sure you want to correct
as soon as possible. A Returned Check is a matter of bank and supplier records
which people try to keep clear of such history.

Further, we are hereby informing you via Certified Mail of this Returned Check and
we are giving you 15 days to make good this debt by sending us a replacement check
or money order.

Also, we are holding your Returned Check containing the bank stampings and other
data as evidence of the facts reported above so we can fully document the exact
nature of this transaction. Your Returned Check will be sent to you after we get
a good check or money order from you for the above amount.

Thank you for your order.

Very truly yours,

Bad Check Law

An Act Regulating The Issuance of Checks, Drafts
And For The Payment of Money . . .

"Be it enacted by the Senate and House of Representatives
of the United States of America in Congress . . . that any
person . . . who, with intent to defraud, shall make, . . .
or deliver any check . . . for payment of money upon any
bank . . . knowing . . . that the maker or drawer has not
sufficient funds . . . with such bank . . . for the payment of
such check . . . in full upon its presentation shall be guilty
of a misdemeanor and punishable by imprisonment for
not more than one year, or be fined not more than $1,000,
or both. . . . a check . . . which is refused by the drawee
because of insufficient funds of the maker . . . shall be
prima facie evidence of the intent to defraud . . . within five
days after receiving notice in person or writing that such
draft or order had not been paid. . . ."

Figure 12-7

zations will write the deadbeat, outlining the risk they're taking. It will help you collect more.

5. Hire a collection agency. While you'll get only half of the amount collected, half is better than nothing. And it is pleasant to know that you beat the deadbeat!

6. Report the deadbeat to the credit reporting agencies. While such agencies won't help you collect on the bad check, having such a check listed on a person's credit report is enough to hamper their getting future credit. Some will even make good on the bad check, just to have the black mark removed from their credit report. Again, *you* get paid, instead of being ripped off.

7. Another effective technique is to report the person to the local police station "Bunco" squad. They may gently remind the person that there's a severe penalty for not making good on a bad check. About 80 percent of the people who are called by the bunco squad will pay you—which is all you really want!

Using the various methods given here you *can* get paid *every* time! Is it worth the effort? I think so. Why? Because when you get a deadbeat to pay you teach him or her a valuable lesson, namely:

> *It's wrong to rip off a business. And if you try to commit such a fraud, the consequences for you can be severe. So start living your life right—pay for what you want. It will make you feel a lot better. And your life will be much more productive and fulfilling.*

To show you that what I say above is correct, try renting a list of deadbeat names. They're for rent from a number of mailing-list brokers. You'll often find that such deadbeats buy and buy. And the checks they send you don't bounce! Why?

Because many deadbeats have revised their life style. They're paying for what they want—with a good check or a valid credit card. So you *can* make money from deadbeats—both your own and those from other firms.

Just be sure that when you rent a list of deadbeats that they're real deadbeats, and not a *compiled* list. The difference between a deadbeat customer list and a compiled list is this:

- With a customer list, the person either sent money or ordered an item or service by mail or phone
- With a compiled list, a mailing-list house went through standard listings of various types available to them and put the names on a list.

As a general guide, compiled lists seldom pull as well as customer lists—even if the customers were deadbeats at the start! Further, the same is true, even if the customers paid with good checks or valid credit cards.

Compiled lists, though, *do* have their place. They're excellent for business-to-business selling—that is, when you're selling a product or service to another business. And only compiled lists can give you the names and addresses of 14 million businesses in the United States. And only they can give you such unusual listings as these which I've selected at random!

- 760 baseball clubs
- 54 basketball clubs
- 444 feed grinding companies
- 837 music publishers
- Etc.

So you see, if you have a specialized product or service to sell, a compiled list may be just what you need. Just be sure to keep in mind the difference between *customer* lists and *compiled* lists! It will really put money into your bank—the best place for it!

Know Your Profit Numbers

Mail order is a numbers business! It is easier to figure your profit in mail order than in any other business. Why? Because in mail order:

1. You know *all* your costs associated with any sale

because you have your bills for everything in front
of you.
2. Knowing your costs, you can easily figure your profit
because you also have your sales income in front of
you.

Let's see how this works. Let's say you take a full-page
ad in a magazine that costs you $2,000 (a typical cost
these days). You're selling a product or service for $20.
The item or service you're selling costs you $5.00. You
sell 320 of the items from your ad. Your profit will then
be:

Ad cost for each sale = Cost of ad/Number sold

Or, for this item or service:

Ad cost for each sale = $2,000/320 = $6.25

Now if your packing and mailing costs run $3.00 per
item, your total cost will = ad cost + item cost + packing
and mailing cost. Or for this item,

Total cost = $6.25 + $5.00 + $3.00 = $14.25

Your profit will be sale price – total cost, or $20 – $14.25
= $5.75. Since you sold 320 items, your total profit = total
number of units sold × profit per unit. Or 320 × $5.75
= $1,840.

But don't stop here! You now have 320 *customer* names.
And if you keep bringing out new items or services, as
we suggested earlier, you'll probably be able to sell half
these customers one or more things—for more profit.

As you gain experience with your mail–order business,
you'll begin to find that your average customer buys a
certain dollars' worth of products or services from you.
For example, in my mail-order business:

*Our average customer buys more than $200 worth of
products from us. So if we get 2,000 new customers in
any year, we know that we'll eventually receive some
$400,000 from these customers. How do we ensure this
will happen? In two ways: (1) By constantly looking for,*

and getting, new customers, and (2) by regularly finding and introducing new products to keep our customers "turned on" to sending us their orders.

When you promote by direct mail instead of by publication ads, you figure your profit in much the same way. Thus, if you made a mailing that cost $2,000 total, you would use the same equations as you did above. And your profit would be the same, if you sold the same number of units with an identical mailing cost.

You'll often hear people in mail order talk about the "Cost per inquiry." How do you figure it? It's easy. Let's say you run an ad (or a mailing) that costs you $3,000. You don't try to sell from the ad. You just ask the people to send for more information. It is this information that does the selling. You get, we'll say, 500 inquiries from your ad or mailing. Your item sells for $100.

Your cost per inquiry = cost of ad or mailing/number of inquiries received. For this offer,

Cost per inquiry = $3,000/500 inquiries = $6.00

"This seems high," you say? Not so, good friend! People pay $15, $20, $30 for each inquiry these days. And they're happy—if they can convert 25 percent, or more, of their inquiries to sales. Let's see how this might work out for your item which sells for $100.

If you convert (that is, sell to) 25 percent of your inquiries, you will make 0.25 × 500 = 125 sales. At $100 per sale, your income will be $100 × 125 sold = $12,500. Yet your ad or mailing cost only $3,000. So you've brought in $12,500/$3,000 = 4.17 times your ad or mailing cost! You can easily get rich this way. And your *cost per order* = $3,000/125 orders = $24.00—a small amount.

And joy of joys, you still have 500 – 125 = 375 names that you can keep trying to sell to! Or you can rent these names out to other companies and make money from them. You would add your list rental income to the $12,500 you've already brought in from the ad or mailing.

Be sure to use the *cost per order* approach to evaluating your ad and list mailing results. Why? Because:

*Some beginners use **percentage response** as a way of evaluating ad or list mailing costs. While your response percentage **is** important, you'll often see that a higher percentage response—say 12 percent—will have a larger per-order cost than a lower percentage response! So be sure to look at both numbers. But remember that it's the cost per order that you must pay. You can't spend response percentages—you **can** spend the dollars you get for an order.*

Grow Rich with Ride-Alongs

When you get an order from a customer you must ship the item or service ordered. But smart mail-order pros send more than what's ordered. Thus, you'll usually send:

- A copy of the general catalog showing the company's other products
- Flyers on products or services too new to be in the general catalog
- Any new special offers the firm may have

These items are called *ride-alongs* or inserts. Thus, in my highly successful mail-order business we:

- Include a copy of our 48-page catalog with every book and course we ship to a customer
- Include at least four inserts in every issue of our monthly newsletter *International Wealth Success*
- Generate large sums of income from these ride-alongs at relatively little extra cost

The theory behind ride-alongs or inserts is simple:

1. You've already decided to invest in the shipping cost to send the book or other item or service your customer ordered.
2. So the cost of the ride-along is small (usually just printing) compared to the potential income such an insert can generate for you.

3. Especially if including the ride-along or insert does not increase your postage or shipping cost.
4. Further, a happy customer is much more inclined to order again than is a new customer who has not yet seen an example of the great items you offer!

Figures 12-8 and 12-9 show examples of two inserts we use in our newsletter. The cost of printing these is pennies. Yet they pull in many thousands of dollars of business each year.

So be sure to use ride-alongs or inserts whenever you can. When your business is new you probably won't have more than a few products. At this stage it's wise to promote products from other people, even if your profit on each is lower than it would be from your own product.

Why is this? Because it's smart to get your customers into a *buying* mood from the very start. Since some customers will stay with you for years if you keep adding new offerings, it's smart to let them know that you expect them to keep buying. Your products or services will make your customers happy while their money will keep your accountant happy!

You can even have your supplier *drop ship* the items you sell that aren't your own. In this arrangement you:

1. Send your supplier a typed label with the name and address of the customer, plus what was ordered.
2. Include a check in payment for what was ordered. This will usually be 50 percent (one-half) of the list price of the item ordered. Thus, you'd send $50 for an item for which you were paid $100.

Drop shipping is great when you can rely on the supplier. But some of the suppliers in business today have more excuses for *not* shipping on schedule than they have products. And if *your* customer doesn't get what was ordered in a timely fashion, *you* are the "bad" person—not your supplier. So you must be extremely careful in picking a supplier.

HOW TO GET
GUARANTEED LOAN MONEY

"I ALMOST LOST MY HOME BEFORE
FINDING THIS INSTANT CASH PLAN!"

I NEEDED MONEY BADLY--to pay my bills so I could get rid of the bill collectors banging on my door--day and night!

BUT THE LENDERS WOULDN'T EVEN TALK to me since my credit was so bad! "Get lost!" is what they said, or told me in their eyes. I was desperate. My kids hardly had any food; my car wouldn't go a block without breaking down; the landlord was ready to throw us out of our tiny, unheated house.

I FRANTICALLY RAN AROUND, looking for money. Yet everywhere I turned I got a NO along with a cold, cold shoulder. I couldn't--it seemed--raise a thin dime to pay my bills. What could I do? My wife was ready to leave me, taking our kids with her!

THEN ONE NIGHT, WHILE LYING AWAKE IN BED, I discovered the idea of GUARANTEED LOAN MONEY. I jumped up and madly searched for a pencil and paper to jot down the ideas pouring out of my mind. It seemed like the perfect answer to anyone who:

    **Has bad credit
    **Has been turned down for a loan
    **Doesn't have a good job history
    **Needs money so badly "he can smell it"
    **Needs personal, business or real estate
        loans to make money

BUT BEFORE I STARTED FEELING GOOD I decided to test out my GUARANTEED LOAN MONEY METHOD to see if it would work. To give it an "acid test" I went back to several lenders who had turned me down in the last few weeks.

TO MY GREAT SURPRISE EACH LENDER SAID YES! That meant each would lend me the money I needed--with almost NO QUESTIONS! I was stunned! The method really does work. Joy hit me!

TO BE DOUBLY SURE THE GUARANTEED LOAN MONEY METHOD WORKS, I had some of my "bad-credit" friends try it. They got the money they needed in hours! After they had been turned down just a few days earlier!

RIGHT AWAY I KNEW I WAS ON TO SOMETHING GOOD. But to be sure, I called friends 3,000 miles away and told them about my GUARANTEED LOAN MONEY METHOD. "Try it out this way," I told them. "Let me know what results you get!"

WITHIN HOURS I GOT EXCITED CALLS saying "It works! It works! I got the first loan I've ever been able to get in 15 years. And it only took 20 minutes! I love you for what you've done for my family and myself! You should put this method into a book!"

AFTER THREE OTHER PEOPLE TOLD ME THE SAME, I decided it was the thing to do--that is, put the method into a book. Now it's available from IWS--the entire method.

USING THIS METHOD YOU SHOULD BE ABLE TO GET:
    **Unsecured signature loans for personal use
    **Business loans of any type
    **Real estate loans of any type
    **Any other type of loan needed
    **Financing that's "tough to get"

SO IF YOU NEED ANY KIND OF LOAN you should get a copy of my big, helpful, get-out-of-hock GUARANTEED LOAN MONEY METHOD! And if you order now I'll include FREE a copy of "Diversified Loan Sources" which gives YOU hundreds of money sources for this great Method!

BE POOR NO MORE! Get the cash you need NOW! Let me show you how to get GUARANTEED LOAN MONEY sooner than you ever thought possible. Send or call TODAY!

Here's $100. Send me my copy of GUARANTEED LOAN MONEY METHOD, along with my bonus copy of "Diversified Loan Sources". Or if you wish, you can call Ty Hicks day or night at 516-766-5850 to order by credit card. Or enter your credit card number below and send this coupon to: IWS, Inc., 24 Canterbury Rd, Rockville Centre NY 11570. Start NOW!

NAME_____ CARD NO._____

ADDRESS_____ Apt/Suite # _____ EXPIRES_____

CITY_____ STATE_____ ZIP_____

Figure 12-8

Get Credit Now!
Have You Been Rejected For Credit?
Our Five New Credit Power Reports Will Help You Solve Your Credit and Debt Problems!
$19.95
CREDIT POWER
How to Get a Visa and or MasterCard Credit Card
Report #1...How To Get a VISA and/or MASTERCARD CreditCard!
Report #2...How To Increase Your Credit Limits Plus Sophisticated Credit Power Strategies!
How to Repair Your Credit
Report #3...How To Repair Your Credit!
Report #4...How To Reduce Your Monthly Payments
Report #5...How To Wipe Out Your Debts Without Bankruptcy!
Each tape duplicates a Report; Price $19.95 per tape.
Credit Power Reports Also Available On Audio Cassettes!
Each REPORT is a convenient 6 in. X 8.75 in. Pocket Size for EASY USE ANYWHERE!
Each Report is Attractively spiral bound for easy use.
Report #1: Names, Addresses of Banks Offering Secured Credit Cards; Unsecured Card Issuers (over 2,000); Credit Bureau Info; Many Letters You Can Copy; 192 fact-filled pages.
Report #2: Secrets of getting larger & larger signature loans; how to prepare credit card applications; banks with no annual fees. 208 pages.
Report #3: Your legal rights; how to protect your rights; getting bad data removed from credit reports. 256 pages.
Report #4: How to consolidate debts & reduce your monthly payments; lower your interest rate; how to pay interest only. 192 pgs.
Report #5: How NOT to go bankrupt! Stop foreclosure; stop sheriffs & marshals; help others. 152 pages.
Use these reports to help yourself or others! Earn big fees as a credit consultant! Order NOW!
FREE BONUS! How to Get A Mortgage Regardless of Your Credit Rating--when you buy ANY REPORT or TAPE!
Please send me these Reports, No. __, __, __, __, __, or these Cassettes, No. __, __, __, __, __, for which I enclose $______. Or call Ty Hicks at 516-766-5850 day or night to order by credit card. Or send your order to IWS, Inc., 24 Canterbury Rd, Rockville Centre NY 11570.
NAME ____ Card No. ____ Expires ____
ADDRESS ____ Phone No. ____
CITY ____ STATE ____ ZIP ____

Figure 12-9

If you find a supplier with great products or services who's unreliable from a shipping standpoint, take these steps:

1. Estimate how many units of this supplier's products or services you'll sell in a given time.
2. Order this number, or slightly less, from your supplier to inventory in your place of business.
3. You ship when you get an order. Then you'll know the item or service went out on taime. There won't be any "bad" person because your customer will have what was ordered in a reasonable number of days.

What I'm telling you is this: Take advantage of another firm's creative output but *you* control the shipping. Then everyone will be happy—you, your customer, and your supplier!

Track Every Ad and Mailing

The world's greatest business is also the easiest to control because every sales effort you make is traceable. How can you trace your sales efforts? That's easy—you *key* each ad and mailing.

When you key an ad or mailing you use some way to identify where the ad ran, or which mailing contains a certain coupon. By keeping track of the sales made by each ad or mailing you know:

1. Which publication ads pull best for you
2. Which mailing lists give you the lowest cost per order

And by comparing your results for a new ad or mailing with a *control* ad or mailing, you can determine which ads, publications, or mailings are best. Your control ad or mailing is one which has pulled the strongest for you. So you use it to compare the results of all future ads or mailings.

When you start your business you won't have a control ad or mailing. But you will soon develop one as you advertise or mail more. So don't worry now about a control—you'll have one soon!

To key an ad or mailing you can use any number of methods. Typical popular keys are:

1. Add a letter to your address or Post Office box number to identify the ad or mailing from which the person is either ordering or inquiring. Before you take this step you *must* check with your Post Office to see if using a letter as part of your address will be acceptable. You will seldom have any difficulty getting permission to use such a key. And the Post Office officials will probably have some suggestions for letters to avoid when setting up your key. Thus, stay away from any letters that might change the part of town in which your mail is to be delivered. (For example, don't use the letter *S* if your address is in the northern part of town!)

2. When you receive mail at a mailbox center you can usually add a key code to your address without trouble. But, again, get permission from the owner of the center. You don't want your mail returned marked "Unknown"!

3. When you first start your business and you run it under your own name or an assumed company name, you can vary the name in each ad or mailing so you know where the response came from. Thus, if your firm name is *Ajax Enterprises* you can change this to *Afax, Agax, Ahax, Aaax,* etc., to show which ad or mailing the response is from. Likewise, with your own name, you can vary from *A Jones* to *B Jones, C Jones,* etc. Each first initial will show a different ad, publication, or mailing. Again, be sure the mail will be delivered to you! No sense losing orders if your mail deliverer can't leave it in your mailbox.

4. Another popular way to key ads and mailings is to use a Suite Number, Room Number, Department Number, Desk Number, etc. as part of the ordering address. With a classified ad, using such a key may increase your ad cost. Why? Because you're using an extra word or two to key the ad. But many mail-

order pros feel the extra cost is worth the added sales information you obtain.

5. An almost unbeatable way to key an ad is to use a product number that contains data on the ad or mailing. Thus, if you're selling product No. 123, you can add a key letter which indicates where the buyer saw your ad. Thus, with an ad in magazine "A," you can say "To get this great carving knife, order Product No. 123A." You immediately know which magazine your customer is ordering from. You can use the same method for mailings, also.

6. For space ads containing a coupon, use a code key that shows the publication and the date of the ad. Thus, our ad in Figure 12-10 shows a key in the righthand corner of the coupon which tells us which magazine and on what date (month and year) the ad appeared. Why do we do this? Because it tells us what revenue each ad brings in so we can figure our profits from it. And—two years from now when we get a stray order—we'll know which publication and which issue it came from. (That's the great feature of full-page-ads—you get orders from them for years and years. And the money is just as welcome years later as it was when the ad first appeared!)

There are plenty of other ways to make *your* millions in mail order today. Our next chapter gives you a number of these hands-on ideas so you'll get richer sooner in the world's best business. Let's see what these tips are—right now!

CHAPTER 13

MORE TIPS ON MAKING YOUR MILLIONS IN MAIL ORDER TODAY

To keep today's mail-order customers happy you must take some extra steps. Why? Because, as we saw earlier, today's customers seek faster delivery of everything they order from you. Meeting these demands is easy—if you know what works best. Here are a number of methods that work for me and help keep the money flowing in every week.

Use the Best Delivery Methods

Today you have a number of options open to you for best delivery of any item ordered from you. Thus, you have:

- The United States mail service—the best in the world— for low-cost delivery of the usual products sold by mail order—books, magazines, tools, food, etc.
- United Parcel Service for delivery of virtually the same items handled by U.S. mail. Known as UPS, this service may have certain advantages over U.S. mail. Much depends on your location, what you're shipping, etc. These aspects are discussed later.
- Courier services for ultra-fast delivery of letters and packages on weekdays at reasonable cost. Typical of these services are Federal Express, DHL, Purolator, etc.

Let's take a quick look at each of these delivery services and see which is best for you. I'll share some of my experiences with you so you can save time and money.

The U.S. Mail Is Better than You Think

Our firm, IWS, Inc., mails millions of items around the world. And the mail *does* go through! Don't let anyone tell you differently. Most people who criticize the post office mail just a few letters each year. They have no idea of the billions of pieces of mail the U.S. Post Office handles each year efficiently and at low cost.

To mail our books we, like all publishers, use the Special Fourth Class Book Rate. It saves you a lot of money over regular Fourth Class Parcel Post. So be *sure* to use book rate if you sell books by mail.

Since having a record of *every* shipment is important, we use Postal Service Form 3827, titled *Firm Mailing Book*, which you can get free of charge from your post office. Figure 13-1 shows a typical page from this book.

On such a page we mark, in the lefthand column, what was sent, using an abbreviation for the title. Next, the name and address of the customer is entered, followed by the postage and special handling cost, if any. Each page becomes a Certificate of Mailing for the entries on it. The page is stamped by the post office after the number of parcels and the names and addresses are verified by the post office clerk.

Each page gives us our *evidence of mailing*. Thus, if a customer calls and asks when such and such was sent, we refer to our post office book. Here's what I tell the customer:

- Thanks for calling. And thank you very much for your order. Here are the details of your order; please do *not* interrupt me while I speak.
- Your order was shipped by United States mail on _____. It was sent to the following address:

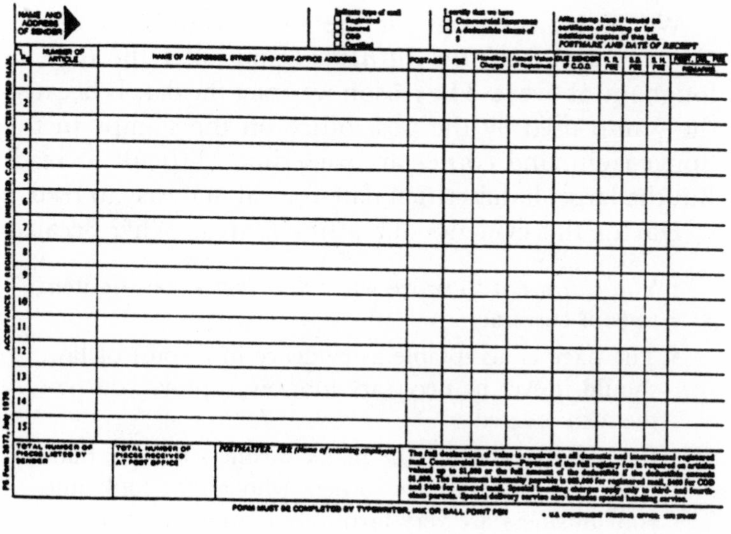
NAME AND ADDRESS OF SENDER

NUMBER OF ARTICLE | NAME OF ADDRESSEE, STREET, AND POST-OFFICE ADDRESS | POSTAGE | FEE | Handling Charge | Actual Value if Registered | DUE SENDER if C.O.D. | R. R. FEE | S.D. FEE | S. H. FEE

1 2 3 4 5 6 7 8 9 10 11 12 13 14 15

TOTAL NUMBER OF PIECES LISTED BY SENDER

TOTAL NUMBER OF PIECES RECEIVED AT POST OFFICE

POSTMASTER, PER (Name of receiving employee)

POSTMARK AND DATE OF RECEIPT

FORM MUST BE COMPLETED BY TYPEWRITER, INK OR BALL POINT PEN

Figure 13-1

_____. You will be getting your ordered item(s) soon.

• Again, thank you for your order. Our post office records are very reliable.

The reason why we ask the customer not to speak while we're reading details of the order is because it gives us a chance to tell the caller *exactly* where the order was sent. Then the customer knows that the order went to the correct address. This is very reassuring to the customer.

We stamp the page in the lower righthand corner *Certificate of Mailing Furnished* and enter the date in longhand above it. The reason we enter the date is because the stamp used by the post office on the stamps in the upper righthand corner are sometimes difficult to read. But the large, handwritten date is clear and easy to read.

Having this evidence of mailing is great. Why? Because

• You can use it to prove when you sent a specific item to your customer

• The page is acceptable as evidence in a court of law, should it ever be necessary for you to prove you sent the item ordered

• Regulatory agencies, the Better Business Bureau, State Attorneys General, and others who might look into your business are very favorably impressed when you send them a photocopy of your Form 3827 page showing the date and method of mailing. Your business immediately acquires a highly favorable image.

As you might imagine, our firm, International Wealth Success, does lots of overseas mailings. Why? Because we have customers throughout the free world. Here are our proven overseas mailing policies which *do* get the products into the hands of our customers—safely and quickly:

1. Use *registered mail* when sending valuable products to third world countries. The economies of these countries are in such a sorry state that pilferage of the mail is a strong possibility. If this occurs you lose what you sent and you have a disgruntled

customer on your hands. So pay the cost of registered mail, passing it on to your customer.

2. Use *insured mail* where such insurance is available in the country to which you're shipping. You'll find information on this in the free post office bulletin on *International Mail*. Some people use both registered and insured mail for the same item. Decide this by figuring the value of what you're shipping and the impact of a loss on your firm.

3. For the developed nations in Europe, for Canada, and for Australia/New Zealand we use only the Certificate of Mailing for surface mail packages. Why? Because the mail systems in these countries are highly reliable with almost no pilferage at all. Further, the surface postage (which we pay) is nominal. But when we ship by air mail to these countries we use registered mail. Why? Because the postage bill for our Kits— many of which weigh 8 pounds or more—is often in the $55.00 range. If the mail were to be pilfered, we would lose both the product and the $55.00 in postage. But when the item is sent by registered mail it *does* arrive safely. We charge the customer for air mail postage because the cost is so high. Almost all our customers are happy to pay it because they want their Kit *now*

4. Where you mail large numbers of parcels overseas, check with your Postmaster on the International Air Lift service. It can save you bundles of money!

For domestic mail you should consider using special handling when you want an item to move through the mail system faster. Though it costs more, the special handling gets your package out of the post office at first class speed, even though you're using parcel post or book rate. Your Postmaster will give you full data on this excellent service.

UPS Is Popular with Mail-Order Houses

UPS—short for United Parcel Service—gives excellent service to thousands of mail-order houses. Some of the advantages of UPS are:

1. You can have your packages picked up every day at a small extra cost to you.
2. Some UPS rates are lower than the post office rates to the same address.
3. Insurance is automatically included (up to $100.00) on all UPS shipments.
4. UPS will accept your company check in payment for the shipping. This is not always so at the post office.
5. UPS will deliver COD (Cash on Delivery) orders and accept a check in payment.
6. For local delivery UPS seems to be faster than some other types of delivery.
7. You can use a page listing of parcels similar to Form 3827 for the parcels UPS picks up from you. There is a savings in your time when you can use a page entry such as that shown in Figure 13-2.

To save the individual parcel pickup charge you can bring your items to your local UPS office. Service at such local offices is quick and efficient. Hand trucks are provided free of charge to get parcels into the shipping area.

Courier Services Give Speedy Delivery

I wish you could answer my phone for a few hours and get the flavor of today's delivery demands. As they say, "Everyone wants everything yesterday"! The answer? One or more of the courier services listed earlier—Federal Express, DHL, Purolator, etc. Such services:

1. Will pick up at your place of business—be it an office, factory, or your home.
2. Provide automatic insurance coverage of each item you send to a customer.
3. Give overnight or second-day service, depending on what you want.

Courier services tend to charge higher prices than Express Mail from the U.S. Post Office. Further, if your

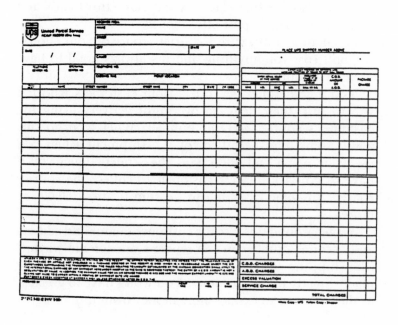

Figure 13-2

customer wants weekend delivery with a courier service, the extra charge can be in the $50 range. Compare this with the *no extra charge* for Express Mail delivery by the U.S. Post Office. Most people don't know what a great buy Express Mail is—especially the weekend delivery aspect.

Another little-known fact about courier services and UPS is that they won't deliver to post office boxes. So if your customer gets his or her mail only at a post office box, you can't use a courier service. You must use Express Mail despite what your customer may want! Of course, you can also use first class, second class, third class and fourth class mail to post office boxes.

Open an account with a courier service of your choice. It won't cost you anything and it's always good to have such an account.

You'll sometimes get orders from customers who tell you to ship their item via overnight delivery using the customer's courier account number. When you do this you'll sometimes be billed for the shipment when you use your name and address as the sender. Then you'll have to go back to your customer to collect the courier charge. In some cases it can be significant—$60.00, or more.

To get around this, use the customer's name and address and account number in the sender's area of the waybill (the shipping ticket). Then the shipping charge will be made directly to the customer. You won't have to go back to the customer to extract more money from him or her!

Deal Quickly with All Regulators

If you're in the mail-order business you will—sooner or later—get a letter or visit from a regulator. This could be the United States Postal Inspection Service (The "Postal Inspectors"), the Federal Bureau of Investigation, your State Attorney General, the Federal Trade Commission

(FTC), etc. These regulators can write or visit you for any number of reasons, such as:

- Failing to make a requested refund
- Complaints from a disgruntled customer
- Questions about an ad you ran
- A review of the products you offer
- Etc.

Don't—like some mail-order operators—think you're above regulations! You *must* respect and comply with the regulations issued by the post office, your Attorney General, the FTC, etc. Why? Because if you don't obey the regulations you might be put out of business. *Never* leave yourself open to such a risk! To deal effectively with any regulator:

1. Answer every letter, visit, or phone call immediately. Don't put off until tomorrow what you can do today!
2. When responding by mail, use Certified Mail, Return Receipt Requested. Why? Because then you'll have court-acceptable evidence that: (a) You *did* respond, (b) date and place of your response, (c) name of person receiving your response, (d) date response was received, and (e) place where your response was received.
3. If asked to respond by phone, do so—immediately. Then write a short note using Certified Mail, Return Receipt Requested, stating:"I called you on ___date___ and spoke to you (or to ___name, title___ if you could not reach the caller) and we agreed ___name the action agreed on___ . This letter confirms our conversation of the above date." Again, it locks in the fact that you <u>did</u> respond to the regulator in a timely and complete fashion.
4. Be polite to every regulator! Don't take the attitude that you're a businessperson and the regulator should bow to you. Not so—regulators are extremely powerful. They expect you to respect their office, their title, and their agency. Show disrespect for any of these and you can have real trouble on your hands!
5. Learn from every regulator. These people are full of

useful information which they'll gladly share with you. You simply must be polite, cooperative, and willing to do as you're told. Pick a fight with a regulator and you'll regret it for life!

6. You can, of course, disagree with a regulator. But if you do, you *must* get immediate advice from a competent professional who knows the business and any regulations or laws that cover it. And in disagreeing with a regulator, do it sensibly. Thus, don't say: "That's crazy, I can't agree to that!" Instead say, "Thank you for your opinion and recommendation. Would you mind if I refer this to our accountant (or attorney) before I give you a final answer? It won't take long and I'll be back to you in ___time___."

7. Make every talk or meeting with a regulator helpful for your future business. Pump him or her for information, ideas, methods, and other data that can be helpful to your business. You'll get a fast "college education" in what you can—and can't—do. And in what you *should* do, too!

In my years in the world's greatest business I've learned a lot about the regulators in various agencies. This is what they've taught me:

- Regulators are fair—they won't ask you to do the impossible.
- Regulators enjoy talking. They can give you the limits on what you can—and cannot—do. But they'll often tell you in "roundabout" terms. So you *must* listen carefully to *everything* they say.
- Regulators expect respect. Give it to them!

Let me give you a few real-life examples of how regulators have helped me be more successful:

- As you know, our newsletter, *International Wealth Success*, publishes millions of words on business and real-estate loans, borrowing methods, etc. We constantly recommend that our readers *not* pay advance fees or "front money" of any kind. A regulator, seeing this in our newsletter, volunteered to write—*free of any charge*—an up-to-date article on front-money schemes he ran into all over the country. As an expert he probably knows more about such schemes than anyone in the world.

- Another regulator asked me to testify for the United States government in a case it prosecuted against some front-money scam operators. I went to Atlanta, Georgia, and gave my testimony. The Government won its case.
- A third regulator told me how to stay out of trouble with advertising. "Never guarantee anything," he said. What he meant was, never guarantee anything over which you have no control. But he said it so forcefully that I've kept our ads out of trouble by thinking of him every time I review a new ad!

Control Your Business with Good Records

Mail order is a very simple business. It's so simple that some BWBs forget to keep accurate records. Then they find they have problems. I don't want *you* to have such problems. So I'll show you a simple way to build a million-dollar business with just pieces of paper!

You start with your order. It can come to you in any of three different ways:

1. By mail—U.S., courier, or hand-delivered
2. By telephone—through your business or personal phone
3. In person—by someone showing up at your place of business and asking to buy one or more of your products or services

When you get an order by mail, it must be processed. Figure 13-3 shows the sequence we use. Since it works well you might want to look it over, punch holes in it, and come up with a better method! (Some BWBs think they know more than the experienced pros. Perhaps they do. We can *all* learn from each other.)

The mail stream arrives at our office every day. It's opened using an electric slitting machine and separated into three streams:

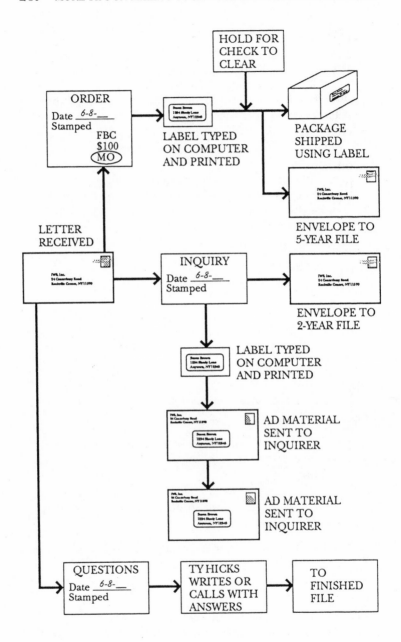

Figure 13-3

1. Orders with payments or company purchase orders
2. Requests for sales information
3. Questions to be answered by Ty Hicks

Each order envelope is date-stamped with the arrival date. Then the item ordered is marked on the outside of the envelope, along with the amount enclosed, and the type of payment—i.e., a check or money order. (We discourage sending cash through the mail; hence, we receive very little of it.)

Envelopes containing money orders go to the computer entry clerk, who enters the information on a customer record. Then a shipping label is printed out and applied to the package containing the item ordered. The package is then shipped via U.S. mail or UPS, depending on the fastest way for delivering the item.

Envelopes containing regular checks are set aside to allow time for each check to clear. Local checks require less clearance time than checks drawn on distant banks. So local checks get quicker shipment.

The purpose of waiting for checks to clear is to prevent being ripped off by the "paper" artists who try to get something for nothing. What these idiots don't realize is that they can be sent to jail for one year and fined heavily if it can be proven that they knowingly sent a bad check through the mail. It gives us a nice charge to beat the bad-check artists.

But don't get me wrong. There really aren't that many bad-check artists around! So you won't often be ripped off. Yet a good businessperson takes every step he or she can to prevent losing money. Be sure you do, too!

Once the check clears, the order is entered on computer, the same as for money orders. A shipping label is printed and the order shipped. Then all envelopes containing orders are filed and saved for five years. With such a file we can easily reconstruct any order, should a person claim they sent money and did not receive what they paid for.

Telephone orders are handled as shown in Figure 13-4. The customer calls in and orders one or more items,

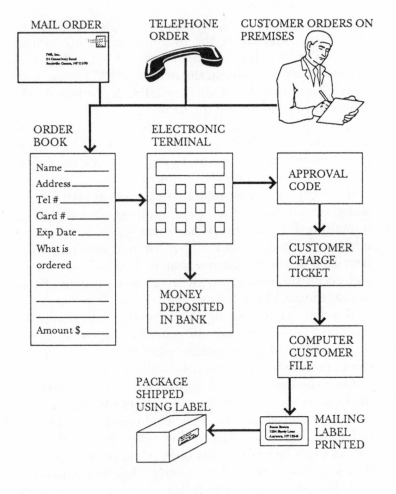

Figure 13-4

paying by credit card. Information on the customer (name, address, telephone number, credit-card number, and expiration date) is obtained by the person answering the phone.

Next, the card number, expiration date, and amount of the charge is keyed into the Electronic Data Capture terminal. Instant approval, or disapproval, is obtained, along with the authorization number for approved transactions. A charge ticket is prepared for mailing to the customer. Then the order is entered on computer, as before, and the order is shipped. At the end of the day the EDC terminal is used to deposit the day's charges into the bank.

Doing business this way has many advantages:

1. The customer gets his or her order sooner. So you have happier customers who are likely to order again.
2. You have fewer bad debts and *no* bounced checks because you get instantaneous approval of your charges.
3. Your business bank account is credited faster. And there's *no* waiting on long lines to put your money into the bank.

When a customer shows up at your place of business to buy an item or service, you'll be paid in cash, by check, or by credit card. For such sales you have your cash register transaction tape which gives you a record of the day's sales. Data from this tape are transferred to your income statement and summarized each week. Your accountant will help you set up books which are best suited for your type of business.

The whole key is to have good records. Why? Because without them your business can run wild. You won't be able to control it—especially as your orders begin to pour in. Getting 8 or 10 orders a day is easy to handle and control. But when your orders jump to 800 or 1,000 per day, you won't be able to keep track of them without good records.

Sales Record Sheet		
Date: __March 31, 19--__ Week No. ___12___		
	Sales, Units	Sales, $
Product No. 1	32	3,200
Product No. 2	12	600
Total Sales	236	$45,821

Ad Cost vs Sales Cost							
Medoa Used	Ad Cost, $	No. of inq.	Ad cost/ inq., $	No. of sales	Ad cost/ sale, $	Income, $ from ad	Income before direct & indirect costs, $
Publication #1	4,200	510	8.24	128	32.81	12,600	8,400
Publication #2							

Figure 13-5

Figure 13-5 shows portions of several sales record sheets. Such records help you evaluate your total income and the results produced by the ads you run and the mailings you make. If an ad or mailing doesn't produce profitable results you'll probably switch your money to other magazines or mailing lists. Good records will tell you when to do this.

At our firm, IWS, Inc., we keep our income records on a weekly basis. Each week we compare the week's income with the income for the same week in the previous year. Likewise, we compare the cumulatve income for the year through the particular week with the previous three years. With such comparisons we can quickly tell "how we're doing." If any actions are needed to boost sales we know early on what to do.

Run Your Office Efficiently

You are—remember—in the world's best *business*. So you must run your affairs in a businesslike and efficient manner if you want to earn more. In your office you'll need:

1. Files for correspondence, advertising outlets, data on competitors, costs, etc.
2. Records detailing both your sales and expenses. Be sure to have such records set up by a qualified accountant. Why? Because it will then be much easier to prepare your income-tax returns. Further, if you're ever audited, your records will show that you're carefully organized and you're reporting every penny of income you get from your business.
3. Files for your bank deposit tickets. They'll show exactly how many checks and how much cash you deposited each day. Don't siphon off cash for your own use! It's illegal to do this, unless you report the cash as part of your income on your tax return. It's much better to deposit all the cash you receive, along with the checks and money orders. An auditor seeing

regular cash deposits into your business bank account
will be much less likely to use a heavy hand in the
audit. Why? Because the bank records show the
company is not skimming off cash to line the pockets
of its owners.
4. A printed invoice, Figure 13-6, to bill your larger
customers. (For one-item buyers we recommend that
you get payment with order—it saves time, energy,
and money.) With a snap-set printed invoice you can
quickly bill your customers and get faster payment.
Snap sets allow you to bill in triplicate without
mailing extra photocopies. Today, most firms
demand bills in triplicate.

At the start, you can run your mail-order business out
of a low-cost three-drawer file. But as your business grows
you'll need more office and storage space. Don't get
discouraged! The more space you need, the larger your
sales and profits. That's exactly what we all seek in this
business!

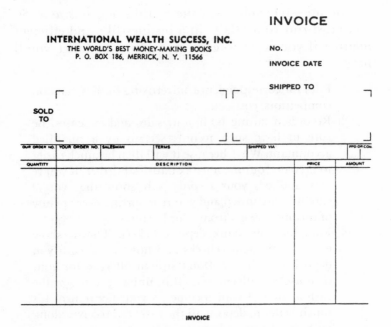

Figure 13-6

Give the "Personal Touch" to Everyone

When I first started my mail-order business, 100 percent of my orders came by mail. Today only 70 percent of the orders come by mail—the other 30 percent come by phone. Someday soon I expect to see 50 percent of my orders arriving by phone. To give the personal touch to your business, consider using these methods:

1. Answer your own telephone. It puts *you* in direct contact with your customer. You know what he or she wants. And you'll learn—directly—how you and your staff can better serve your customers so they send you *more* money—the whole objective of this exercise!

2. Send notes to your customers when it will help in any way. Thus, if a customer asks for special service of some kind, include with the item or service a note saying: "Here's the special item (or service) you ordered. We're happy to send this to you. And we thank you for your order. If we can help in any other way, please call or write us."

3. Supply any special invoices a customer requests. Some firms can't pay unless they have an invoice (bill) in hand. And many overseas customers can't get their bank to release money unless a *pro forma* invoice is presented to the bank. A pro forma invoice is your regular invoice form with the words "Pro forma" typed at the top. While supplying an invoice before you're paid may seem a chore, it can get you lots of sales. Some of our best overseas customers started with our supplying the requested pro forma invoice. In a short time we had thousands of dollars in payments from some of these customers. So the time and energy needed to prepare the pro forma or any other special invoice can be repaid many times over!

4. Save all your incoming orders. You will often be able to impress a customer who calls and says: "Two months ago I sent you guys $100 for _____. I still don't have it. What's the matter? Don't you read your mail?" To answer such a question you just go to the envelope in which the order arrived and read the

postmark date. Often you'll find that the customer's "two months" is ten days! So you say to your customer: "Thanks so much for calling. I'm checking the postmark on your order—we save *every* piece of mail for five years—and it shows that you mailed your order ten days ago. We received it four days ago and your order was shipped today!" With such an answer even the surliest customer is turned into a friend. Yes, the personal touch *does* get results!

5. Use a handwritten note for "hard sells." Let's say you publish a newsletter, like I do. When a person's subscription comes up for renewal you send them several printed forms over a period of months. Some will ignore your notices. What can *you* do? Try a handwritten note sent via first-class mail in a plain white envelope! It can work wonders, especially if you say something personal in your note. Is it worth the effort? Yes, yes, yes! The personal note "grabs" the customer since most think you're too busy to even consider them. And the plain envelope—without a return address—gets their interest. They just *have* to open it to see what's inside!

6. Talk directly to your potential customers. How? Via audio or videotape. Thus, my good friend Jay Reiss— one of the most talented ad copywriters in business today—sends a free audio tape about starting your own mail-order business to prospects. They listen to this tape and hear directly from Jay. Since his voice is pleasing and his message is full of useful suggestions, prospects give him their full attention. Sales are more likely to result when you approach prospects this way. *Note:* A videotape can be even more convincing. But before investing in this type of promotion, be sure (a) Your customers or prospects *do* have VCRs, and (b) They are likely to be sold by such an ad message. Videotapes are expensive and you'll waste money if you're using them to market any product costing less than $100. And prices from $300 to $1,200 are much more likely to show a profit for you and your firm than $100 is.

7. Keep in touch with your customers and prospects. Thus, another mail-order friend of mine—Lee

Howard of Selective Books—publishes a quarterly newsletter he circulates to his book dealers. This newsletter gives tips on selling books by mail, offers details on new books available, and has ads book dealers can use free of charge in selling items to their customers. Receiving this four times a year gives Lee's customers a good feeling. They know he stands behind them—all the way!

8. Assume that your customer is *always* right—even though this is often not the case! But by assuming your customer *is* right you treat him or her better. Result? More sales and better relations with your customers. Why turn your business days into a daily war when by a simple change in attitude you can turn them into a happy experience that's both challenging and fulfilling?

9. Adopt a positive slogan for your business. Pick a slogan that tells what you do in a way that will pique people's interest. Thus, my firm's slogan is: "The World's Best Money-Making Books." These six words tell you *WHAT* we do (publish books on making money), and *WHY* we think they're worth buying (the world's best). While you might argue with our opinion of our books, you'd be the only person in nearly 25 years who did so. I respect your opinion and will fight to protect your right to express it. But I still think our books are rather good!

10. Develop a *Unique Selling Proposition* for as many of your offers as you can. Also called your USP, this concept covers (a) what you offer for sale, (b) how you offer it (payment with order, credit-card charge, bill with order, 10 days free examination, etc.), (c) which benefits you offer your buyer, (d) why the buyer should not be afraid (ironclad money-back guarantee), (e) how the buyer can easily—and quickly—get this excellent item or service you're offering, etc. Your USP sets you apart from your competitors. And it can give you the advantage when your competitors have little to offer to beat your carefully planned products or services.

11. Offer *continuity programs* to give your readers more of the great products or services they so avidly buy

from you. A continuity program is an offering in which you have an ongoing series of products related by a common theme that you offer customers. Thus, you might have a series of books on the history of the world. Your customers buy one book sent to them every six weeks on an *option* basis. With a *negative option*, your customer agrees to accept each book sent to him or her, unless the customer informs you that he or she does *not* want the book. Your customer has a stated time interval—usually three weeks—in which you are to be informed of the negative decision. If you don't hear from the customer, you ship the book (or other product or service) directly to your customer. Continuity programs are popular with mail-order pros because they can give you a predictable source of income over a long period of time. Such programs are popular ways of selling books, collectible items (like model cars, coins, etc.), plates, records (or tapes), etc.

Giving the personal touch will set your mail-order business way above any others. Be sure to teach your staff the importance of treating *every* customer the way they would want to be treated. Being nice to customers ensures everyone's job and advancement. Besides, it makes business much more fun!

Save Money Every Day of the Week

Your successful mail-order business will pile up heaps of cash in your bank. Unless you manage this cash carefully you'll be losing some bottom-line income. And remember, it's bottom-line income that makes *you* and your firm rich! So the more you can carry to that beloved bottom line, the richer you'll get in this, the world's greatest business.

How do you build your bottom line? By controlling your costs so you save every penny you can on:

• Postage and shipping

- Printing and copying
- Advertising and promotion
- Labor and office staff
- Rent, light, and heat

Your best way to reduce costs and save money is to start at the beginning of your sales cycle. Then go through every step in your business and see how you can save money. Typical areas of concern are:

1. Cost of product—can you get it cheaper from another supplier? Often, by going to a different supplier you'll learn a lot about how you can reduce your costs. And this information is usually free!
2. Advertising and promotion—can you get the same, or better, results by advertising in other outlets using different media? Thus, card decks may pull better for you than space ads. But you won't know until you test one way against another. Testing, remember, is the key to success in spending your ad dollar.
3. Postage and shipping costs—these can eat up your profits if you don't control them. Try shipping the cheapest way. Often the difference in delivery time will just be a day or so. But your savings can amount to one-third, or more, of the higher shipping cost.
4. Bank and credit-card costs—often significant if you don't seek ways to reduce them. Thus, instead of leaving a large sum of cash in your business checking account to keep your bank happy, consider using a money market account in which you're allowed to write checks. This way, your checking account will be earning interest for your business. Sure, it may be less than your daily or weekly income. But it *will* be extra money your business money is earning! Many mail-order business pros say that their interest income is a significant portion of their total income from their business.
5. Labor costs—these can be your highest expense if you let them get out of hand. So at the start you'll find that the more you can do yourself, the larger will be your bottom-line profit. As your business grows, you'll do less of the manual work and more of the

supervision and planning. But keep in mind at all times that you may have to return to manual labor if your business starts to decline. Better to do more work than to lose the business entirely!

6. Printing, postage, shipping, etc.—keep looking for ways to save money. Always pass the shipping cost on to your customer where special service (like air, courier, etc.) is requested. You should never be expected to absorb this specially requested cost unless it is a very small portion of the total cost. Thus, a friend of mine who sells unset diamonds at prices from $5,000 to $100,000 gladly pays the postage and insurance when sending an item to a customer. Why? Because the shipping cost, including insurance, is so small compared to the amount he gets for one sale. A diamond weighing just a few ounces can bring in multi-thousands of dollars. Yet the shipping and insurance cost can be under $100!

7. Postage meter—use one for your mailings. It will save postage costs and give your mailings a more professional appearance. But be sure to shop around for the best meter rental price! Some of the old-line companies will sock it to you, renting you a meter at a sky-high price. Don't accept the first meter rental price offered to you. Tell the rep "I'm shopping around. I'll let you know in a few days if your offered rental fee is acceptable. Meanwhile, why don't you sharpen your pencil and see if you can come up with a better price?" You'll be surprised at how a little competition can get your price reduced!

Get Good Legal Advice

Part of earning more in mail order is doing the right thing. While you can pretty well "do your own thing" in mail order, there are certain no-nos you must observe. Thus:

- Chain schemes of all types are forbidden
- Lotteries, games of chance, etc., are outlawed

- Misrepresentation of your product or service can get you into trouble

As a businessperson you are not expected to be an expert on mail-order law. But you *are* expected to consult a competent professional who *does* know the law. And you *are* expected to follow this person's advice as to what is acceptable and unacceptable in your business.

As a general guide, be sure to deliver what you promise your various customers. And if a customer asks for a refund after returning the item in good condition within any time limits you specify, make an instant refund. Using these two guides will almost certainly produce a trouble-free business for you. But *be sure to consult a competent attorney* anyway!

Save Money with Standardized Printing

When you first start you can use standardized printing, which is usually black ink on white paper. Once sales begin to mount you can go to colored inks, special papers, and other costly refinements—if tests show that this approach pulls better for you.

A new mail-order business usually sends its sales materials in a No. 10 envelope—the standard business size. You can save buckets of money by having the printer's standard corner card with your firm's name and address in black ink on the upper lefthand corner of the envelope. Don't use any teasers (like Open Here for Your Future Wealth) on the outside of the envelope because they will just add to your printing cost.

Likewise with printed address labels—stick to black ink at the start. Most people don't pay too much attention to package labels. So your choice of black is fine—as long as it gets the package to the designated address.

But, by all means, be certain to use printed envelopes and labels. To use handwritten materials marks you as a beginner and causes lost sales. Would you order from someone who couldn't afford printed advertising materials?

There are a number of mail-order printers who will produce as few as 250 envelopes for your first order. With this small a number, your printing bill will be so tiny almost anyone can afford it.

When you're ready to place space ads you'll want to have an ad agency letterhead so you save 15 percent of the space cost. Such a letterhead *must* be printed. But standard black on white will get you the same 15 percent agency discount as red, white, and blue will. So save money while still getting the results you seek.

After you start to make money in your business you can spend some of your profits for teasers on your mailing envelopes. A teaser might say "Open here for the greatest mail-order bargain of the century!" You can also spend money for colored inks other than black, more expensive papers, etc. But at the start you'll keep *all* your costs as low as possible!

Know Seasonal Sales Patterns

If you sell consumer-type products or services in your business, you will see seasonal patterns in your sales. These patterns will:

- Give you your largest sales in February
- Produce your lowest sales in June
- Give you sales of smaller, or greater, numbers in other months

Figure 13-7, based on data from Dependable Lists, Inc., shows how sales vary from month to month in typical consumer-type mail-order businesses. This graph gives you the ratio of replies from one month to another to mailings you make to prospects. So if you received 130 replies in February from a mailing, you'd get 85 replies from the *same size* mailing in June. The same is true

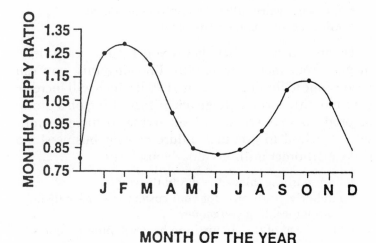

Figure 13-7. Typical mail-order reply ratios.

for the identical ad run in the same magazine in these two months.

But if you're selling items or services to markets other than consumers, you'll probably find that your seasonal sales patterns are somewhat different. Knowing such patterns can help you understand why your business is down in one month and up in another. Some retail businesses make 40 percent of their annual sales between Thanksgiving and Christmas. Owners of such businesses know this and don't get worried when sales are down in June.

To make your millions in mail order today, develop or find products which are less subject to seasonal variations. Thus, we find that our products and services aimed at small businesspeople:

- Have almost *no* seasonal swings
- Answer people's needs year-round
- Sell better when other product sales are down
- Allow us to promote year-round

Having such products helps you keep a nearly level income from month to month. Knowing this, you can devote time to finding new items to sell which will increase your monthly income. Remember: Just sitting on a group of products or services without trying to increase your sales can lead to eventual failure of your business! To make mail-order millions today you must:

- Keep pushing sales *every* day of the year
- Find new "turn-ons" for your customers to have them continue sending you money
- Stay ahead of the competition by developing products or services answering the newest needs of your customers

This constant push may seem a grind. But it really isn't. Why? Because it keeps *you* young, making you more interesting to yourself and to others! Not only that—it makes your bank account grow faster. Could there be any better reason for breaking new ground every day?

To overcome the seasonal nature of the consumer mail-order business, try to offer products that will sell any time of the year. One of my secret answers you can use is to run classified ads that have 365-day appeal to prospects. Here are a few of the classified ads that bring in money every day of the year that the mail is delivered. They even bring in orders—via credit card—on mail holidays! Read these ads and you'll see why they pull year-round—in summer's heat and six-foot snowfalls.

GET BUSINESS LOANS FAST! Low-cost directories show how, where. ABC, 123 Main, Anytown 00000.

MAKE BIG MONEY IN REAL ESTATE! Complete, easy-to-understand guide shows how, where. ABC, 123 Main, Anytown 00000.

SELL MONEY! Make money helping others find money. Send today for complete info. ABC, 123 Main, Anytown 00000.

MAKE MAILBOX MILLIONS—quickly, easily. Big kit shows you how—starting now! ABC, 123 Main, Anytown 00000.

GET RICH IN IMPORT-EXPORT! Easy international mail-order business can make you rich. ABC, 123 Main, Anytown 00000.

BE A 2ND MORTGAGE BROKER and make big money! Complete guide shows how, where. ABC, 123 Main, Anytown 00000.

PUBLISH YOUR OWN NEWSLETTER and get rich! Easy and fun to do. Full info. ABC, 123 Main, Anytown 00000.

MAKE MONEY IN LOCAL REAL ESTATE! Big guide shows you how, where. ABC, 123 Main, Anytown 00000.

HELP OTHERS BUILD GOOD CREDIT while you get rich! Full info, ABC, 123 Main, Anytown 00000.

BE A BIG-EARNING LEASE BROKER for business equipment. Kit shows how, where. ABC, 123 Main, Anytown 00000.

LEASE AUTOS & TRUCKS FOR BIG COMMIS-SIONS! We show you how—fast. ABC, 123 Main, Anytown 00000.

MAKE YOUR FORTUNE WITH ZERO CASH! Start with no money and grow rich. ABC, 123 Main, Anytown 00000.

There you have 12 classified ads that can make you rich! If you'd rather have other ads and you can't write them yourself—or you want to run full-page ads year-round—try a professional copywriter such as my mail-order expert friend, Jay Reiss, Figure 13-8. A good

Figure 13-8

copywriter can prepare selling ads that will put money in your bank—every day!

Yes, mail order *is* different today. The tips in this chapter show you how to cash in quickly and easily on the ever-expanding mail-order market. Do what you think is right and you too can be a mailbox millionaire!

CHAPTER 14

LITTLE-KNOWN SECRETS FOR BUILDING YOUR MAIL-ORDER MILLIONS

MAIL ORDER IS changing—constantly. So you must keep up-to-date if you want to go on building your wealth. In this chapter we give you a number of the most frequently asked questions about making mailbox millions today.

We hope *your* question is among those here. But if it isn't, don't fret. You can call me *free of charge* on my 800 number and I'll answer your question directly. Since I'm at the phone from 8:00 A.M. to 10:00 P.M. daily, it shouldn't take long for you to get your answer!

Mail-Order Advertising

Q. Do I need an advertising agency for my mail-order company?
A. At the start, no. But as your firm grows you should work with one of the many ad agencies serving mail-order companies. The typical fee you'll pay is 15 percent of the ad cost. But a good agency will earn you a lot more than its fee! To pick the right agency for your business, ask several to make presentations to you, after they've looked

over your business and its product line. Pick the agency that will do the best job for you.

Q. How often should I run space and classified ads?

A. The more often you advertise, the stronger the response you'll get from your ads. While an ad is an expense at the time you run it, you'll soon find that an ad is also an investment. Why? Because a good ad will pull in orders or responses for months—sometimes even for years. So advertise as often as your budget will allow.

Q. How much money should I spend on advertising?

A. There's no single answer to this question. But you'll find that successful mail-order firms spend at least 5 percent of their sales income on advertising. And some firms will spend as much as 10 to 15 percent on ads. Thus, if you're selling $100,000 worth of items in a year, your advertising expenditures will run from a low of $5,000 to a high of $15,000.

Q. Do color and ad position really make much difference?

A. Ads with two or more colors usually pull better than black-and-white ads. But ads with color cost more. And ads nearer the front or back of a publication will often pull better. But such positioning—especially front and back covers—costs more. So you have to trade off your extra cost versus the stronger pull. And the only way you can tell is by testing. When you're first starting your business, ask to have your ads placed as close to the front of the publication as possible. But don't spend extra money until you know your ad pulls in the orders or responses. Then figure out how many extra sales you must make to recover the higher cost of the special-position ad. For example, if you're selling a $50 product and the special position costs $600 over the "run of the paper" space,

You must sell $600/$50 = 12 *more* products to recover your extra cost

Only you can decide, based on your experience with the publication, if you can sell the 12 extra items. You apply the same type of test for the higher cost of an extra color in your ad.

Q. What's the easiest way to rent mailing lists?

A. Work with a *list broker*. There are hundreds of mailing list brokers in business today. You'll find them in any large-city Yellow Pages. Call several brokers, tell them about your business, and ask for their recommendations of lists you might use. Brokers can be highly valuable to you. Why? Because they will reflect a much broader view of what's working in the mail-order field than any individual business owner. So you get a cross-section of the results other mail-order firms are achieving. And list brokers will tell you which of their lists will do best for what you're selling. So *use* list brokers—they can give you the competitive edge that will make you mailbox millions!

Q. How often should I follow-up on an inquiry?

A. As a general guide, you should follow-up at least once, after your initial response to a prospect. Many mail-order pros follow-up six times, after their first mailing. Some reduce the price or vary the offer with each follow-up. The key concept however is:

> *A prospect is more likely to buy than a suspect. So spend your time and money to convert prospects (a person who called or wrote for more information on your offer). With high-priced products or services you can follow-up dozens of times and still make money!*

Q. Where can I get information on the cost of advertising?

A. At the start you'll have to rely on your own research. To determine the cost of various size ads, call or write the publications that interest you. Ask for their *Rate Card*. This card shows the cost of various size ads, as shown in Figure 14-1. To get the address and telephone number of any domestic publication, consult a copy of *Standard Rate & Data* at any large public library. This publication gives much useful information on magazines and newspapers of all kinds.

Q. What is a *till-forbid* order?

A. This is an advertising term which tells a publication to run your ad on a continuous basis until you forbid them to run it any longer. So the ad runs until you say *Stop*!

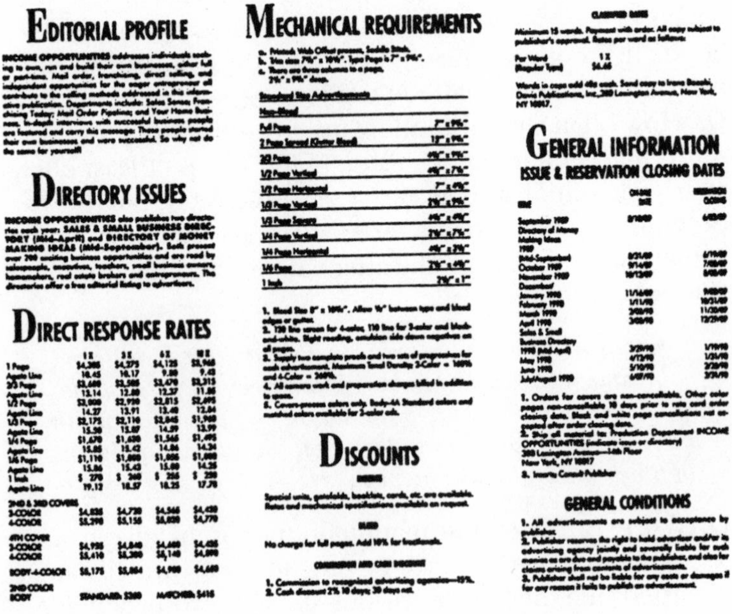

Figure 14-1. Portion of a typical rate card. (Courtesy Davis Publications, Inc.)

Q. What are bill and package stuffers?

A. These are printed ads on a full-size page, or in a smaller format, that are inserted with bills or packages by either your own firm or another company. You pay for the printing of the stuffers. A small fee is charged by the outside company in whose bills or packages your ad is stuffed. Thus, the fee might be $50 per 1,000 stuffers. When the stuffing fee is combined with the printing cost, the total is still less than mailing the ad yourself. However, the response may be lower than you'd get with your own mailing.

Q. Is it wise to use testimonials in my ads?

A. Yes, it *is!* Testimonials are powerful convincers with potential buyers. So use as many testimonials as you can in each ad. Just be sure that you have written and signed permission from the person giving the testimonial to use it in advertising. If you don't want to get permission—or can't—you can use the person's initials instead of their name. In general, get written permission for *every* testimonial you use. Keep every written testimonial on file forever. *Never* throw a written testimonial away! You may need the written document to prove that the testimonial was (and is) real.

Q. Should my ads be tested?

A. Yes, *every* ad must be tested! Testing is the name of the game in money-making mail order. Without testing you're flying blind. And that's how crashes occur. So keep this rule in mind at all times:

> *Test every* ad, even the least expensive. Keep accurate records of the cost of the ad, the number of orders or responses, and the conversion rate of the responses—i.e., the percentage of the responders who buy something from your company. Such records will quickly tell you if your ads are giving you the results you seek. Test, test, test— the three secrets of successful mail order!

If you're doing mailings from rented lists you can test by using only a portion of a list—say 500 names out of 5,000 names. The response you get from these 500 names will tell you if you should *roll out*—that is, mail to all 5,000 names.

Q. How are guarantees different today?

A. Successful mail-order pros offer a full money-back guarantee on all items they sell. The guarantee helps remove whatever doubt may be in a buyer's mind. But to reinforce the guarantee you'll often see a *Sworn Statement* attached to an ad or catalog. This Sworn Statement, furnished by the accountant or attorney for the owner of the firm, says:

> *As the Certified Public Accountant for XYZ Company, I hereby swear that the owner, _____, is a millionaire.*

Or

> *As Certified Public Accountant for XYZ Company, I hereby swear that the income statements cited in this advertisement are accurate and are verified by the bank records of XYZ Company.*

Or

> *As the Attorney for XYZ Company I hereby swear that the legal items cited above are based on the laws noted. Full disclosure is available in the files of XYZ Company*

The Sworn Statement adds credibility to the money-back guarantee. Often, the Sworn Statement will convince the worst doubter to send money. And that, good friend, is the purpose of most ads run by mail-order pros!

Q. Is the ad headline important?

A. It sure is! Some experts say the headline is 80 percent of your ad. That is, if the headline "grabs" the reader, the remainder of the ad will probably be read. But if the headline does not catch the reader's attention, there's very little chance that the remainder of the ad will be read. So concentrate on writing—or having written—aggressive headlines that induce your readers to read every word in your ad. Only then will they act and send you money! You'll even find that catalogs today strive to use a strong headline for each product. The effect is to make the catalog a powerful selling

device that reaps profits for the mail-order firm issuing
it.

Q. Is "dense" body copy needed in every ad?

A. In recent years many mail-order ads featured "dense"
body copy—that is, the reader was given fact after fact.
For self-help books the ad started with the author's date
of birth and went on in great detail from there. For product
ads—especially products in the electronics field—it seems
that every physical law involved is cited. Why such dense
copy? Because such ads sell! Mail-order buyers like long
copy. They love to pore over an ad, reading every word
in it several times. This is why many mail-order pros stick
with fact-filled, dense copy. Figure 14-2 shows a typical
dense-copy ad. As you'll see when you read it, the ad gives
detail after detail about what's being sold.

Recently there's been a switch by some mail-order pros
to less dense ads. These pros think they can sell just as
effectively with an ad having less copy. While the jury is
still out as to whether these ads pull as well—or better
than—dense-copy ads, the people running them still seem
to be eating regularly! What I'm suggesting to you here
is that dense body copy is not needed for every space ad.
Look around you in the publications serving your field
of sales and you'll see that what I say is true. If such ads
would fit your product or service, consider *testing* one or
two. Then decide what's best for you!

Q. How are decoys used in direct mail?

A. When you rent a mailing list there will be a few names
in it that are decoys. This is called "salting a list." The
decoys are names put on the list by the firm renting you
the names. These decoy names are regularly checked by
the list renter to see that they are used only once. Of course,
if you're allowed to mail to a list more than once (this
does not happen often), the renter will still check to see
that you mail only the allotted number of times.

When you rent your mailing list to others, you too should
salt it with decoy names. If you work with a list broker,
such names can easily be inserted. Then you can check

YOU HAVE ALWAYS KNOWN YOUR FUTURE IS IN YOUR HANDS,

but did you know you could re-visit the past to change the future? That's right the past. Once you have acquired the skills necessary to locate and purchase distressed property you will be able to roll back the hands of time and purchase both real estate and personal property at yesterday's prices.

There is no quicker way to make big profits in real estate than by purchasing distressed property. Now is the best time for you to acquire distressed property, and soon you can enjoy financial independence.

These new tapes by Cliff Leonard author of **"License to Steal"** will provide you with information on a variety of methods for acquiring property with very little down, no qualifying and much more

Every day we hear about how much better the economy is getting. Even with our "better" economy the facts show that there are still thousands and thousands of property owners that are in financial trouble. Distressed property sales occur everyday throughout the U.S. There will be a profit made at each of these sales and that profit will go to the individual that has learned how to acquire it. That profit could be yours.

This profit can be made by purchasing property from various sources that includes: sheriff sales, foreclosure sales, trustee sales, bankruptcy sales, and IRS sales to name a few. You will learn:

- How to locate the distressed property.
- How to approach the owner.
- How to locate pre-foreclosures.
- The legal steps used in foreclosures, trustee sales, IRS sales, Bankruptcies, Sheriff sales, etc.
- How to discount liens
- Numerous methods for locating distressed personal property for sale.
- And much more

I Guarantee that no where in the market place will you be able to purchase a tape program on distressed property that covers so many areas for such a low price. Most distressed property tape programs are selling for 2 to 4 times this price. There are even books for only foreclosures that sell for more than this tape program. And this program covers all kinds of distressed property including foreclosures.

I'll bet that some of you are saying right now "I sure wish I had started purchasing distressed property five years ago." Well for goodness sakes don't say that five years from now. I want you to be able to say, "I'm glad I did rather than I wish I had."

After you have purchased your first piece of distressed property you'll wonder why you waited so long.

This tape program is for you if:

- You want to make a profit as soon as you buy

- You would like to cash in on the distressed real estate market.
- You want to gain financial independence

This program includes a workbook that outlines the steps presented in the tape program. In addition the workbook includes copies of many forms used in the foreclosures and trustee sales and the addresses of various agencies that conduct distress property sales.

If you want to start making a profit **when you buy** real estate and personal property -- then learn to invest in distressed property. If you want to take advantage of today's market then fill out the, coupon below and order **"Foreclosures and Other Distressed Property Sales"** for $49.95 plus $2.00 for postage.

"If not for the help in your excellent program I would not have the many rental properties I now own. I recommend you to anybody."
M.S. Jacksonville, FL

"I really enjoyed your tapes. They have already helped me several times to purchase items significantly below market value."
M.M. Tallahassee, FL

I want to learn how to purchase real and personal property below market value. Please rush me **"Foreclosures and Other Distressed Property Sales."** for $49.95 plus $2.00 postage.

Tapes ordered _____ = $49.95 = _____

Postage for _____ Tapes x $2.00 ea. = _____

TOTAL ORDER _____

Enclosed is my check or money order.

Charge my: VISA   MasterCard

Card No. _____ Expiration Date _____

Name _____ Apt/Suite # _____

Address _____

City _____ State _____ Zip _____

Signature _____

INTERNATIONAL WEALTH SUCCESS, INC.
The World's Best Money-Making Books
24 Canterbury Rd, Rockville Ctr NY 11570

Figure 14-2

to see that the firms renting your list use it only the number of times specified in the rental agreement.

Decoy names can also be used to verify that the renter is sending the ad material that was submitted as a sample. You don't want the people on your mailing list receiving objectionable material from a mailer to whom you rented your names. Decoys will quickly reveal any switching of ad materials.

Q. How can I estimate what results I'll get from my advertising?

A. The best ways to estimate the results you'll get from your advertising is to sit down with pencil and paper and face reality. Here are some guidelines for various types of ads:

> *Full-page space ads*: Look for at least twice your ad cost. Thus, if your ad costs $2,000, you should bring in $4,000 in direct sales. If you bring in three times, or more, your ad cost, you can look to retire in just a few years, if every ad you run does this well! (These numbers are for space ads in which you ask the reader to send you money directly for your product or service. At the start, *never* run a full-page ad that doesn't ask for money—unless you want to go broke.)
>
> *Two-step ads of any size*: Here you ask the ad reader to inquire about your offer. You may ask for $1 or $2 to pay postage and handling. In today's market this is not a large amount for these expenses. Expect to *convert*—that is, sell—25 percent of the people asking about your offer. Thus, if you get 1,000 inquiries, some 250 of these people will buy what you offer. But you'll still have 750 names to "hit" again with your offer, or to rent out to the other firms for a handsome profit.
>
> *Classified ads of any size*: You really can't expect to sell from classified ads. Yet people keep trying to do it, again and again. But their ads soon disappear. What does this mean? Just one thing—they ain't selling nothing! Use classified ads to generate inquiries. You should be able to convert 15 to 20 percent of them. Then you can try them again and later rent the names out.
>
> *Catalog ads:* Full-page ads in your catalog will usually

pull better than smaller ads. Seek to generate at least eight times your catalog cost-per-page from each full-page ad. This is a minimum income per page. With our 48-page catalog we seek to make sales of 20 times its cost. Thus, at a cost of $2,200 for 5,000 copies of this black-and-white catalog, we seek to make sales of $44,000. Many times we far exceed this sales level. But the 20-times-cost is our goal. As a beginner the 8-times-cost will put you in the black. But aim a lot higher!

Direct-mail promotion: Seek to bring in at least three times the total cost of your mailing. Thus, if it costs you $1,000 for postage, printing, list rental, envelope stuffing, etc., seek to make $3,000 in sales from this mailing. With such a result you'll be able to get rich and drive the best car in town!

Deck mailings: Some people try to sell from a deck card. But there really isn't enough space on a card to deliver a very convincing sales pitch. So I recommend that you do two-step selling with deck mailings. Use the deck to generate inquiries. Send these people your sales material and make the sale. Your conversion rate should run in the 20 to 25 percent range.

Using the above guidelines you can estimate what results you might get from your advertising. Keeping careful records of each sale allows you to track your results so you know if your estimates are accurate. Each time you estimate what results you'll achieve you will be more accurate, as you "crank in" the results of previous ads. Recognize here and now that you'll never be 100 percent accurate. But as long as your sales exceed your estimates you'll be happily inaccurate!

To track your ad results, set up a customer file for each buyer on your business computer. There are a number of low-cost software programs available for mail-order operators. Using such a program you can easily accumulate data on the results of each ad in terms of number of sales and dollar revenue. And when you want to make another mailing or rent your list to an outside firm, you just press a few keys and your computer will print out the names quickly and easily. Your "dumb secretary" will clatter away day and night, making money for you!

Your computer will even help you evaluate *split runs* where you run one version of your ad in one part of a publication's circulation, and another ad version in a different part of the circulation. Such split runs will quickly tell you which ad pulls better. Knowing this you can junk the poor puller.

Q. Who should write the copy for my ads?

A. You should! Why do I say this? For a number of practical reasons shared by dozens of my mail-order friends all over. These pros tell me—again and again—that their experience agrees with mine in that:

- The best ads for my products are the ads I write myself, even though I may later have my copy polished by a professional copywriter.
- It takes me longer to explain to a copywriter what I want to say than it does for me to write the copy myself. Besides, when I write the copy it's accurate. When someone else writes the copy I usually have to spend lots of time making it right.
- No one knows your product line like you do. So you're the best person to write about it—even if you're not the world's best copywriter.
- Some of the most successful mail-order pros still write all—or most of—their ad copy. If such pros do it, so too can you. Don't be afraid of writing your own ads— it's fun and rewarding. And you'll have the satisfaction of knowing that it's your own words that are bringing in those big bucks!
- You can always take your ads to a professional copywriter and have them polished. But the cost of doing this will be a lot less, and it will be much faster, than if you went to a copywriter with just a few ideas and had that person develop the entire ad.
- Some people write their ad first and then develop a product to fulfill the promises made by the ad! This can be great fun and can make your banker the best friend you ever had.
- Study the ads that run consistently in various publica-

tions serving your field. These ads are pulling sales. If they weren't, they'd stop running. Notice what appeals these ads have. Then be sure your ad has similar appeals to the people in your market. Without such appeals your ad won't have much chance of making money for you. And the *only* reason you should ever write an ad is to make money!

Q. How long should I run a successful ad?
A. Run any ad until it stops paying for itself. This means that once you drop below bringing in twice your ad cost, you should consider stopping the ad. But you have to work out the numbers of each ad, product cost, shipping, etc.

Sometimes you'll find that if you stop an ad for a few months you can bring it back and it will start pulling again. Why? Because a new audience has come along and is ready to buy. But the only way you'll ever learn this is to test, test, test!

Products that Make Profits

Q. Why are "one-shot" products unattractive?
A. Because with a one-shot product you sell your customer once and have nothing else to sell him or her. Successful mail-order pros know that:

- The real profits in mail order come when you make your second, third, fourth, or fifth sale to a customer who likes your product line.
- A line of products or services will induce a customer to spend more money with you than just one product will.
- With one product you don't have any "back-end"—that is, orders generated by a happy experience with the first item or service ordered.
- One-shot products keep you spinning your wheels looking for new customers to sell to. With a line of products, additional sales come to you automatically if you use a catalog of your other items and send it out with each item purchased.

Now there are plenty of mail-order pros that make it big with just one product. My good friend Joe Karbo made millions with his *Lazy Man's Way to Riches*. But Joe had a line of similar books he wrote before he published *Lazy Man*. So he really had a line of excellent products.

My own mail-order business has made me millions also because I have a line of products and services that:

1. Start with a low-cost newsletter—just $24 per year for 12 information-packed valuable issues,
2. Move on to big, useful books that are modestly priced but give dollar-laden information, and
3. Cap all this with powerful kits and courses that get you started making money in just days. Thus, one reader who ordered our *Loans By Phone Kit* ($100, see the back of this book) writes: "I ordered your kit and have had it for about two months and I have a projected income of over $100,000 for the next two months. I have already made $16,400." Another reader writes, "I am using your *Financial Broker/Finder/ Business Broker Kit*. I have done absolutely no advertising and yet I already have (in less than 30 days) five clients seeking loans from $5,000 to $50,000. I am currently working with a gentleman on setting up an Import/Export business, again with one of your kits. Ty, I have never been so busy or had so much fun since I found the friend I have found in you. Again, thanks!" Each of the two kits mentioned by the above customer is priced at $99.50 and was sold to the person after he bought a lower-priced item.

Q. Which products will make me the most money?
A. The products you develop yourself to serve a certain need you see will usually make you the most money. The same is true of services you develop for a need you see. Yes, you *can* make money selling products you buy from others (our *Directory of High Discount Merchandise Sources* [see the back of this book] lists thousands of products you can buy from other firms and re-sell to your customers). But you won't make as much money on such products as you will on the items or services you dream up yourself

and either make on your own or hire someone to make for you. Why can't you make as much on resale products or services? Because:

- The firm you're buying from is making a profit on its sale to you.
- *You* price the product or service so *you* make a profit on its sale to others
- The customer has to pay more because *two* profits are being sought on the one product or service
- The resulting high price reduces your sales. So your overall profit is lower!

When you develop your own product or service, *you* are the only one seeking a profit. So you can price the product more competitively. This means that your sales will be larger, giving *you* a higher profit. So when you're deciding which product or service to sell, give preference to those *you* develop—they'll make much more money for you. And since you "dreamed up" the product or service, it will probably have unique features which make it highly saleable to anyone needing it.

Q. How can I piggy-back my offerings for greater profits?
A. Offer related items (products or services) so your buyer can order several items at once, instead of sending a one-shot order. Thus, people interested in boating will—over the years—buy hundreds of products in the boating field. So when you approach buyers via the mail, a catalog, or on electronic media, offer dozens of piggy-back items. Your sales will soar!

Q. Won't I sell more at lower prices than higher prices?
A. No! You'll often sell *more* at *higher* prices if your product or service is:

1. Unique—that is, different from any others.
2. Complete—that is, all your customer needs to accomplish the task for which he or she bought your product or service.
3. Of suitable bulk—that is, worth the price in terms of weight, size, service rendered, etc. For a product priced at $100 (an excellent price for the next many years)

you should have a weight of at least 3 pounds (1.5 kilo) if it is not a gemstone, gold, or some other precious material having an intrinsic high price of its own.

4. Backed up by personal consultation—that is, having a phone number and name to call to get answers to questions and other help.

Develop products having these characteristics and price them at $100 to $150 and you can sell 20 to 30 units a week. This means you'll be grossing $2,000 to $4,500 a week. This is a nice starting income. Further:

• With higher priced unique products you won't be putting yourself through a wringer shipping hundreds of items each week.

• Instead, you'll have a nice, relaxed business in which the money flows steadily into your bank account while you enjoy a non-frenzied life!

So develop the unique, the unusual, the helpful, the complete, backed by personal service. This way you'll avoid the greatest pricing fallacy of all—that low mail-order prices will make you a millionaire. Today high prices—with full service behind a unique product—will make you millions faster than you could ever imagine!

Q. Is there any easy way to convert inquiries into sales?

A. Yes, there is! How do you easily convert inquiries into sales? You:

1. Send ad material to *every* person who inquires about your products or services. Never ignore handwritten inquiries. Never ignore post-card inquiries. Never ignore "flaky" inquiries. Why? Because they can *all* produce one of your largest sales ever. We've had post-card inquiries that produced over $2,000 in sales!

2. Do your inquiries first—that is, send out your sales literature first thing in the day. Why? Because your inquiries represent your *future* sales. You *must* build for the future. Without doing so, your business may decline over time.

3. Be sure your ad material contains lots of offerings. Thus, we send an 8-page (less than 1 ounce of weight

to conserve postage costs) flyer to *all* inquiries. It contains offerings on 43 different, but related, items. Such a flyer easily converts inquiries into sales.

4. And if the inquiries don't buy the first time, we follow up on them five times more. Eventually, a large number of these inquiries buy a useful product or service from us that helps them build their riches in a business of their own.

Q. How can I get names of new prospects to sell my products or services?

A. One of the best ways to get new prospect names is to have your customers recommend others who might want, or need, what you're selling. Another way is to allow your customers to sell your products or services and earn a commission on each sale.

Why are these methods good? For a number of reasons:

1. They don't cost you much. So you save on your ad and promotion costs.

2. Your customers find "hot ones" for you—that is, people who are interested in what you're selling. Your cost of getting *prospects* instead of suspects is much lower when your own customers recommend you to their friends.

3. With unique products—which I urge you to develop—you might almost become an "in" type company where it's smart to buy from *you* because you have so many unusual features to offer your customers. You and your company become a cult—bringing in big sales! Remember: Being an "in" company will bring *you* big profits from products and services you offer.

Q. Should I give free samples of my products?

A. Yes, if you're in the retail business where people come to you. But in mail order the cost of delivering a sample to anyone is constantly rising. And it seems that for every prospect that asks for a sample, you have ten suspects that ask! So your cost of giving free samples can shoot your advertising expenses through the roof. Here's a sensible approach on samples that works well for me:

1. Don't give samples free. Instead, charge a nominal amount that covers your product or service cost, postage, packaging, etc. Then you'll attract more prospects—people willing to pay for a look at what you offer.
2. Where possible, include a brief sample in your ad materials. You can't do this, of course, if you're selling gas-powered lawnmowers by mail. But if you're selling printed materials, as I do, you can give a sample page of a publication to show your prospect what he or she will be getting.
3. Be sure your sample represents the end product your customer will get when an order is placed. This means your sample should not be better than what the customer finally gets after placing an order with you.

Q. What should I look for in the products or services I will sell?
A. There are a number of features you should seek in products or services you either develop or buy to sell to others. Always:

- *Try for the highest quality* possible. Customers will be impressed by quality and they'll buy from you again and again.
- *Develop new* items or services to solve problems that lots of people have. Your new solution to a common problem will find a large market with big sales.
- *Offer* products or services for serious use, as opposed to fads. While a fad can make you a lot of money quickly, fads come and go just as quickly. Items or services needed in personal or business activities sell for longer and will ultimately earn more for you.
- *Keep* an eye on customer progression—that is, selling a person one item, then another, and another. This way you make more on each sale because you already have the customer on your list. Selling a line of items instead of a one-shot will give you customer progression—and happiness!
- *Never* "marry" any product—be ready to sell what moves. Trying to push a product or service your customers don't

want is a sure way to lose buckets of money. Don't let this happen to you!

Build a Happy Customer List

Q. What makes a happy customer in mail order today?
A. There are a number of elements that make a happy customer. You should:

1. *Deliver speedily* what's ordered. As we saw earlier, today's world is in a hurry. Getting an item or service quickly builds a strong bond with your customer.
2. *Ensure high quality* for top marks with customers. So sell only the best—it will light up your customer's lives!
3. *Wrap safely* to prevent damage to what you sell. Remember: In this business, *everything* is marketing. Even the way you wrap what you sell gives an unspoken message to your customer. It tells whether you really care about him or her. Companies that care have happy customers!
4. *Include the cost of shipping* as part of the price of what you sell. This makes it much easier for your customer to order and gets you extra sales. Why? Because your customer is happy he or she doesn't have to do complex figuring of shipping costs.
5. *Offer service* to your customers—that is, be ready to answer questions, solve problems, etc. The more you help a customer, the more he or she will buy from you—if you have a complete product line to offer. Service given freely and in a friendly way always builds happy customers!
6. *Answer complaints immediately.* Don't let them lie around to haunt you. Call your customer on the phone. Explain what happened to cause the complaint. Then give *exact* details as to what steps you'll take to rectify the situation. Follow up with a written response. Unhappy customers can be made into the most loyal buyers you've ever had—if you respond to complaints immediately!

7. *Make refunds rapidly.* Don't diddle around! Make the refund and go out and earn ten times as much—you'll be better off and you'll have a happy customer.

Q. How should I keep my customers' names on file?
A. Today there's just one practical way—on a computer. While you can use manual methods at the start, you *must* quickly move to a computer. Why? Because:

- A computer allows you to contact your customers more often. *Remember:* Mail-order customers *enjoy* getting a mailing from you. It gives them a chance to order more of your excellent products or services!
- A computer allows you to earn extra income renting out your customer or prospect lists. And you're in this business to make money—right?
- A computer allows you to put up each customer on a file that gives you valuable information like:
  * Where the customer was obtained
  * What the customer bought
  * How much the customer spent
  * When the customer buys (time of year)
  * Etc.

So don't be afraid of computers! They're fun to work with and they'll return their cost over and over again.
Q. What other steps can I take to keep customers happy and buying?
A. Keep in personal touch with as many customers as possible. The personal touch will make your customers friends. For instance, I often have my customers out on my yacht during the summer. They enjoy the trip while they try to pick my brain for new ideas.

And I call customers daily. They can call me and get a quick opinion on a question they have. Such personal contact continues to build my business. While it *is* work, it's also fun—and very rewarding in many ways!

Try to offer your customers unique services if you're selling products. Or offer unqiue products if you're selling services. Thus, at IWS, Inc., my firm, we sell products and offer free services as follows:

- Our main products are books, newsletters, and kits (which are collections of books and manuals in a self-teaching format)
- Our *free* services offered to readers of our books, newsletters, and kits are:
  * Copies of our 48-page catalog
  * Business and real-estate loans from IWS at low interest rates with liberal repayment terms and no credit check
  * 800-number consultation (toll-free) with me whenever a reader has a business or real-estate question (and mail order *is* a business, remember!)
  * Personal meetings with myself when the reader needs some face-to-face advice and help

Now I know that if you're selling dress patterns by mail (a great money-maker), such services will not fly for you. But I'm sure that there are some services that will. What? Try fashion consulting, wardrobe advice, etc. It may just work! The whole key, though, is to offer more than your competition does. Then you'll build a happy customer list— quickly and easily.

Q. What is the most important way a prospect judges my offers?

A. The most important way a prospect judges your offers is through your mailings and ads. Here are a number of things you can do to convince a prospect your offers will really help him or her:

- Use plain, direct language—it convinces a prospect faster and shows that you really want to help him or her
- Present *your* view in all your mailings and ads to let the prospect know that your firm is interested in him or her
- Choose short sentences, punchy words, and clear descriptions in simple language to show your prospect that you want to talk directly to him or her in quickly grasped terms
- Qualify your firm by telling the prospect how long you've been in business, what organizations you belong to, what qualifications your staff has

- Support your quality claims with testimonials from earlier satisfied customers
- Stand behind everything you sell—give written guarantees where they will help sales
- Give a bonus for ordering items you want to sell strongly. Just be sure the bonus item is valuable to your buyer and will motivate a person to send you the order you want
- Give clear, simple ordering instructions. Don't ask your buyer to do anything but order! It's the order that pays your bills—not silly questions generated by a confusing coupon or ordering instructions!

Show your prospect that you want his or her business because you have something great to offer. If you convince any prospect of this, the orders will pour into your mailbox, making you a millionaire sooner than you think!

Get to Know Your Post Office

Q. Why is it important for me to understand the post office?
A. There are a number of key reasons why understanding the post office can make you a better business person while becoming a mailbox millionaire. These reasons are:

1. You will always use the post office in mail order! No matter how many competing delivery services may come on the scene, you will still use the post office for most of your mailings. So you *must* understand how to mail at the lowest cost—efficiently.
2. There are a number of mail-order laws that the post office upholds. You don't want to violate any of these laws because you can find yourself in a difficult position. As a general guide, do *not* promote lotteries, chain schemes, gambling, etc. via the mails. Why? Because it's against the law. Figure 14-3 gives a quick summary of some of the practices you *must* avoid if you're to succeed in mail order. But be safe—get yourself an attorney familiar with postal law and have each

Mail-Order Offers to Avoid

Chain schemes of all kinds—letters, sales scams, charities, money-raising offers, etc. Steer clear of pyramid schemes, also.

Lotteries and games of chance—no matter for what type of beneficial purpose should *not* be offered by mail.

Simulated billings which are really sales pieces—a bill is a bill. Don't try to make a sales piece look like one!

"Front Money" Advance Fee Schemes—in which a person puts up a sum of money to get a loan. Charging a fee *after* you get a person a loan is permissible. Front money creates problems. *Never* charge front money or work with anyone who does!

"Miracle" cures of all kinds—avoid these like a deadly disease because they could be the death of your business! And stay away from magic reducing diets, skin creams, potency pills, and similar scams. They only lead to trouble.

Home work plans—envelope stuffing, newspaper clipping, envelope addressing, etc. often causes problems if people don't earn what's promised to them.

Phony religions, cults, charities—can extract money from people without a legitimate reason. Getting involved can lead to many different problems for you.

Any other product or service which doesn't deliver what is promised—can lead to customer complaints and eventual investigation by the authorities. It will just waste your time and could lead to severe penalties. Give such items a wide berth!

Figure 14-3

offer you make reviewed by your attorney. Then there's little chance that you'll have problems.

3. Helpful and free post office seminars run at large facilities will enable you to save money on every large mailing you make. Since postal costs are rising, it's important that you keep up with the ways in which

you can hold the line on the increases. While your postal costs *are* provable and tax-deductible to your business, it's senseless to waste money when there are ways of saving it.

Q. How else will I benefit from understanding the post office?
A. There are a number of permits, rules, and guidelines which allow you to save money. Using these will build your profits while showing your customers that you are an efficient mailer. Typical of these are:

- Bulk mail permit allows you to mail at third class rates to save money on mail that's not time-sensitive or can be delivered over several days without affecting its usefulness to your buyer
- First Class Presort Permit allows you to save on first class mail if you pre-sort it according to post office requirements. You get speedy delivery with a saving!
- Fourth Class Book Rate saves you a lot of money over Fourth Class Parcel Post. If you don't believe me, just compare the cost of mailing a 5-pound book across the country via Book Rate and Parcel Post Rate!
- Post Office boxes cost much less to rent than the same size boxes in privately run mail centers. Also, your post office box will get the mail sooner than an outside box. Why? Because the post office box is right in the same building where the mail is received!

In years of dealing with the post office I have consistently found the people who work there to be sincere, helpful, and courteous. I have made it a point to get to know everything I can about the post office and its people. It has really paid off for me in postal savings, better service, quicker delivery, and more fun in business! You can do the same.

To help understand postal rules better, get a free subscription to *Memo to Mailers*. Figure 14-4 gives details. You'll enjoy reading it.

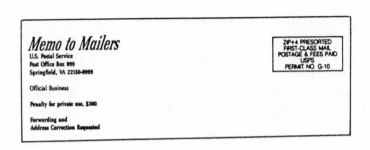

Figure 14-4

Financing Your Mail-Order Business

Q. How can I finance my mail-order business?
A: There are many different ways to finance your new mail-order business. Remember that mail order *is* a business! So you follow regular practices in financing your business. These are:

1. Prepare a business plan. Without such a plan you don't have much hope of finding the money you seek.
2. Contact the bank you regularly do business with and ask if they'd be interested in making a business loan to you. Show your business plan to the loan officer—it will help in getting your loan.
3. Request a loan application from my firm, IWS, Inc., if you're a reader of, or a regular subscriber to our newsletter, *International Wealth Success.* We're always interested in new mail-order businesses to finance. And I promise you we will *not* try to go into your business! We're very happy with our publishing and lending

businesses. They keep us busier than anyone we know. At the same time they provide a good income—far more than we can ever spend. That's why we offer our excess IWS, Inc. corporate funds at moderate interest rates to up and coming businesses of all kinds. While we cannot—and do not—guarantee that we'll be able to make every loan requested, we *do* guarantee to review your loan proposal at *no* cost of any kind. If we can't make the loan to you, we'll recommend some lenders who might be able to work with you. And we'll give you a fast answer once we receive your filled-out loan application.

4. Apply at the Small Business Administration (SBA). They either make, or guarantee, many loans for mail-order businesses. And SBA can give much faster answers today—in as little as three days for some loans. So don't use the tired excuse of "Oh, it takes too long with SBA!" That's *not* so these days.

5. Seek venture-capital funding if your mail-order business has a really large potential. Venture funds need not be repaid—they're an investment in your firm. But you do give up a portion of your ownership of your firm. So there's a trade-off. As the man said— "There are *no* free lunches in this world."

6. Use any of the many other sources of business funding given in Figure 14-5. If you have trouble understanding any of these, just give me a ring on the phone and I'll explain them in greater detail—if you're a 2-year, or longer, subscriber to our newsletter, mentioned earlier.

Q: Do Beginning Mail-Order Wealth Builders ever run ads on credit and then pay for the ad with sales they make from it?

A: This *is* done. But it's very risky—unless you know from past experience what sales revenue you can safely expect from the ad. I know of plenty of mail-order pros who run full-page ads without paying for them up front. They pay for the ad 30 days after it runs. By this time they've brought in enough money to pay for the ad. But these people are walking a tightrope with each ad. If an ad doesn't pull,

Fig. *14-5* *Sources of Financing for Your Mail-Order Business*

1. Check ads in your local paper under "Capital Available."
2. Look under "Funds/Funding Available" in your IWS* newsletter.
3. Look for "Money Available" ads in industry magazines and newspapers.
4. Write, or call, local or national banks. Ask for loan info.
5. Write, or call, local or national finance companies. Ask for loan info.
6. Write, or call, local or national mortgage companies. Ask for loan info.
7. Write, or call, local or national credit unions. Ask for loan info.
8. Write, or call, local savings & loan associations (S&Ls).
9. Write, or call, local building & loan associations (B&Ls).
10. Run classified ads (free to subscribers) in *IWS* for "Lenders Wanted."
11. Run classified ads in national papers seeking lenders.
12. Co-broker with financial brokers having lenders available.
13. Contact local and national real-estate brokers.
14. Work with franchisors who can supply lenders for buyers.
15. Work with equipment lease brokers having contacts with lenders.
16. Explore overseas lenders through local branch offices.
17. Check federal government loans—there are hundreds available.
18. Contact your state or city government for loans—there are many.
19. Use credit card lines of credit as loan sources.
20. Get finders to locate suitable loans for you.
21. Seek out private lenders among business associates.
22. Work with big-ticket item funders for boats, planes, etc.
23. Contact insurance companies for large real-estate loans.
24. Work with surety-bond firms, using lenders acceptable to them.

* *IWS* is the abbreviation for *International Wealth Success,* the monthly newsletter published by the author.

Fig. 14-5 *Sources of Financing for Your Mail-Order Business*

---

25. Attend lender meetings to get an inside track on their loan needs.
26. Contact local professionals (MDs, DDSs) seeking investments.
27. Write or call attorneys and accountants, asking for lender names.
28. Contact large firms making loans to suppliers.
29. Ask stockbrokers for clients who want to make loans.
30. Get business associates to take out home equity loans.
31. Ask your bank to recommend other lenders to you.
32. Deal with specialty lenders—ship, aircraft, truck, etc.
33. Work with nonprofit lenders—see your "Yellow Pages" for names.
34. Get loans from SBICs—Small Business Investment Companies.
35. Contact local business development companies.
36. Borrow on the cash value of an insurance policy.
37. Apply to pension funds for large real-estate loans.
38. Get accounts receivable financing (AR) from AR lenders.
39. Borrow on commercial paper you issue through your corporation.
40. Use a banker's acceptance (BA) to get import-export loans. See your bank.
41. Get venture-capital firms to lend money to your company.
42. Get loans from tax-haven lenders—usually banks.

---

they're likely to go tumbling into a real credit problem, unless they have reserve funds on hand—or can borrow money to pay for the ad. So, while you *can* operate this way, it's best to pay for your ad in advance. Then you'll get a 3 percent cash discount. And you won't be in a cash bind if the ad doesn't pull as strongly as you planned.

Q: Is it harder to finance a mail-order business than another type of business?

A: No—a mail-order business is easier to finance than many other types of businesses. Why? For these very strong reasons:

• Cash flow is strong in a mail-order business. Your

customers don't hang you up for months before they pay for what you shipped.

- Requiring payment with order eliminates being ripped off by customers who never pay. Such people are commonly met in many other types of business—but not in mail order.
- Mail-order is a *daily* cash business. So you have money every day of the week which you can use to repay any loans you got to start your business. (I wish you could be with me for just one day as we open the mail. Checks and money orders pile up on the desk as the slitting machine does its job of opening the envelopes. You'd quickly get the picture of a daily cash business—even though 99 percent of the payments coming in are either checks or money orders. (With the accelerated check processing banks have today, these payments are almost cash, anyway.) In mail order you get paid *every* day— not once a month, as in some businesses. All this adds up to easy financing of any mail-order business!

Q: What ways can I use to bring in more money every day so I can pay off my startup loans faster?

A: You can use a number of the little-known secrets for making big sales with just pennies for "convincers." These low-cost convincers bring in thousands of times what you lay out—allowing you to repay loans fast. Powerful convincers to consider for your mail-order business are:

- *Broadsides* — a newspaper-size collection of ads for your products or services. Broadsides can be mailed, given away on street corners, stuck under auto windshield wipers, put on store checkout counters, etc. The key to bringing in big bucks with a broadside is the attention its large size gets from prospects. Yet the newsprint used is probably the cheapest paper around. So your ads get into the hands of potential buyers for almost nothing!
- *Bouncebacks*—a low-cost ad you enclose with your regular mailings that promotes one or more items different from your main offering. Thus, your bounce- backs give your prospect another group of choices in case he or she isn't interested in your main product or service. For example, if you're selling jewelry by mail

(a great business), your bounceback might offer a new hair or skin care product that gives miracle-like results. So if your prospect has enough jewelry at the moment, he or she can turn down your great offers (foolishly, of course), and opt for better looking hair or skin. Note that the person who buys lots of jewelry usually enjoys being looked at. So a hair or skin product will "grab them" and get them to send you big bucks for a 3 × 5 inch bounceback you can print for about two-tenths of a cent! And the weight of a bounceback is so little that it will never increase your postage cost.

- *Involvement device*—a stamp, plastic disk, coin, bill, or other item that requires some action on the part of your buyer to indicate a desire to purchase what you offer. You've seen, no doubt, an involvement device such as a postage-size stamp with the line: "If you want us to send you one of our big 100-hour outdoor flashlights, just paste this stamp in the YES box and return this card containing your name and address, using the enclosed envelope. Be sure to include your check or money order for $89.95!" Involvement devices can increase both the number of sales, and the amount of your sales. Why? Because the device gives your buyer a feeling of power when doing what he or she is told to do. Crazy? Sure. But involvement devices *do* work! Ask any successful mail-order pro and you'll hear dozens of stories of how a particular involvement device pulled in millions of dollars. Haven't you ever subscribed to a magazine by taking a small stamp-size picture of its cover and pasting it in a box to show which publication *you* want? You were using an involvement device. Try them in your business and watch your bank account balloon!
- *Lift letter*—written by a top person in your firm (that could be *you*, as President) to convince the prospect to buy. Your letter gives a lift to the informational material you send the prospect about how great your products or services are, what wonderful things they'll do for your buyer, etc. You steer clear of product specifics in your lift letter. Instead, you concentrate on benefits the buyer will obtain from anything he or she gets from you. A lift letter will often be the final convincer in a sale. Why?

Because it appeals to the buyer's emotions, instead of cool, clear logic. Remember: People buy from an emotional basis and then defend their decision with logic!

- *Free-standing inserts*—are your *broadsides* (see above) inserted in the Sunday newspaper between sections. So when someone buys the Sunday paper and looks for the sports section (we'll say), he or she comes on your free-standing insert. Pulling it out, the person glances over it and decides if it should be read further. Since the Free-Standing Insert (FSI for short) is separate from the paper, it usually gets more attention than an ad in one of the regular sections of the newspaper. To use an FSI, contact your local paper having the readership you want to reach. You'll be nicely surprised that the cost of an FSI is a lot less than you might think! And they *do* generate strong sales for lots of mail-order pros.

- *Contests and sweepstakes*—both can pull strongly for your business. But you *must* have superb legal advice for any contest or sweepstakes promotions you plan. Why? Because both federal and state authorities rigidly police these kinds of sales promotions. As a guide, follow these easy steps:

  1. Do *not* require any purchase of a prospective contestant. You are not allowed to require a person to buy something to be eligible to enter your contest. That's why you'll often hear the line: "No purchase required" when a contest is being publicized.

  2. Be certain *not* to charge a fee to enter a sweepstakes drawing. Again, it isn't allowed! Anyone who's interested in what you're offering should be eligible to submit an entry.

  3. Get good legal advice for each type of promotion. There are legal firms that specialize in advising clients running contests or sweepstakes. Contact such a firm and tell them what you want to do. Just be certain to discuss your plans fully *before* you make any offers to the public. You don't want your efforts to be reduced to nothing because you overlooked one important (or even unimportant) rule governing contests and sweepstakes. Your

attorney can show you how to avoid these kinds of problems.

4. Be sure to tie your contest into future sales. Do the same for sweepstakes. The goal of every contest or sweepstake drawing is to generate more sales of your products or services. You're not running either program for its own sake! You're running one or the other (or both) to generate more sales. Some highly successful contest and sweepstake pros I know include their entry blank along with product or service mailings. Though *No Purchase is Required,* many of the people getting the mailing will buy anyway. Their reasoning: If I buy something and send the order in with the entry blank for the contest or sweepstakes, my chances for winning will be much higher! Let that be a key idea for you, namely: Never mail a contest or sweepstake entry to a prospect without including plenty of sales material—such as your catalog. You'll find that about 75 percent of the people you send the entry to will order something—*if* you include your sales material! A word to the wise should be enough to put *you* into this millionaire-building business of sales promotion contests and sweepstakes. When it comes to prizes, you can often have these contributed free of charge to your firm. How? By arranging to give the contributing company plenty of free advertising when you promote the contest or sweepstakes. Thus, if you'll be giving a certain type of computer as a prize, the computer manufacturer might be willing to give you the computer(s) free for the publicity you give the computer firm in your ads featuring the prizes. When this happens, as it has to me, your only cost of promoting your contest or sweepstakes is the advertising you do. Can't you see why mail order is the world's best business!

The Ultimate Mail-Order Success Secrets

Q: How can I really make it in mail order today?

A: There are a number of *proven* guidelines which, if followed, are almost certain to earn you millions in mail order. These guidelines are:

1. *Pick products or services* that are currently selling for others. Sure, you *can* break through new frontiers—after your business is established and profitable. But at the start sell items that are making millions for others. Just be sure to offer improved, cheaper, or faster products or services. Then you really can't miss making those millions for yourself.

2. *Deliver your product or service* as quickly as possible, consistent with protecting yourself against possible ripoffs by the paper artists.

3. *Always include additional sales materials* with every item shipped or service rendered. This way you'll sell a customer while he or she is ready to buy.

4. *Treat every customer with kindness and attention.* Never ignore any customer! *Do* what you promise to do. Be a person who keeps his or her word.

5. *Get good legal and accounting advice.* Pay all taxes that are due—on time. Be aware of postal regulations and FTC requirements. Avoid getting too close to outlawed products and practices. It's much easier to make money legally and legitimately selling acceptable products or services!

6. *Set annual goals for your business* in terms of sales you'll achieve. Plot out how and where you'll advertise to achieve your sales goals. Then go all-out to reach your goals.

7. *Concentrate on making maximum sales to all customers.* Go back again and again to existing customers to sell them more. Rent out your mailing lists to bring in more money. Sell your inquiry envelopes to get them out of the office and to wring every penny from your business.

8. *Make full use of Express Mail and the courier services* to deliver products and services quickly to your

customers. Fast delivery is one of the most highly valued services you can offer your customers.

9. *Use bonus items, gifts, and other "freebies"* to weld a strong bond with your customers. People love a free gift, no matter how little it costs. Shower your customers with thoughtful freebies and they'll love you forever.

10. *Everything is marketing!* Remember those three words and you'll understand Ty Hicks' mail-order secret! And I'm here—ready to help you in every way I can. With advice, financing, guidance, etc. Try me and see!

BIBLIOGRAPHY

Other Profit-Building Tools from Tyler Hicks' *INTERNATIONAL WEALTH SUCCESS* Library

As the publisher of the famous *INTERNATIONAL WEALTH SUCCESS* newsletter, Ty Hicks has put together a remarkable library of dynamic books, each geared to help the opportunity-seeking individual — the kind of person who is ready and eager to achieve the financial freedom that comes from being a SUCCESSFUL entrepreneur. Financial experts agree that only those who own their own businesses or invest their money wisely can truly control their future wealth. And yet, far too many who start a business or an investment program of their own do not have the kind of information that can make the difference between success and failure.

Here, then, is a list of publications hand-picked by Ty Hicks, written especially to give you, the enterprising wealth builder, the critical edge that belongs solely to those who have the *inside* track. So take advantage of this unique opportunity to order this confidential information. (These books are *not* available in bookstores.) Choose the publications that can help you the most and send the coupon page with your remittance. Your order will be processed as quickly as possible to expedite your success. (Please note: If, when placing an order, you prefer not to cut out the coupon, simply photocopy the order page and send in the duplicate.)

IWS-1   **BUSINESS CAPITAL SOURCES.** Lists more than 1,500 lenders of various types — banks, insurance companies, commercial finance firms, factors, leasing firms, overseas lenders, venture-capital firms, mortgage companies, and others. $15. 150 pgs.

IWS-2   **SMALL BUSINESS INVESTMENT COMPANY DIRECTORY AND HANDBOOK.** Lists more than 400 small business investment companies that invest in small businesses to help them prosper. Also gives tips on financial management in business. $15. 135 pgs.

IWS-3   **WORLDWIDE RICHES OPPORTUNITIES,** Vol. 1. Lists more than 2,500 overseas firms seeking products to import. Gives name of product(s) sought, or service(s) sought, and other important data needed by exporters and importers. $25. 283 pgs.

IWS-4 **WORLDWIDE RICHES OPPORTUNITIES,** Vol. 2. Lists more than 2,500 overseas firms seeking products to import. (Does NOT duplicate Volume 1.) Lists loan sources for some exporters in England. $25. 223 pgs.

IWS-5 **HOW TO PREPARE AND PROCESS EXPORT-IMPORT DOCUMENTS.** Gives data and documents for exporters and importers, including licenses, declarations, free-trade zones abroad, bills of lading, custom duty rulings. $25. 170 pgs.

IWS-6 **SUPPLEMENT TO HOW TO BORROW YOUR WAY TO REAL ESTATE RICHES.** Using government sources compiled by Ty Hicks, lists numerous mortgage loans and guarantees, loan purposes, amounts, terms, financing charge, types of structures financed, loan-value ratio, special factors. $15. 87 pgs.

IWS-7 **THE RADICAL NEW ROAD TO WEALTH** by A. David Silver. Covers criteria for success, raising venture capital, steps in conceiving a new firm, the business plan, how much do you have to give up, economic justification. $15. 128 pgs.

IWS-8 **60-DAY FULLY FINANCED FORTUNE** is a short BUSINESS KIT covering what the business is, how it works, naming the business, interest amortization tables, state securities agencies, typical flyer used to advertise, typical applications. $29.50. 136 pgs.

IWS-9 **CREDITS AND COLLECTION BUSINESS KIT** is a 2-book kit covering fundamentals of credit, businesses using credits and collection methods, applications for credit, setting credit limit, Fair Credit Reporting Act, collection percentages, etc. Gives 10 small businesses in this field. $29.50. 147 pgs.

IWS-10 **MIDEAST AND NORTH AFRICAN BANKS AND FINANCIAL INSTITUTIONS.** Lists more than 350 such organizations. Gives name, address, telephone, and telex number for most. $15. 30 pgs.

IWS-11 **EXPORT MAIL-ORDER.** Covers deciding on products to export, finding suppliers, locating overseas firms seeking exports, form letters, listing of firms serving as export management companies, shipping orders, and more. $17.50. 50 pgs.

IWS-12 **PRODUCT EXPORT RICHES OPPORTUNITIES.** Lists over 1,500 firms offering products for export — includes agricultural, auto, aviation, electronic, computers, energy, food, healthcare, mining, printing, and robotics. $21.50. 219 pgs.

IWS-13   **DIRECTORY OF HIGH - DISCOUNT MERCHANDISE SOURCES.** Lists more than 1,000 sources of products with full name, address, and telephone number for items such as auto products, swings, stuffed toys, puzzles, oils and lubricants, CB radios, and belt buckles. $17.50. 97 pgs.

IWS-14   **HOW TO FINANCE REAL ESTATE INVESTMENTS** by Roger Johnson. Covers basics, the lending environment, value, maximum financing, rental unit groups, buying mobile-home parks, and conversions. $21.50. 265 pgs.

IWS-15   **DIRECTORY OF FREIGHT FORWARDERS AND CUSTOM HOUSE BROKERS.** Lists hundreds of these firms throughout the United States which help in the import/export business. $17.50. 106 pgs.

IWS-16   **CAN YOU AFFORD NOT TO BE A MILLIONAIRE?** by Marc Schlecter. Covers international trade, base of operations, stationery, worksheet, starting an overseas company, metric measures, profit structure. $10. 202 pgs.

IWS-17   **HOW TO FIND HIDDEN WEALTH IN LOCAL REAL ESTATE** by R. H. Jorgensen. Covers financial tips, self-education, how to analyze property for renovation, the successful renovator is a "cheapskate," property management, and getting the rents paid. $17.50. 133 pgs.

IWS-18   **HOW TO CREATE YOUR OWN REAL-ESTATE FORTUNE** by Jens Nielsen. Covers investment opportunities in real estate, leveraging, depreciation, remodeling your deal, buy- and lease-back, understanding your financing. $17.50. 117 pgs.

IWS-19   **REAL-ESTATE SECOND MORTGAGES** by Ty Hicks. Covers second mortgages, how a second mortgage finder works, naming the business, registering the firm, running ads, expanding the business, and limited partnerships. $17.50. 100 pgs.

IWS-20   **GUIDE TO BUSINESS AND REAL ESTATE LOAN SOURCES.** Lists hundreds of business and real-estate lenders, giving their lending data in very brief form. $25. 201 pgs.

IWS-21   **DIRECTORY OF 2,500 ACTIVE REAL-ESTATE LENDERS.** Lists 2,500 names and addresses of direct lenders or sources of information on possible lenders for real estate. $25. 197 pgs.

IWS-22   **IDEAS FOR FINDING BUSINESS AND REAL ESTATE CAPITAL TODAY.** Covers raising public money, real estate financing, borrowing methods, government loan sources, and venture money. $24.50. 62 pgs.

IWS-23   **HOW TO BECOME WEALTHY PUBLISHING A NEWSLETTER** by E. J. Mall. Covers who will want your newsletter, planning your newsletter, preparing the first issue, direct mail promotions, keeping the books, building your career. $17.50. 102 pgs.

IWS-24   **NATIONAL DIRECTORY OF MANUFACTURERS' REPRESENTATIVES.** Lists 5,000 mfrs.' reps. from all over the United States, both in alphabetical form and state by state; gives markets classifications by SIC. $28.80. 782 pgs., hardcover.

IWS-25   **BUSINESS PLAN KIT.** Shows how to prepare a business plan to raise money for any business. Gives several examples of successful business plans. $29.50. 150 pgs.

IWS-26   **MONEY RAISER'S DIRECTORY OF BANK CREDIT CARD PROGRAMS.** Shows the requirements of each bank listed for obtaining a credit card from the bank. Nearly 1000 card programs at 500 of the largest U.S. banks are listed. Gives income requirements, job history, specifications, etc. $19.95. 150 pgs.

IWS-27   **GLOBAL COSIGNERS AND MONEY FINDERS ASSOCIATION.** Publicize your need for a cosigner to get a business or real estate loan. Your need is advertised widely under a Code Number so your identity is kept confidential. $50.

IWS-28   **WALL STREET SYNDICATORS.** Lists 250 active brokerage houses who might take your company public. Gives numerous examples of actual, recent, new stock offerings of start-up companies. $15. 36 pgs.

IWS-29   **COMPREHENSIVE LOAN SOURCES FOR BUSINESS AND REAL ESTATE LOANS.** Gives hundreds of lenders' names and addresses and lending guidelines for business and real estate loans of many different types. $25; 136 pages. 8½ × 11 in.

IWS-30   **DIVERSIFIED LOAN SOURCES FOR BUSINESS AND REAL ESTATE LOANS.** Gives hundreds of lenders' names and addresses and lending guidelines for business and real estate loans of many different types. Does not duplicate IWS-29. $25; 136 pages; 8½ × 11 in.

IWS-31   **CREDIT POWER REPORTS**—five helpful reports to improve your credit rating and credit line. Report No. 1: *How to Get a Visa and/or Mastercard Credit Card*; $19.95; 192 pages; 5 × 8 in. Report No. 2: *How to Increase Your Credit Limits, Plus Sophisticated Credit Power Strategies*; $19.95; 208 pages; 5 × 8 in. Report No. 3: *How to Repair Your Credit*; $19.95; 256 pages; 5 × 8 in. Report No. 4: *How to Reduce Your Monthly Payments*; $19.95; 192 pages; 5 × 8 in. Report No. 5: *How to Wipe Out Your Debts Without Bankruptcy*; $19.95; 152 pages. Each book is also available on a cassette tape which duplicates the entire content of the report. The tapes are priced at $19.95 each and run 60 minutes. Please specify which tape you want when ordering; the tape title duplciates the report title.

IWS-32   **GUARANTEED MONTHLY INCOME** gives you a way to earn money every month via mail order selling books and kits to people seeking a business of their own. With this plan the money comes to you and you keep a large share of it for yourself. $15; 36 pages; 8½ × 11 in.

Newsletters

IWSN-1   **INTERNATIONAL WEALTH SUCCESS,** Ty Hicks' monthly newsletter published 12 times a year. This 16-page newsletter covers loan and grant sources, real-estate opportunities, business opportunities, import-export, mail order, and a variety of other topics on making money in your own business. Every subscriber can run one free classified advertisement of 40 words, or less, each month, covering business or real-estate needs or opportunities. The newsletter has a worldwide circulation, giving readers and advertisers very broad coverage. Started in Jan., 1967, the newsletter has been published continuously since that date. $24.00 per year; 16 pages plus additional inserts; 8½ × 11 in.; monthly.

IWSN-2   **MONEY WATCH BULLETIN,** a monthly coverage of 100 or more active lenders for real estate and business purposes. The newsletter gives the lender's name, address, telephone number, lending guidelines, loan ranges, and other helplful information. All lender names were obtained within the last week; the data is therefore right up to date. Lender's names and addresses are also provided on self-stick labels on an occasional basis. Also covers venture capital and grants. $95.00; 20 pages; 8½ × 11 in.; monthly; 12 times per year.

Success Kits

K-1   **FINANCIAL BROKER/FINDER/BUSINESS BROKER/CON-SULTANT SUCCESS KIT** shows YOU how to start your PRIVATE business as a Financial Broker/Finder/Business Broker/Consultant! As a Financial Broker YOU find money for firms seeking capital and YOU are paid a fee. As a Finder YOU are paid a fee for finding things (real estate, raw materials, money, etc.) for people and firms. As a Business Broker YOU help in the buying or selling of a business—again for a fee. See how to collect BIG fees. Kit includes typical agreements YOU can use, plus 4 colorful membership cards (each 8 × 10 in.). Only $99.50. 12 Speed-Read books, 485 pgs., 8½ × 11 in., 4 membership cards.

K-2 ***STARTING MILLIONAIRE SUCCESS KIT*** shows YOU how to get started in a number of businesses which might make YOU a millionaire sooner than YOU think! Businesses covered in this big kit include Mail Order, Real Estate, Export/Import, Limited Partnerships, etc. This big kit includes 4 colorful membership cards (each 8 × 10 in.). These are NOT the same ones as in the Financial Broker kit. So ORDER your STARTING MILLIONAIRE KIT now—only $99.50. 12 Speed-Read books, 361 pgs., 8½ × 11 in., 4 membership cards.

K-3 ***FRANCHISE RICHES SUCCESS KIT*** is the only one of its kind in the world (we believe). What this big kit does is show YOU how to collect BIG franchise fees for YOUR business ideas which can help others make money! So instead of paying to use ideas, people PAY YOU to use YOUR ideas! Franchising is one of the biggest businesses in the world today. Why don't YOU get in on the BILLIONS of dollars being grossed in this business today? Send $99.50 for your FRANCHISE KIT now. 7 Speed-Read books, 876 pgs., 6 × 9 & 8½ × 11 in. & 5 × 8 in.

K-4 ***MAIL ORDER RICHES SUCCESS KIT*** shows YOU how YOU can make a million in mail order/direct mail, using the known and proven methods of the experts. This is a kit which is different (we think) from any other—and BETTER than any other! It gives YOU the experience of known experts who've made millions in their own mail order businesses, or who've shown others how to do that. This big kit also includes the Ty Hicks book "How I Grossed More Than One Million Dollars in Mail Order/Direct Mail Starting with NO CASH and Less Knowhow." So send $99.50 TODAY for your MAIL ORDER SUCCESS KIT. 9 Speed-Read books, 927 pgs., 6 × 9 & 8½ × 11 in.

K-5 ***ZERO CASH SUCCESS TECHNIQUES KIT*** shows YOU how to get started in YOUR own going business or real estate venture with NO CASH! Sound impossible? It really IS possible—as thousands of folks have shown. This big kit, which includes a special book by Ty Hicks on "Zero Cash Takeovers of Business and Real Estate," also includes a 58-minute cassette tape by Ty on "Small Business Financing." On this tape, Ty talks to YOU! See how YOU can get started in YOUR own business without cash and with few credit checks. To get your ZERO CASH SUCCESS KIT, send $99.50 NOW. 7 Speed-Read books, 876 pgs., 8½ × 11 in. for most, 58-minute cassette tape.

K-6 **REAL ESTATE RICHES SUCCESS KIT** shows YOU how to make BIG money in real estate as an income property owner, a mortgage broker, mortgage banker, real estate investment trust operator, mortgage money broker, raw land speculator, and industrial property owner. This is a general kit, covering all these aspects of real estate, plus many, many more. Includes many financing sources for YOUR real estate fortune. But this big kit also covers how to buy real estate for the lowest price (down payments of NO CASH can sometimes be set up), and how to run YOUR real estate for biggest profits. Send $99.50 NOW for your REAL ESTATE SUCCESS KIT. 6 Speed-Read books, 466 pgs., 8½ × 11 in.

K-7 **BUSINESS BORROWERS COMPLETE SUCCESS KIT** shows YOU how and where to BORROW money for any business which interests YOU. See how to borrow money like the professionals do! Get YOUR loans faster, easier because YOU know YOUR way around the loan world! This big kit includes many practice forms so YOU can become an expert in preparing acceptable loan applications. Also includes hundreds of loan sources YOU might wish to check for YOUR loans. Send $99.50 NOW for your BUSINESS BORROWERS KIT. 7 Speed-Read books, 596 pgs., 8½ × 11 in.

K-8 **RAISING MONEY FROM GRANTS AND OTHER SOURCES SUCCESS KIT** shows YOU how to GET MONEY THAT DOES NOT HAVE TO BE REPAID if YOU do the task for which the money was advanced. This big kit shows YOU how and where to raise money for a skill YOU have which can help others live a better life. And, as an added feature, this big kit shows YOU how to make a fortune as a Fund Raiser—that great business in which YOU get paid for collecting money for others or for yourself! This kit shows YOU how you can collect money to fund deals YOU set up. To get your GRANTS KIT, send $99.50 NOW. 7 Speed-Read books, 496 pgs., 8½ × 11 in. for most.

K-9 **FAST FINANCING OF YOUR REAL ESTATE FORTUNE SUC-CESS KIT** shows YOU how to raise money for real estate deals. YOU can move ahead faster if YOU can finance your real estate quickly and easily. This is NOT the same kit as the R.E. RICHES KIT listed above. Instead, the FAST FINANCING KIT concentrates on GETTING THE MONEY YOU NEED for YOUR real estate deals. This big kit gives YOU more than 2,500 sources of real estate money all over the U.S. It also shows YOU how to find deals which return BIG income to YOU but are easier to finance than YOU might think! To get started in FAST FINANCING, send $99.50 today. 7 Speed-Read books, 523 pgs., 8½ × 11 in. for most.

K-10 **LOANS BY PHONE KIT** shows YOU how and where to get business, real estate, and personal loans by telephone. With just 32 words and 15 seconds of time YOU can determine if a lender is interested in the loan you seek for yourself or for someone who is your client — if you're working as a loan broker or finder. This kit gives you hundreds of telephone lenders. About half have 800 phone numbers, meaning that your call is free of long-distance charges. Necessary agreement forms are also included. This blockbuster kit has more than 150 pages. 8½ × 11 in. Send $100 *now* and get started in one hour.

K-11 **LOANS BY MAIL KIT** shows YOU how and where to get business, real estate, and personal loans for yourself and others by mail. Lists hundreds of lenders who loan by mail. No need to appear in person — just fill out the loan application and send it in by mail. Many of these lenders give unsecured signature loans to qualified applicants. Use this kit to get a loan by mail yourself. Or become a loan broker and use the kit to get started. Unsecured signature loans by mail can go as high as $50,000 and this kit lists such lenders. The kit has more than 150 pages. 8½ × 11 in. Send $100 *now* to get started in just a few minutes.

K-12 **REAL-ESTATE LOAN GETTERS SERVICE KIT** shows the user how to get real estate loans for either a client or the user. Lists hundreds of active real estate lenders seeking first and junior mortgage loans for a variety of property types. Loan amounts range from a few thousand dollars to many millions, depending on the property, its location, and value. Presents typical application and agreement forms for use in securing real estate loans. *No* license is required to obtain such loans for oneself or others. Kit contains more than 150 pages. 8½ × 11 in. Send $100 *now* to get started.

K-13 **CASH CREDIT RICHES SYSTEM KIT** shows the user three ways to make money from credit cards: (1) as a merchant account, (2) helping others get credit cards of their choice and (3) getting loans through lines of credit offered credit card holders. Some people handling merchant account orders report an income as high as $10,000 a day. While this kit does not, and will not, guarantee such an income level, it *does* show the user how to get started making money from credit cards easily and quickly. The kit has more than 150 pages. 8½ × 11 in. Send $100 *now* to get started soon.

K-14   ***PROFESSIONAL PRACTICE BUILDERS KIT*** shows YOU how to make up to $1,000 a week part time, over $5,000 a week full time, according to the author, Dr. Alan Weisman. What YOU do is show professionals — such as doctors, dentists, architects, accountants, lawyers — how to bring more clients into the office and thereby increase their income. Step-by-step procedure gets you started. Provides forms, sample letters, brochures, and flyers YOU can use to get an income flowing into your bank in less than one week. The kit has more than 150 8½ × 11 in. pages. Send $100 *now!* Start within just a few hours in your local area.

K-15   ***VENTURE CAPITAL MILLIONS KITS.*** Shows how to raise venture capital for yourself or for others. Gives steps for preparing an Executive Summary, business plan, etc. You can use the kit to earn large fees raising money for new or established firms. $100. 200 pgs.

K-16   ***GUARANTEED LOAN MONEY.*** Shows how to get loans of all types—unsecured signature, business, real estate, etc.—when your credit is not the strongest. Gives full directions on getting cosigners, comakers, and guarantors. $100. 250 pgs.

K-17   ***IMPORT-EXPORT RICHES KIT*** shows you how to get rich in import-export in today's product-hungry world. This big kit takes you from your first day in the business to great success. It gives you 5,000 products wanted by overseas firms, the name and address of each firm, procedures for preparing export-import documents, how to correspond in four different languages with complete sentences and letters, names and addresses of freight forwarders you can use, plus much more. Includes more than 6 books of over 1,000 pages of useful information. $99.50.

K-18   ***PHONE-IN/MAIL-IN GRANTS KIT.*** This concise kit shows the reader how to jump on the grants bandwagon and get small or large money grants quickly and easily. Gives typical grant proposals and shows how to write each so you win the grant you seek. Takes the reader by the hand and shows how to make telephone calls to grantors to find if they're interested in your grant request. You are given the actual words to use in your call and in your proposal. Also includes a list of foundations that might consider your grant application. $100; 200 pages, 8½ × 11 in.

K-19   ***MEGA MONEY METHODS*** covers the raising of large amounts of money—multimillions and up—for business and real-estate projects of all types. Shows how to prepare loan packages for very large loans, where to get financing for such loans, what fees to charge after the loan is obtained, plus much more. Using this kit, the BWB should be able to prepare effective loan requests for large amounts of money for suitable projects. The kit also gives the user a list of offshore lenders for big projects. $100; 200 pages; 8½ × 11 in.

K-20 **FORECLOSURES AND OTHER DISTRESSED PROPERTY SALES** shows how, and where to make money from foreclosures, trustee sales, IRS sales, bankruptcies, and sheriff sales of real estate. The kit contains six cassette tapes plus a workbook containing many of the forms you need in foreclosure and trustee sales. Addresses of various agencies handling such sales are also given. $51.95; 80 pages and 6 cassette tapes. 8½ × 11 in.

K-21 **SMALL BUSINESS LOAN PROGRAM** is designed to obtain loans for small and minority-owned businesses doing work for government agencies, large corporations, hospitals, universities, and similar organizations. The small business loan program pays up to 80% on accounts receivables within 48 hours to manufacturers, distributors, janitorial services, building contractors, etc. Startups acceptable. You earn a good commission getting these loans funded, and receive an ongoing payment when the company places future accounts receivable with the lender. $100; 200 pages; 8½ × 11 in.

K-22 **PHONE-IN MINI-LEASE PROGRAM** helps you earn commissions getting leases for a variety of business equipment—personal computers, copy machines, typewriters, laser printers, telephone systems, office furniture, satellite antennas, store fixtures, etc. You earn direct commissions of 3% to 10% of the cost of the equipment up to $10,000. You get immediate approval of the lease by phone and the lender finances the equipment for the company needing it. Your commission is paid by the lender directly to you. $100; 150 pages; 8½ × 11 in.

K-23 **INTERNATIONAL FINANCIAL CONSULTANT KIT** shows how to make money as an international financial consultant working with large lenders who finance big projects. Gives the agreements and forms needed, fee schedule, lender who might work with you, sample ads, sample letters, plus much more. With this kit on hand, the beginner can start seeking large deals using overseas funding sources. The kit provides a variety of lenders for international deals in all parts of the world. $100; 200 pages; 8½ × 11 in.

K-24   ***INTERNATIONAL BANKING KIT*** shows the reader how to form
an international bank to receive deposits, make loans, handle credit
cards, issue certificates of deposit, send money bank-to-bank, plus
much more. Forming an international bank may be the answer to *your*
funding needs because you will receive funds to invest. You may become a banker when you use the information in this kit. But it will
take time and energy to get your offshore bank started. This kit tells
you how and helps you get started sooner. $100; 200 pages; 8½ ×11 in.

ORDER FORM

Dear Ty: Please rush me the following:

☐ IWS-1	*Business Capital Sources*	$15.00	_____
☐ IWS-2	*Small Business Investment*	15.00	_____
☐ IWS-3	*World-wide Riches Vol. 1*	25.00	_____
☐ IWS-4	*World-wide Riches Vol. 2*	25.00	_____
☐ IWS-5	*How to Prepare Export-Import*	25.00	_____
☐ IWS-6	*Real Estate Riches Supplement*	15.00	_____
☐ IWS-7	*Radical New Road*	15.00	_____
☐ IWS-8	*60-Day Fully Financed*	29.50	_____
☐ IWS-9	*Credits and Collection*	29.50	_____
☐ IWS-10	*Mideast Banks*	15.00	_____
☐ IWS-11	*Export Mail-Order*	17.50	_____
☐ IWS-12	*Product Export Riches*	21.50	_____
☐ IWS-13	*Dir. of High-Discount*	17.50	_____
☐ IWS-14	*How to Finance Real Estate*	21.50	_____
☐ IWS-15	*Dir. of Freight Forwarders*	17.50	_____
☐ IWS-16	*Can You Afford Not to Be . . . ?*	10.00	_____
☐ IWS-17	*How to Find Hidden Wealth*	17.50	_____
☐ IWS-18	*How to Create Real Estate Fortune*	17.50	_____
☐ IWS-19	*Real Estate Second Mortgages*	17.50	_____
☐ IWS-20	*Guide to Business and Real Estate*	25.00	_____
☐ IWS-21	*Dir. of 2,500 Active Real Estate*		
	Lenders	25.00	_____
☐ IWS-22	*Ideas for Finding Capital*	24.50	_____
☐ IWS-23	*How to Become Wealthy Pub.*	17.50	_____
☐ IWS-24	*National Dir. Manufacturers' Reps*	28.80	_____
☐ IWS-25	*Business Plan Kit*	29.50	_____
☐ IWS-26	*Money Raiser's Dir. of*		
	Bank Credit Card Programs	19.95	_____
☐ IWS-27	*Global Cosigners and*		
	Money Finders Assoc.	50.00	_____
☐ IWS-28	*Wall Street Syndicators*	15.00	_____
☐ IWS-29	*Comprehensive Loan Sources for*		
	Business and Real Estate Loans	25.00	_____
☐ IWS-30	*Diversified Loan Sources for*		
	Business and Real Estate Loans	25.00	_____
☐ IWS-31	*Credit Power Reports*		
	Report No. 1	19.95	_____
	Report No. 2	19.95	_____
	Report No. 3	19.95	_____
	Report No. 4	19.95	_____
	Report No. 5	19.95	_____
☐ IWS-32	*Guaranteed Monthly Income*	15.00	_____
☐ IWSN-1	*International Wealth Success*	24.00	_____
☐ IWSN-2	*Money Watch Bulletin*	95.00	_____
☐ K-1	*Financial Broker*	99.50	_____
☐ K-2	*Starting Millionaire*	99.50	_____
☐ K-3	*Franchise Riches*	99.50	_____
☐ K-4	*Mail Order Riches*	99.50	_____
☐ K-5	*Zero Cash Success*	99.50	_____
☐ K-6	*Real Estate Riches*	99.50	_____
☐ K-7	*Business Borrowers*	99.50	_____
☐ K-8	*Raising Money from Grants*	99.50	_____
☐ K-9	*Fast Financing of Real Estate*	99.50	_____
☐ K-10	*Loans by Phone Kit*	100.00	_____

Order form is continued on back of this page

☐ K-11	*Loans by Mail Kit*	$100.00	_____
☐ K-12	*Real Estate Loan Getters Service Kit*	100.00	_____
☐ K-13	*Cash Credit Riches System Kit*	100.00	_____
☐ K-14	*Professional Practice Builders Kit*	100.00	_____
☐ K-15	*Venture Capital Millions Kit*	100.00	_____
☐ K-16	*Guaranteed Loan Money*	100.00	_____
☐ K-17	*Import-Export Riches Kit*	99.50	_____
☐ K-18	*Phone-in/Mail-in Grants Kit*	100.00	_____
☐ K-19	*Mega Money Methods*	100.00	_____
☐ K-20	*Foreclosures and Other Distressed Property Sales*	51.95	_____
☐ K-21	*Small Business Loan Program*	100.00	_____
☐ K-22	*Phone-in Mini-Lease Program*	100.00	_____
☐ K-23	*International Financial Consultant Kit*	100.00	_____
☐ K-24	*International Banking Kit*	100.00	_____

Total Amount of Order _____

I am paying by: ☐ Check   ☐ MO/Cashier's Check   ☐ Visa/MC

Name: _____

Address: _____

City: _____ State: _____ Zip: _____

Visa/MC#: _____ Exp: _____

Signature: _____

Send all orders to: Tyler Hicks, Prima Publishing and Communications
P.O. Box 1260 HE, Rocklin CA 95677

Or with Visa/MC, call orders at (916) 624-5718 Mon.–Fri. 9 AM–4 PM PST

INDEX